Language Learners with Special Needs

SECOND LANGUAGE ACQUISITION
Series Editor: Professor David Singleton, *Trinity College, Dublin, Ireland*

This series brings together titles dealing with a variety of aspects of language acquisition and processing in situations where a language or languages other than the native language is involved. Second language is thus interpreted in its broadest possible sense. The volumes included in the series all offer in their different ways, on the one hand, exposition and discussion of empirical findings and, on the other, some degree of theoretical reflection. In this latter connection, no particular theoretical stance is privileged in the series; nor is any relevant perspective – sociolinguistic, psycholinguistic, neurolinguistic, etc. – deemed out of place. The intended readership of the series includes final-year undergraduates working on second language acquisition projects, postgraduate students involved in second language acquisition research, and researchers and teachers in general whose interests include a second language acquisition component.

Other Books in the Series
Language Learners in Study Abroad Contexts
 Margaret A. DuFon and Eton Churchill (eds)
Early Trilingualism: A Focus on Questions
 Julia D. Barnes
Cross-linguistic Influences in the Second Language Lexicon
 Janusz Arabski (ed.)
Motivation, Language Attitudes and Globalisation: A Hungarian Perspective
 Zoltán Dörnyei, Kata Csizér and Nóra Németh
Age and the Rate of Foreign Language Learning
 Carmen Muñoz (ed.)
Investigating Tasks in Formal Language Learning
 María del Pilar García Mayo (ed.)
Input for Instructed L2 Learners: The Relevance of Relevance
 Anna Nizegorodcew
Cross-linguistic Similarity in Foreign Language Learning
 Håkan Ringbom
Second Language Lexical Processes
 Zsolt Lengyel and Judit Navracsics (eds)
Third or Additional Language Acquisition
 Gessica De Angelis
Understanding Second Language Process
 ZhaoHong Han (ed.)
Japan's Built-in Lexicon of English-based Loanwords
 Frank E. Daulton
Vocabulary Learning Strategies and Foreign Language Acquisition
 Višnja Pavičić Takač
Foreign Language Input: Initial Processing
 Rebekah Rast
Morphosyntactic Issues in Second Language Acquisition
 Danuta Gabryś-Barker(ed)
Investigating Pragmatics in Foreign Language Learning, Teaching and Testing
 Eva Alcón Soler and Alicia Martínez-Flor (eds)

For more details of these or any other of our publications, please contact:
Multilingual Matters, St Nicholas House, 31-34 High Street,
Bristol, BS1 2AW, England
http://www.multilingual-matters.com

SECOND LANGUAGE ACQUISITION 31
Series Editor: David Singleton, *Trinity College, Dublin, Ireland*

Language Learners with Special Needs
An International Perspective

Edited by
Judit Kormos and Edit H. Kontra

MULTILINGUAL MATTERS
Bristol • Buffalo • Toronto

Library of Congress Cataloging in Publication Data
Language Learners with Special Needs: An International Perspective/Edited by Judit Kormos and Edit H. Kontra. 1st ed.
Second Language Acquisition: 31
Includes bibliographical references and index.
1. Language and languages–Study and teaching. 2. Students with disabilities.
I. Kormos, Judit. II. Kontra, Edit H.
P53.818.L36 2008
371.9'0446–dc22   2008012756

British Library Cataloguing in Publication Data
A catalogue entry for this book is available from the British Library.

ISBN-13: 978-1-84769-090-6 (hbk)
ISBN-13: 978-1-84769-089-0 (pbk)

Multilingual Matters
UK: St Nicholas House, 31-34 High Street, Bristol, BS1 2AW.
USA: UTP, 2250 Military Road, Tonawanda, NY 14150, USA.
Canada: UTP, 5201 Dufferin Street, North York, Ontario M3H 5T8, Canada.

Copyright © 2008 Judit Kormos, Edit H. Kontra and the authors of individual chapters.

All rights reserved. No part of this work may be reproduced in any form or by any means without permission in writing from the publisher.

The policy of Multilingual Matters/Channel View Publications is to use papers that are natural, renewable and recyclable products, made from wood grown in sustainable forests. In the manufacturing process of our books, and to further support our policy, preference is given to printers that have FSC and PEFC Chain of Custody certification. The FSC and/or PEFC logos will appear on those books where full certification has been granted to the printer concerned.

Typeset by Techset Composition Ltd.

Contents

The Contributors vii

Introduction
Judit Kormos and Edit H. Kontra 1

1 L1 and L2 Literacy, Aptitude and Affective Variables
   as Discriminators Among High- and Low-achieving
   L2 Learners with Special Needs
   Richard L. Sparks, Leonore Ganschow and Jon Patton 11

2 Writing Abilities in First and Second Language Learners
   With and Without Reading Disabilities
   Katherine Ndlovu and Esther Geva 36

3 Second Language Assessment in Dyslexia: Principles
   and Practice
   Turid Helland 63

4 Input, Processing and Output Anxiety in Students with
   Symptoms of Developmental Dyslexia
   Ewa Piechurska-Kuciel 86

5 Vocabulary Learning in Dyslexia: The Case of a
   Hungarian Learner
   Ágnes Sarkadi 110

6 An Experiment with Direct Multisensory Instruction
   in Teaching Word Reading and Spelling to Polish Dyslexic
   Learners of English
   Joanna Nijakowska 130

7 Deaf EFL Learners Outside the School System
   Ágnes Bajkó and Edit H. Kontra 158

8 Hungarian Teachers' Perceptions of Dyslexic
   Language Learners
   Judit Kormos and Edit H. Kontra 189

9 Teachers' and Trainers' Perceptions of Inclusive Education within TEFL Certificate Courses in Britain
    Anne Margaret Smith 214

Index 234

The Contributors

Ágnes Bajkó graduated at the Faculty of Arts and Faculty of Pedagogy and Psychology of Eötvös Lóránt University, Budapest. She wrote her MA dissertation about teaching English to Deaf EFL learners. She would like to pursue further her studies on Deaf education and intends to teach English to Deaf learners.

Leonore Ganschow, EdD (Professor Emerita, Miami University, OH) taught courses in educational psychology, learning disabilities and gifted education from 1981 to 1998. After retirement she was Acting Editor of *Annals of Dyslexia* for two years and editor of a newsletter for the *International Academy for Research in Learning Disabilities* (IARLD) for six years. She has published over 70 book chapters and articles on language difficulties in L1 and L2. Currently, she directs a Literacy Task Force, which sponsors research-based instruction in reading/spelling for volunteer tutors in her community.

Esther Geva, who trained in Israel, the United States and Canada, is Professor in the Department of Human Development and Applied Psychology, University of Toronto. Professor Geva conducts research in the areas of language and literacy development in normally developing and struggling second language and bilingual students. She published numerous chapters and articles in these areas, and presented her work internationally. Professor Geva, a Minerva Scholar, has served on numerous advisory and review committees in the United States and Canada concerned with research on literacy development in minority children, a recent one being the US-based National Literacy Panel that conducted a comprehensive review of the research on the development of literacy among language minority children and youth.

Turid Helland is an Associate Professor in Logopedics at the Department of Biological and Medical Psychology, University of Bergen, Norway. Her research interests are language and dyslexia, and she has published and reviewed articles in different national and international journals. She is a member of two research groups, 'Learning and cognition' and 'Cognitive Neuro Science', and is the leader of the 'Speak up!' project, a longitudinal study of children at risk for developing dyslexia. The project has followed children from five to eight years of age using linguistic and cognitive tests, fMRI and different principles of intervention.

Edit H. Kontra is Associate Professor at the Department of English Applied Linguistics of Eötvös Loránd University, Budapest. Her main research interest lies in individual differences, language testing and the methodology of teaching EFL.

Judit Kormos is a Senior Lecturer at the Department of Linguistics and English Language, Lancaster University. She formerly worked at Eötvös Loránd University, Budapest. Her research interests include second language speech production, the psychological processes of second language acquisition and the role of cognitive factors in learning foreign languages. Together with Edit H. Kontra she is currently involved in a research project that investigates the language learning processes of dyslexic and Deaf learners in Hungary.

Katherine Ndlovu is currently pursuing her doctoral studies in the School and Clinical Child Psychology programme at the Ontario Institute for Studies in Education of the University of Toronto. Her research interests include the language and literacy development of children learning to speak English as their second language. Her doctoral dissertation is an analysis of the story-writing abilities of children in Grades 4–6 (9–12 years of age) who may be at risk for academic difficulties. Her clinical interests include psycho-educational assessment and intervention for children from diverse cultural and linguistic backgrounds who have learning disabilities.

Joanna Nijakowska holds a PhD in linguistics from the University of Lodz, Poland. She specialises in psycholinguistics, foreign language teaching and learning difficulties (especially dyslexia). An author of three books and over 30 research papers, she has been invited to research and teach at many European academic centres, including Manchester University, the University of York and the University of Tampere. In Poland, she runs teacher training courses for ELT practitioners and specialists. She is organiser of a newly launched conference series on the relationship between behaviour, cognition and language.

Jon Patton is a mathematician by training and has been working with Miami University since 1983. He has extensive experience with Mathematical and Statistical Modelling. He also holds a Visiting Professor position with the Decision Sciences and Computer Science Departments and has taught several courses in these department over the years. He has a BS in Civil Engineering from Ohio State, an MA in mathematics from the University of Alabama in Huntsville, and an MS in Industrial Engineering and a PhD in Mathematics from Purdue University. He has authored and co-authored over 30 papers in Operations Research and Language Learning.

The Contributors

Ewa Piechurska-Kuciel is Assistant Professor in the Department of English, Opole University, Poland. She specialises in applied linguistics, especially the role of affect in language acquisition.

Ágnes Sarkadi is PhD student at Eötvös Loránd University, Budapest, and together with Judit Kormos and Edit H. Kontra she works as co-investigator in the Equal Rights in Foreign Language Education Research Project in Hungary. She teaches a course about dyslexic language learners to future teachers of English at Eötvös Loránd University. She also teaches English to dyslexic teenagers and adults in one-to-one setting.

Anne-Margaret Smith studied Linguistics and Language Teaching at York and Lancaster Universities and has worked with language learners of all ages in several different countries. She is also a qualified teacher of dyslexic learners and this led to her PhD research, which was an investigation of how well English language teachers are prepared during initial training to manage diverse and inclusive classrooms. Currently she is exploring ways of assessing the support needs of overseas students in a Further Education college. She also offers workshops for teachers who would like to know more about including disabled language learners in their classes.

Richard L. Sparks received his EdD from the University of Cincinnati. He is currently Professor at the College of Mt St Joseph in Cincinnati, Ohio, where he teaches courses in reading, learning disabilities, assessment and research. His research interests are foreign (second) language learning, reading disabilities and hyperlexia. He has published numerous papers in both native language and foreign language journals. Dr Sparks also has a private practice in which he conducts psycho-educational evaluations and consults with professional organisations.

Introduction

JUDIT KORMOS and EDIT H. KONTRA

This edited volume is about language learners with special needs, but more importantly, it is *for* them. When sending out the call for papers, the editors' main objective was to put those language learners into the limelight who endure various disadvantages and are frequently subjected to discrimination because they are different; to disseminate information about learning disabilities and people with special needs in order to make the learning of foreign languages more accessible for all.

By language learning we mean studying another language in order to communicate with members of different linguistic and ethnic groups, and to speak, read and write in a language that is not one's own. In this sense, and with a little exaggeration, we might say that in our globalised world everyone is a language learner: children and adolescents as well as mature adults. Individuals, families and whole communities migrate for economic, social and political reasons, and for them learning another language is a matter of survival. Most children who go to school, and many students who go to college, have to satisfy a foreign language requirement. Graduates wishing to work abroad also study languages, and those who stay in their home countries are likely to have a better chance of getting a good job if they have a working knowledge of a foreign language. 'Use it or lose it', as the saying goes, and people who are long out of school also continue to be language learners in the sense that they need to practice by reading foreign texts or watching foreign TV channels in order to keep up their knowledge. Foreign languages play an important role in our lives, and this is particularly true for people within the European Union. Maintaining political and social relations, mobility in work and education, foreign trade, international companies, projects and cultural events, foreign travel and tourism all require that people have a shared language by means of which they can understand each other.

Many people learn foreign languages with ease and gain as much pleasure from the process itself as from the results. For many others, however, learning a foreign language is a struggle, an endless series of failures and frustrations. Methods and materials usually serve the needs of the majority, and little attention is devoted to discovering the needs of those who could and would also learn a foreign language but need different methods and materials, differently prepared teachers, more guidance and a much more supportive learning environment.

Though not everyone is interested in languages, everybody is aware that knowing a foreign language is a passport to a world 'out there': to knowledge and up-to-date information, to science and technology, to a world of art, literature and culture. If some choose to place their priorities elsewhere, they have every right to do so, but no citizen of any country should be deprived of this valuable tool owing to their different-than-average educational needs. It is therefore the duty of the society of the majority to be aware of those special needs and also to raise the awareness of others; to conduct research that can lead to a better understanding of special educational needs, and to investigate the possibilities of catering to them.

We chose the expression 'learners with special needs' in order to be able to include as many different types of learners as possible: people who have language and learning disorders, those with physical disabilities, and also those who are often considered impaired but who see themselves as members of a linguistic and cultural minority: the Deaf. In our call for papers we opened the gates as wide as possible, and we are pleased to be able to present here a good selection of research papers that cover quite a wide area of disabilities and special needs.

Definitions of Special Needs and Learning Disabilities

The first international consensus document on learners with special educational needs was drawn up by UNESCO in 1994 and is commonly known as the Salamanca guidelines. These guidelines state that 'every child has unique characteristics, interests, abilities and learning needs' and that 'education systems should be designed and educational programmes implemented to take into account the wide diversity of these characteristics and needs' (UNESCO, 1994: viii). In the guidelines 'the term "special educational needs" refers to all those children and youth whose needs arise from disabilities or learning difficulties' (UNESCO, 1994: 5). In line with the Salamanca guidelines, the Organisation for Economic Co-operation and Development, representing most European countries, distinguishes between three major groups with special educational needs: students with disabilities (including sensory and motor impairment as well as mental disorders); students with difficulties, representing the group of students with learning disabilities; and those with disadvantages (meaning primarily social and economic disadvantages) (OECD, 2002 – cited in Gordosné Szabó, 2004). Therefore in many countries of Europe, special educational needs (SEN) may involve all kinds of disabilities besides learning difficulties. In the United Kingdom, however, SEN refer only to learning difficulties (1996 Education Action cited in Orton, 2004). In the United States this term is not even used, and students with learning difficulties are called 'learning disabled'.

Learning disabilities (LDs) are difficult to define for two reasons: first they represent an underlying concept that is not directly observable, and second, they are dimensional, that is, they can be placed on a continuum ranging from mild to severe (Fletcher et al., 2007). The first definition of learning disabilities, which dominated the international field of special education up to the 1990s and is still in use in many countries, is based on the discrepancy between students' aptitude, primarily measured with the help of IQ tests and standardised tests of achievement. An example of this conceptualisation of LDs is the Hungarian definition of dyslexia, which states that 'dyslexia is a type of developmental disorder in which students experience difficulties in reading despite adequate intellectual capacities' (translated from Gordosné Szabó, 2004: 112). This definition, however, has come in for serious criticism due to the inherent bias of IQ tests in favour of certain ethnic and social groups and also because it was found to under-identify students with LD (for a review see Fletcher et al., 2007). The main question that arose was: How is it possible to identify LDs that are not due to mental disorders or retardation without reference to intellectual abilities? One possible solution was to introduce the concept of unexpectedness, that is, the common-sense observation that LDs occur despite adequate cognitive skills, appropriate socio-economic circumstances and high-quality literacy instruction. The most recent conceptualisation of learning disabilities views unexpectedness as the student's failure to respond to appropriate and high-quality instruction (Response to Intervention Model – Fuchs & Fuchs, 1998). An alternative definition of learning disabilities was provided by the so-called Intraindividual Differences Model (Kavela & Forness, 2000). In this model learning disabilities are seen as specific impairments in cognitive and neuro-psychological functioning. The model received its name because of its assumption that individuals show variability in cognitive strengths and weaknesses.

LDs include dyslexia and other difficulties related to various literacy and academic skills. LDs have been categorised in many different ways (for a review see Fletcher et al., 2002), and here we will present the most recent and empirically best supported classification, proposed by Fletcher et al. (2007). LDs can affect three main domains: reading, mathematics and written expression. Reading disabilities can be further subcategorised into reading disabilities manifested in word recognition and spelling, which are commonly called dyslexia, and into reading disability affecting global comprehension and reading disability primarily causing problems in the fluency and automaticity of reading. Mathematics disabilities are also known as dyscalculia; students with this type of LD have difficulties in performing arithmetic operations. Disabilities in written expression, which involve problems with handwriting and composition, have also been found to exist independently of reading disabilities (e.g. Abbott & Berninger, 1993). The different types of LDs affecting various domains of academic performance can be present both in isolation and in combination in any individual student. Moreover, LDs might also co-occur with attention deficit disorder and attention hyper-activity disorder (ADHD), which in themselves are not classified as learning disabilities but as behavioural disorders.

The causes of learning disabilities have been widely researched in the past hundred years, and a large number of theories have been proposed to account for what lies at the heart of the most common LD: developmental dyslexia. In one of the most widely held views, the cause of reading disorders is phonological processing deficit (Frith, 1985; Liberman & Shankweiler, 1985; Stanovich, 1988), which primarily involves difficulties with speech perception and sound-discrimination (for a review see Joanisse et al., 2000). This view has recently been challenged as a number of children identified as LD were found to have no deficit in sound-discrimination, but in comparison with non-LD students, they were slower in processing auditory stimuli (Snowling, 2008). Snowling (2008) reported a series of studies that showed that although most students with LD have phonological processing problems, they frequently exhibit symptoms of visual processing difficulties, attention deficit and language impairment. This finding is in line with the experiences of specialists working with LD students who often find that these students have varying strengths and weaknesses. Since the cause of dyslexia seems to be some kind of language disorder, more specifically receptive language disorder, it is often difficult to distinguish dyslexia from specific language impairment (SLI), which is a failure in oral language development that also causes problems in reading and often co-occurs with phonological processing deficit (Tallal et al., 1988). Recent research, however, has shown that children with SLI tend to have more global speech perception problems than dyslexic learners (see e.g. Joanisse et al., 2000). Nevertheless the difficulties students with SLI experience in learning how to read and spell in their L1 are similar to those of students who merely have phonological deficit, that is, dyslexia in the narrow sense (Kamhi & Catts, 1986). Since the literacy problems of SLI and dyslexic children are analogous, both groups are regarded at risk of LD and therefore have special educational needs both in L1 and L2 instruction.

Individuals with sensory or motor impairments do not by definition have LDs, but, in the broad sense of the term, they too have SEN which must be catered to, for otherwise the right of these learners to equal opportunities in education is violated. On 13 December 2006 the General

Assembly of the United Nations adopted by consensus the 'Convention on the Rights of Persons with Disabilities', which has been signed by 101 nations (United Nations, 2007) including those represented in this volume: the United States, Canada, Hungary, Norway, Poland and the United Kingdom. This document makes detailed recommendations for measures that should be taken to ensure the realisation of full and equal participation of disabled people in education. Besides dealing with individuals with physical disabilities, the articles of the Convention contain specific recommendations about the education of those with visual and hearing impairment. The agreement emphasises the facilitation of the learning of Braille and sign language, and urges signatory states to educate teachers with appropriate awareness of disabilities and to provide adequate training in the use of techniques and materials to support people with disabilities, and to also employ teachers who live with disabilities themselves.

The inclusion of the Deaf among people with disabilities is a highly controversial issue. Those who are born or who grow up without the faculty of hearing identify themselves and want to be recognised by others as members of a minority, that of the Deaf with a capital 'D', who are not bound together by a medical condition but by a shared language and culture. Members of the Deaf community resent being called *hearing impaired* and being pitied as victims (Lane *et al.*, 1996). They refuse to be considered imperfect copies of hearing people and have as little desire to 'become hearing' (Ladd, 2003: 37) as black people under oppression have to become white or women who suffer discrimination to become men. Deaf parents take pride in having Deaf children who can inherit the language and culture of the community and help keep it alive.

The struggle of the Deaf for acknowledgement as a language minority is far from over. Oralism, 'the educational system imposed on Deaf communities worldwide during the last 120 years which removed Deaf educators, Deaf communities and their sign languages from the Deaf education system' (Ladd, 2003: xviii) is still alive and continues to play a dominant role in most countries of the world. Deaf communities differ from other linguistic minorities in the crucial role that education plays for them. According to a rough estimate, 90% of Deaf children are born to hearing parents (Ladd, 2003), which means that the place where the majority of Deaf children can be naturally socialised into Deaf culture is not the family but school, where they can also acquire the natural language that is fully accessible for them: their national sign language (Lane *et al.*, 1996).

The editors of this volume share this cultural-linguistic view of Deafness and include the Deaf in this book not as disabled people but as people who, as learners of foreign languages, have special educational needs which have to be recognised and appreciated by schools, teacher training institutions and educational policy makers as well. They identify with the goals set by the UN Convention: to ensure 'that the education of persons, and in particular children, who are blind, deaf or deafblind, is delivered in the most appropriate languages and modes and means of communication for the individual, and in environments which maximize academic and social development' (United Nations, 2007: 14).

In This Volume

The first four chapters in this volume explore the characteristics and performance of language learners with learning disabilities and the effect of cognitive and affective factors on their second language acquisition processes. The first three chapters also address the issue of the diagnosis and identification of learning disabilities among language learners in naturalistic and foreign language settings. The research reported in these chapters is quantitative in nature, which allows for valid generalisations about the settings the authors work in. The studies represent the cognitive-psychological orientation in the field of second language acquisition research, which is also reflected in the fact that the authors of the first three chapters are psychologists by profession.

In their chapter, Sparks, Ganschow and Patton investigate how literacy skills and cognitive abilities in the first language (L1), foreign language (L2) word decoding and spelling skills, foreign language aptitude and motivation differ across four groups of foreign language learners in the United States: high- and low-achieving students with no apparent learning disabilities, learning disabled students and students with ADHD. Their results indicate that what differentiates these groups of students is writing skills in L1, L2 word reading skills and foreign language aptitude, which are all cognitive as well as literacy-based variables. The major finding of their research is that if these variables are used to classify learners into groups of low-achieving, high-achieving, learning disabled and ADHD students, most students with LD belong to the low-achieving group and learners with ADHD tend to be placed among high-achievers. The authors draw the conclusions that students with LD and ADHD can also succeed in acquiring an L2 and that students who struggle to learn an L2 but have no diagnosis of an LD might have similar underlying cognitive abilities and literacy skills to LD students. They therefore recommend that students who have difficulty in successfully acquiring an L2 should be given appropriate help both by L1 and L2 teachers, no matter what their LD status is.

The main question in the second chapter focusing on language learners with special needs is also how learning disabled students can be distinguished from their normally developing peers. Geva and Ndlovu investigate a different setting: English language learners in a part of Canada where English is the main language of communication. Their concern is the timely diagnosis of learning disabilities among children who speak

English as a second language (ESL). The major issue in the assessment of ESL learners is whether it is possible to diagnose reading disabilities before students' proficiency in English is fully developed. The authors demonstrate that tests of phonological awareness and word-level reading can appropriately distinguish reading disabled (RD) children regardless of their language background. In their study Geva and Ndlovu also compared the writing skills of students along the dimensions of the language and disability status. The most interesting finding of their research is that ESL children who have had at least four years of schooling in Canada performed as well as first language speakers of English (EL1) on the writing test, and it was only RD status that differentiated among students in terms of writing performance. Furthermore, the scores that ESL children with RD achieved in various components of the writing test did not differ significantly from EL1 students. Geva and Ndlovu conclude that ESL children should also be assessed for risks of learning disabilities as early as possible in their school-career and that students with RD should receive targeted instruction to develop their writing skills.

The third chapter of the book, by Helland, describes an assessment tool developed by the author and her colleagues to evaluate dyslexia-related foreign language learning problems in Norway. The great innovation of this measurement instrument is that it unites expertise from the fields of special education, psychology and second language acquisition research and that it offers a test that is suited to the needs of dyslexic language learners. In her chapter, Helland also investigates how the spelling skills of learning disabled and normally developing Norwegian school children differ. Her results indicate that in addition to scoring lower on the spelling test, dyslexic students also exhibit different patterns of spelling errors than their non-dyslexic peers.

Chapter 4, written by Piechurska-Kuciel, explores how anxiety related to foreign language processing changes over a period of three years among Polish teenagers with symptoms of dyslexia and learners with no apparent signs of learning disability. The participants, who were studying English as a second foreign language in secondary school, generally experienced decreasing levels of anxiety as their secondary education proceeded, but students with dyslexia symptoms suffered from higher levels of anxiety than their non-dyslexic peers throughout the three years. The results of this longitudinal research draw attention to the importance of affective factors in the foreign language acquisition processes of dyslexic students.

Chapter 5 represents a bridge between learner-focused studies in the volume and research on instructional practice. In her case study of a successful dyslexic language learner, Sarkadi explores the vocabulary learning difficulties of her participant as well as her reactions to compensatory teaching intended to help her acquire words. The participant of this qualitative investigation is a Hungarian learner of English, who was tutored by the author herself. Sarkadi documents the instances of her student's vocabulary learning problems in detail and thus provides an insider's view of what a dyslexic language learner experiences when studying words. The chapter also gives an account of how multisensory techniques, explicit phonemic awareness instruction and training in language learning strategies can be used in tutoring students with learning disabilities.

The next chapter, by Nijakowska, tests the techniques presented in Sarkadi's chapter in an experimental study conducted with Polish learners of English. Nijakowska examines how the performance of a group of dyslexic learners who received phonemic awareness training with the help of multisensory methods changes in comparison with dyslexic and non-dyslexic students who participated in a traditional foreign language instruction programme. Although the size of the experimental group is small, which limits the generalisability of the findings, the results reveal that the multisensory instructional programme was so successful that students in the experimental group outperformed even the non-dyslexic group on a word-reading and spelling test. The results of the study, though in need of further support, underline the effectiveness of phonemic awareness training and the use of multisensory techniques in teaching foreign languages to students with LD.

The research presented in Chapter 7 is unique in the volume in that it describes how Hungarian Deaf learners acquire English in a course especially designed for them. The chapter, by Bajkó and Kontra, provides an overview of the characteristics of the participating Deaf learners in terms of their language learning strategies and beliefs as well as their motivation. In their qualitative inquiry the authors also describe the teaching methods, tasks and classroom management techniques used by the teacher of the group in detail, giving an insider's perspective of the Deaf language learning classroom. The major conclusion that Bajkó and Kontra draw is that the use of sign language, the L1 of the students, is an invaluable tool in teaching foreign languages to the Deaf.

The last two chapters of the book present research on the teachers' perspective of students with special educational needs. Chapter 8 written by Kormos and Kontra reports on an interview study conducted with foreign language and special education teachers and speech therapists involved in a special compensatory programme for dyslexic language learners in Hungary. The study explores the language teachers' and special education experts' perceptions of the nature of the problems dyslexia causes in foreign language learning at classroom level. The interview data reveal that teachers can recognise the symptoms of dyslexia in almost every aspect of language learning, not just in spelling and reading performance. On the basis of their findings, the authors draw up a model of teachers' perceptions of dyslexia in the process of foreign language learning and show how good practice in teaching foreign languages to students with LD can be based on their model.

In the last chapter, Smith reports a mixed-method study, in which she surveyed and interviewed English language teachers working in public and private institutions in the United Kingdom. Her inquiry focused on the preparation which ESL teachers received for working with students with special educational needs, the support they got from their institutions to foster the inclusion of these students and the actual problems they experienced when working with learning disabled students. Smith's findings draw attention to the inadequacy of the training which teachers receive to ensure the successful inclusion of learners with special needs in language classrooms.

The editors hope that this volume will serve as a small contribution to the achievement of equal rights in education for language learners with SEN. The first step towards this goal is awareness: if educators, policy makers and teacher trainers are aware of the special needs of learners with disabilities, they can initiate the necessary changes. If teachers find out about methods that worked well with some SEN learners, they can further experiment with them and develop them to suit the needs of others. Though the studies included in this book have their limitations, and many of the findings are not generalisable, either because of small sample sizes or owing to the qualitative nature of the investigation, they can definitely be built on in the design of evidence-based therapy. It is also hoped that the research described in this book will motivate researchers in different contexts to further investigate the language learning process of learners with an even wider variety of special needs.

Acknowledgements

The editors are grateful for the support of the Klebelsberg Kunó programme of the Pro Renovanda Cultura Hungariae Foundation in editing this volume. We would also like to thank the blind external reviewers of the chapters, Zsuzsanna Abrams, Lisa Atalianis, Leslie Barratt, Kata Csizér, Margaret Crombie, Zoltán Dörnyei, Ágnes Godó, Robert Hoffmeister, Elaine Horwitz, Stella Hurd, Éva Gyarmathy, Angie Malderez, István Ottó, Bojana Petric, Lynn Snyder and Zsuzsa Tóth for their thorough and helpful reviews. Thanks are also due to the authors of the chapters for their hard-work and cooperation in preparing and revising their chapters and peer-reviewing others. We are indebted to Christopher Ryan for proofreading all the chapters and giving us useful advice concerning issues of wording and expression. Finally, we are most grateful to Tommi and Marjukka Grover from Multilingual Matters, who supported our book project right from the beginning, and David Singleton for his help and encouragement as Series Editor.

References

Abbott, R. and Berninger, V. (1993) Structural equation modeling of relationships among developmental skills and writing skills in primary and intermediate grade writers. *Journal of Educational Psychology* 85 (3), 478–508.

Fletcher, J.M., Morris, R.D. and Lyon, G.R. (2004) Classification and definition of learning disabilities: An integrative perspective. In H.L. Swanson, K.R. Harris and S. Graham (eds) *Handbook of Learning Disabilities* (pp. 30–56). New York: Guilford.

Fletcher, J.M., Lyon, G.R., Fuchs, L.S. and Barnes, M.A. (2007) *Learning Disabilities: From Identification to Intervention*. New York: Guilford.

Frith, U. (1985) Beneath the surface of developmental dyslexia. In K. Patterson, M. Coltheart and J. Marshall (eds) *Surface Dyslexia: Neuropsychological and Cognitive Studies of Phonological Reading* (pp. 301–330). Mahwah, NJ: Lawrence Erlbaum.

Fuchs, L.S. and Fuchs, D. (1998) Treatment validity: A simplifying concept for reconceptualizing the identification of learning disabilities. *Learning Disabilities: Research and Practice* 4 (4), 204–219.

Gordosné Szabó, A. (2004) *Bevezető általános gyógypedagógiai ismeretek* [Introduction to special education]. Budapest: Nemzeti Tankönyvkiadó.

Joanisse, M.F., Manis, F.R., Keating, P. and Seidenberg, M.S. (2000) Language deficits in dyslexic children: Speech perception, phonology and morphology. *Journal of Experimental Child Psychology* 77 (1), 30–60.

Kamhi, A.G. and Catts, H.W. (1986) Toward an understanding of developmental language and reading disorders. *Journal of Speech and Hearing Disorders* 51 (3), 337–347.

Kavela, K.A. and Forness, S.R. (2000) What definitions of learning disability say and don't say: A critical analysis. *Journal of Learning Disabilities* 33 (3), 239–256.

Ladd, P. (2003) *Understanding Deaf Culture*. Clevedon: Multilingual Matters.

Lane, H.L., Hoffmeister, R. and Bahan, B. (1996) *A Journey into the Deaf-world*. San Diego, CA: Dawn Sign Press.

Liberman, I. and Shankweiler, D. (1985) Phonology and the problems of learning to read and write. *Remedial and Speech Education* 6 (1), 8–17.

Orton, C. (2004) Dyslexia in England. In I. Smythe, J. Everatt and R. Slater (eds) *International Book of Dyslexia* (pp. 86–91). Chichester: John Wiley.

Snowling, M.J. (2008) Specific disorders and broader phenotypes: The case of dyslexia. *The Quarterly Journal of Experimental Psychology* 61 (1), 142–156.

Stanovich, K.E. (1988) Explaining the differences between the dyslexic and the garden-variety poor reader: The phonological-core variable-difference model. *Journal of Learning Disabilities* 21 (4), 590–604.

Tallal, P., Curtiss, S. and Kaplan, R. (1988) The San Diego longitudinal study: Evaluating the outcomes of preschool impairments in language development. In S.G. Gerber Mencher (ed.) *International Perspectives on Communication Disorders* (pp. 86–126). Washington, DC: Gallaudet University Press.

UNESCO (1994) The Salamanca statement and framework for action on special needs education. On WWW at http://www.unesco.org/education/pdf/SALAMA_E.PDF. Accessed 15.04.08.

United Nations (2007) Convention on the rights of persons with disabilities. On WWW at http://www.un.org/esa/socdev/enable/rights/convtexte.htm. Accessed 15.04.08.

Chapter 1

L1 and L2 Literacy, Aptitude and Affective Variables as Discriminators Among High- and Low-achieving L2 Learners with Special Needs

RICHARD L. SPARKS, LEONORE GANSCHOW and JON PATTON

Introduction

In 1975 the United States government issued Public Law 94-142, the Education for All Handicapped Children Act, which guarantees individuals aged 3–21 with disabilities the right to a free and appropriate public education. (In the 1990s, the law was renamed the Individuals with Disabilities Education Act, or IDEA.) Students classified as learning disabled (LD) and with attention deficit hyperactivity disorder (ADHD) are covered under this act. Students classified as LD generally receive this classification because they exhibit a discrepancy between their IQ on a standardised measure of intelligence and their reading, writing, and/or math skills on standardised measures of academic achievement. Students diagnosed with ADHD are supposed to meet Diagnostic and Statistical Manual of Mental Disorders-IV (DSM-IV) criteria for this disorder (American Psychiatric Association, 1994). Students can be classified as LD or ADHD as early as first grade and receive services from teachers trained in special education. In the United States the study of an L2 generally does not begin until high school, that is, Grade 9. In most states, the study of an L2 is not required for graduation but is strongly recommended for those students who plan to attend college.

Since the early 1980s the authors have focused their research on studies of the relationship between L1 (native language) and L2 (foreign language) learning, and, especially the impact of L1 skills on L2 learning among students with special needs. Since the study of an L2 generally does not begin until high school (and sometimes continues in college), all of their studies have focused on these older populations. Early searches of the literature yielded few studies on this topic in the L1, L2 or special education literature, whereupon they began collaborating with educators across the disciplines of foreign language, linguistics and special education. There is now a substantial body of research on L1/L2 learning in older L2 learners, particularly students considered to be 'at-risk' for learning an L2. Some students in these studies were classified as LD or ADHD; many other students experienced learning difficulties in L2 classroom settings but were not classified as disabled. In the 1960s L2 educator Paul Pimsleur and his colleagues (Pimsleur *et al.*, 1964) referred to the problem of L2 learners as 'underachievers'; other terms, such as low-achieving and at-risk, have been used to describe students who struggle to learn an L2 in classroom settings. As the review of literature will show, students classified as LD and other at-risk learners enrolled in L2 classes share similar language profiles, whereas ADHD students enrolled in L2 classes, for the most part, do not exhibit language difficulties and often have more in common with not-at-risk L2 learners.

In the present study the authors were interested in further clarifying the nature of L2 difficulties among four distinct student groups of L2 learners in the United States: students classified as LD, students classified as having ADHD, low-achieving L2 learners, and high-achieving L2 learners. The investigation addressed the following question: How accurately does a battery of L1 and L2 tests distinguish the four populations? Decisions about which testing instruments (L1 and L2) to use for the study were based on research on best predictors of performance in L2 courses (see review by Ganschow & Sparks, 2001). A previous study conducted with the same population as the current study is described in the review of literature (Sparks *et al.*, 2008a). However, the emphasis in this earlier study lay on examining similarities and differences among the four groups on the test battery, whereas the present study focuses on the 'legitimacy' of the categorisations of these four distinct groups and the testing measures that best identify group membership.

The Role of L1 for L2 Learning

In 1989, Sparks and Ganschow proposed the Linguistic Coding Differences Hypothesis, or LCDH (Sparks *et al.*, 1989) to explain why students beginning the study of an L2 might have difficulties with learning the L2 in classroom settings. In the L1 literature, it is well documented that most individuals who have difficulty learning to read and spell struggle with certain language rule systems: the phonological (phonological awareness), phonological/orthographic (sound-letter correspondences) and grammar systems (see Rayner *et al.*, 2001). Thus, poor readers/writers/ spellers are inefficient at decoding and encoding words (Snow *et al.*, 1998), which in turn affects reading and writing fluency (Wolf, 2001).

In the LCDH, Sparks and Ganschow speculate that L2 learning is built largely on L1 skills and that problems in L1 will carry over into the L2 (Sparks, 1995; Sparks & Ganschow, 1991, 1993a, 1995a). In the L2 literature, Cummins (1984) has made similar claims with his Linguistic Interdependence Hypothesis. Thus, in both Cummins' hypothesis and the LCDH, proficiency in the L2 is thought to be partially dependent on competence in the L1.

Most of Sparks *et al.*'s studies over the years have focused on verifying the LCDH hypothesis. The studies include short- and long-term prediction studies (Sparks *et al.*, 1995, 1997c, 2006); comparisons of good and poor L2 learners (Ganschow & Sparks, 1995; Ganschow *et al.*, 1991; Sparks & Ganschow, 1993b; Sparks *et al.*, 1998b, 1992a, b); teacher and parent perception studies (Sparks & Ganschow, 1995b, 1996; Sparks *et al.*, 2004a); and studies on the efficacy of direct instructional methods in the phonological and grammatical systems for at-risk learners in the L2 (Ganschow & Sparks, 1995; Sparks & Ganschow, 1993c; Sparks *et al.*, 1992c, 1996, 1997, 1998a).[1] What is clear from these studies is that individuals who have difficulties with the phonological, phonological/ orthographic and syntactic components of the L1 as reflected on tests of word decoding, spelling, phonological awareness and grammar are likely to experience related difficulties in the L2. Low levels of L2 aptitude as reflected in scores on the Modern Language Aptitude Test (Carroll & Sapon, 1959) also differentiate good and poor L2 learners. The origins of L2 learning difficulties of low-achieving students have not been found to lie in the areas of intelligence and vocabulary learning or verbal short-term memory. Other educators have reported similar findings in younger populations. Dufva and Voeten (1999) found that the L1 literacy and phonological processing skills of Finnish children in first grade predicted performance in English in the third grade. Hulstijn and Bossers (1992) showed that individual differences in L2 learning could be accounted for by individual differences in L1 skills among Dutch elementary age students. In two different studies, Kahn-Horwitz *et al.* (2005, 2006) reported that L1 skills in Hebrew were strong predictors of L2 skills in English among elementary age students. Likewise, cross-linguistic studies have also found relationships between L1 phonological/ orthographic skills, especially word decoding, and L2 reading skill. In these studies, L1 phonological awareness has been found to be a good predictor of L2 decoding and reading skills (Cisero & Royer, 1995; Comeau *et al.*, 1999; Lindsey *et al.*, 2003). For a comprehensive review of L2 reading, see Koda (2005).

Commonly Used Predictors of Success in L2 Learning

Specific L2 measures have been instrumental in shaping research on the prediction of L2 performance in classroom settings. In particular, they include measures of L2 aptitude, learning styles and L2 affective factors, such as motivation and anxiety. In the present study the authors used only aptitude and motivation measures, as their earlier studies have shown that anxiety and learning styles instruments have numerous conceptual and measurement problems (Au, 1988; Ganschow & Sparks, 1996; Ganschow *et al.*, 1994; Sparks, 2006a; Sparks & Ganschow, 2007, Sparks *et al.*, 1997b).

L2 aptitude tests were among the earliest predictors of FL proficiency and achievement (Carroll, 1990). One of the most common L2 aptitude tests is the Modern Language Aptitude Test (MLAT) (Carroll & Sapon, 1959). Based on factor analytic studies conducted by Carroll (1962), the MLAT measures four aspects of language aptitude: learning and remembering sound/symbol relationships (phonetic coding), inferring grammar rules (grammatical sensitivity), native language vocabulary (inductive language learning ability) and rote learning capacity (rote memory). In the 1980s, Skehan conducted a longitudinal study of first language development with children initially tested at age three to examine the origins of L2 aptitude and determine whether L2 aptitude was related to L2 achievement (Skehan, 1986). In that study, he used subtests from an elementary version of the MLAT as well as other L1 measures and tests of L2 aptitude. His results showed strong correlations between early indices of first language development and both L2 achievement and L2 aptitude. Further analysis of the data showed that the L2 aptitude measures accounted for most of the success in L2 achievement. More recent findings have suggested that the MLAT is a strong predictor of L2 proficiency and achievement (see e.g. Ehrman & Oxford, 1995; Skehan, 2002; Sparks & Ganschow, 2001).

Non-cognitive variables (anxiety, personality, motivation, attitudes) have been studied extensively in L2 research. Researchers have speculated that motivation, in particular, may play a role in predicting success or failure in L2 learning. Generally, motivation is described as students' attitudes about, interest in, and efforts towards learning a L2 (Gardner *et al.*, 1997). Gardner and his colleagues (Gardner, 1985a; Gardner & Lambert, 1965) have conducted extensive research into the construct of motivation and its relationship to L2 learning. In his socio-educational model of second language acquisition, Gardner proposed that motivation was a good predictor of L2 achievement, a finding that has been supported in subsequent studies (see review by Gardner, 1990). A commonly used test to measure motivation is Gardner's Attitude/Motivation Test Battery (AMTB) to determine students' levels of motivation of L2 learning (Gardner, 1985b). The survey includes questions concerning attitudes towards other language groups, attitudes towards the learning situation in the classroom context and general motivation about learning an L2 (Gardner, 1990). Masgoret and Gardner (2003) conducted a meta-analysis of the contribution of attitudes and motivation to L2 achievement using the AMTB. They found overall correlations ranging from 0.29 to 0.39, depending on the achievement criteria measures. Their findings showed that motivation makes a modest, but significant, contribution to L2 achievement.

Comparison Studies with Disabled and Non-disabled L2 Learners

Much of the work on classified populations and L2 learning has been conducted by the authors, who have compared good and poor L2 learners as well as learners classified as LD, ADHD and LD/ADHD. As might be expected, students classified as LD have been found to perform significantly more poorly than high-achieving L2 learners on the aforementioned L1, L2 aptitude and L2 proficiency measures (see Ganschow et al., 1991; Sparks et al., 1992b). Of particular interest to this investigation were studies comparing students classified as at-risk for learning an L2 with students classified as LD. In several studies the authors found that although the two groups performed significantly more poorly than high-achieving L2 learners, there were few differences between the two populations on L1, L2 aptitude and L2 proficiency measures (e.g. see reviews by Sparks, 2001, 2005). Within groups of students classified as LD there were no differences between those who chose to complete L2 courses and those who elected to take L2 course substitutions (allowable at many universities in the United States) on multiple L1 measures of academic achievement (see Sparks, 2006b; Sparks et al., 1999).

Sparks and colleagues have conducted three studies on ADHD populations and L2 performance. In general, the findings of these studies show that students classified as ADHD enrolled in L2 courses are not likely to experience particular difficulties with L2 learning, as measured by their performance in L2 courses (Sparks et al., 2003, 2004b, 2005). In one study, students classified as both LD and ADHD performed better on measures of L1 achievement than students classified as LD alone.

The authors have conducted one investigation related to the present study that involved the same four populations (Sparks et al., 2008a). In that study they followed these groups over two years of L2 study and compared their performance on a variety of measures, including L1 achievement and cognitive ability administered in elementary school prior to their enrollment in L2 courses, L2 aptitude, L2 decoding and spelling, and oral and written L2 achievement measured at the end of L2 coursework. Findings showed no significant differences between the low-achieving and LD groups and few differences between the high-achieving and ADHD groups; however, significant differences were found between the high-achieving group and the low-achieving and LD groups.

Research Aims and Rationale

The aforementioned studies lead into the primary purpose of the present study; that is, to determine how accurately a carefully selected battery of L1 and L2 instruments discriminates group membership in four specified groups of L2 learners: students classified as LD, students classified as ADHD, students identified as high-achieving by specified criteria, and students identified as low-achieving by specified criteria. If low-achieving L2 learners perform similarly to students classified as LD on L1 and L2 testing measures, might there not be shared membership in both groups? If ADHD students perform similarly to high-achieving L2 learners on the testing measures, might their performance yield shared membership with the high-achieving group? A secondary purpose of this study is to determine whether an affective variable, L2 motivation, is important for determining group membership. Few studies with good and poor L2 learners have used both cognitive (L1 and L2 literacy, L1 cognitive ability, L2 aptitude) *and* non-cognitive (affective) measures as variables in the same study (McCollum, 2003). In addition, most studies with L2 learners have been short-term, covering only one to two years. In the present study, participants' L1 achievement and L1 cognitive ability scores from elementary school were obtained, and they were followed through their entry into L2 courses several years later.

Method

Participants

The participants were 156 students who attended a large, suburban, public high school in a medium-sized, mid-western city in the United States. All of the participants had enrolled in first-year Spanish classes in either their freshman (Grade 9) or sophomore (Grade 10) years. (Students in the United States generally begin to study a second language in high school.) None of the participants spoke a second language or had prior experience in L2 courses. Three different cohorts of students over three different years were used to obtain a sufficient number of high- and low-achieving learners and students classified as LD and ADHD. There were similar numbers of students in each of the three cohorts (Cohort 1 = 45 students, Cohort 2 = 56 students, Cohort 3 = 55 students). There were 86 males and 70 females in the study. The mean age of the students at the beginning of the study was 14 years, 4 months (ages ranged from 14.0 years to 15.4 years). To maintain anonymity, each participant was identified by his/her student identification number used by the school district.

There were four categories of students included in the participant pool: high-achieving L2 learners, low-achieving L2 learners, students classified as learning disabled (LD), and students classified as having attention deficit hyperactivity disorder (ADHD). The authors chose the participants from these four categories to obtain a representative cross-section of students enrolled in Spanish classes at the high school. High-achieving students ($n = 49$) were chosen randomly from a list of those achieving grade A or B in the first semester of the first-year Spanish course. Low-achieving ($n = 55$) students were those who had achieved grade C, D or F in the first semester of the first-year Spanish course. Students classified as LD ($n = 30$) had problems with reading and writing and were receiving special education services through an Individualised Education Plan (IEP). Students classified as ADHD ($n = 22$) had been diagnosed by either the public school district or diagnosticians in private practice (psychologists, psychiatrists) and had an active Section 504 plan.[2] There were more males than females in the study because of the larger number of male students classified as LD and ADHD.

Instruments

There were three L1 literacy measures and one measure each of L1 cognitive ability, L2 aptitude, L2 motivation, L2 word decoding and L2 spelling. (See Appendix 1 for a description of standardised measures.)

L1 literacy

There were three standardised L1 achievement tests used in this study. Each of them included two subtests. The tests were chosen because they measured the language-based, literacy skills that have been found to be predictive of L2 learning and proficiency. The tests were: (1) the fourth grade Metropolitan Achievement Test (MAT) (Harcourt Assessment Inc., 1992), Form S: Reading (MAT Reading) and Language (MAT Language) subtests; (2) the state's fourth grade proficiency test: Reading (Elementary Reading Proficiency) and Writing (Elementary Writing Proficiency) subtests; and (3) the state's ninth grade proficiency test: Reading (Secondary Reading Proficiency) and Writing (Secondary Writing Proficiency) subtests.[3] Data were collected from students' school records to obtain these test scores.

L1 cognitive ability

The measure of L1 aptitude used for the study was the Otis-Lennon School Ability Test-Form 7 (Harcourt Assessment Inc., 1996) that had been administered by the school district when the participants were in the sixth grade. The Otis-Lennon has two subtests, Verbal and Nonverbal, that are combined to yield a total academic aptitude score (Otis-Lennon IQ). The test differs from traditional cognitive ability, or IQ, tests in that it is group-administered and requires both word recognition and reading comprehension because the student must read each item before s/he marks a response. Each student's total score was used for this study.

L2 aptitude

The Modern Language Aptitude Test-Short Form (MLAT) (Carroll & Sapon, 1959) was used to measure students' L2 aptitude. The test is designed to provide an indication of a student's probable degree of success in L2 learning. This measure was chosen because it has been found to be predictive of L2 learning in many different contexts. The Short Form consists of three subtests: (1) Spelling Clues, which measures phonetic decoding and vocabulary; (2) Words in Sentences, which measures grammatical functions of words; and (3) Paired Associates, which measures rote memory. The subtests yield a total score; however, the three subtests were used separately as discriminators for this study.

L2 motivation

In order to measure students' L2 motivation, the authors used selected items from the Attitude/Motivation Test Battery (Gardner, 1985b; Gliksman et al., 1982). The instrument was modified by the authors to use with secondary-level students in the United States. The final instrument, which the authors called the L2 Motivation Survey (L2 Motivation), consisted of 27 items that used a seven-point rating scale with a forced-choice, balanced design format. Students responded to each item with a single answer: strongly agree, moderately agree, agree, neutral, disagree moderately disagree or strongly disagree. In order to make an accurate estimate of a student's level of motivation for L2 learning, local norms were established. First, the authors calculated each student's mean score on the instrument. Then, all of the students' mean scores were transformed into z scores. Each student's z-score was used in subsequent analyses. The reliability of the L2 Motivation instrument was checked by calculating Cronbach's alpha. The reliability coefficient for this instrument was 0.92. The items on the L2 Motivation Survey are included in Appendix 2. The term L2 Motivation is used throughout the remainder of this paper and in the tables.

L2 word decoding

The word decoding measure consisted of a real word list of 20 words and a pseudoword decoding list of 20 words. The real and pseudowords in Spanish were a specific decoding task that involved the use of vowel sounds in Spanish that were not consistent with the vowel sounds in English. The vowel sounds in Spanish used different letter combinations and contained multisyllabic words and words with diacritical markings.

Students read the words aloud and their responses were marked correct or incorrect as they read. For a response to be considered correct, the student had to pronounce the word correctly. If the student spontaneously self-corrected a response, that response was counted as correct. The reliability of the Spanish real word decoding and pseudoword decoding lists was checked by calculating Cronbach's alpha. For both the word decoding and pseudoword decoding lists, the reliability coefficient was 0.80. The two word lists were combined to obtain a measure of L2 Word Decoding for which the maximum score was 40 points. The word lists are provided in Appendix 3.

L2 spelling

The students were also given a spelling test in Spanish (L2 Spelling). The L2 spelling task consisted of 20 words designed to measure a specific encoding task. Like the word decoding tasks, this measure included vowel sounds in Spanish that were not consistent with the vowel sounds in English, used different letter combinations, and contained multisyllabic words and words with diacritical markings. The test was administered by the students' Spanish teachers in the classroom groups. After the teacher read the word aloud, the students wrote the word on a piece of paper. The students were allowed 20 seconds to spell each word. Responses were marked as correct or incorrect. The reliability of the Spanish spelling list was checked by calculating Cronbach's alpha. The reliability coefficient for the list was 0.80. The spelling word list is provided in Appendix C. The maximum total score for the L2 spelling list was 20 points.

Procedures

Data were collected at specific intervals for the three cohorts of students during the course of this study.[4] After a student had been selected for participation in the study, his/her MAT Reading and Language, Otis-Lennon, and state proficiency test scores were obtained from school records. During the first month of the first-year Spanish course, the L2 aptitude measure (MLAT) was administered in the classroom group setting by the L2 classroom teachers. During the last month of the first-year Spanish course, the L2 word decoding and L2 spelling measures were administered by a university professor of Spanish.

Results

Separate multiple analyses of variance (MANOVA) were used to determine if there were significant differences among the three cohorts over three different years on the testing measures used in the study, that is, L1 literacy, L1 cognitive ability, L2 aptitude, L2 motivation, L2 word decoding and L2 spelling. Each of these three cohorts included high-achieving, low-achieving, LD and ADHD students. A MANOVA was conducted on the aforementioned measures specifically to determine whether there were overall differences in the three cohorts' L1 and L2 skills. Findings showed that there were no significant differences among the three cohorts on any of the measures. Table 1.1 reports the scores on the testing measures for

Table 1.1 Means and standard deviations of total group (three cohorts) on the L1 and L2 literacy, L1 cognitive ability, L2 aptitude and L2 motivation measures

Testing measures	M	SD	Range Minimum	Maximum
L1 Literacy				
MAT Reading[a]	104.8	13.8	69	135
MAT Language[a]	104.4	12.5	72	135
Elementary Reading Proficiency[b]	222.8	21.6	152	287
Elementary Writing Proficiency[c]	5.3	1.4	2	8
Secondary Reading Proficiency[d]	225.4	25.4	152	288
Secondary Writing Proficiency[e]	5.6	1.0	2	8
L1 Cognitive Ability				
Otis-Lennon[a]	105.3	15.1	66	150
L2 Aptitude				
MLAT Spelling Clues[f]	8.4	3.6	0	18
MLAT Words in Sentences[g]	11.6	3.7	2	24
MLAT Paired Associates[h]	10.7	5.9	0	24
L2 Motivation[i]	0.0	1.0	−3.1	2.3
L2 Literacy				
L2 Word Decoding[j]	23.9	7.7	1	38
L2 Spelling[k]	8.4	3.6	0	18

[a]Standard scores ($M = 100$, $SD = 15$).
[b]Scaled scores ($M = 211.0$, $SD = 17.3$, range 100–290).
[c]Raw scores ($M = 5.6$, $SD = 1.1$, range 0–8) (in 1.0 increments).
[d]Scaled scores ($M = 226.6$, $SD = 26.6$, range 72–290).
[e]Raw scores ($M = 5.5$, $SD = 0.9$, range 0–8) (in 0.5 increments).
[f]Raw scores (maximum possible score = 50).
[g]Raw scores (maximum possible score = 45).
[h]Raw scores (maximum possible score = 24).
[i]z-Scores.
[j]Raw scores (maximum possible score = 40).
[k]Raw scores (maximum possible score = 20).

the total group. Table 1.2 reports the scores on the testing measures for each of the four groups.

A Discriminant Analysis procedure, a technique used to study the differences between two or more groups with respect to several variables,

Table 1.2 Means and standard deviations on the L1 and L2 literacy, L1 cognitive ability, L2 aptitude and L2 motivation measures for the high- and low-achieving, LD and ADHD groups

Testing measures	High-achieving (n = 49)		Low-achieving (n = 55)		LD (n = 30)		ADHD (n = 22)	
	M	SD	M	SD	M	SD	M	SD
L1 Literacy								
MAT Reading[a]	114.0	11.5	98.3	10.1	99.7	15.7	108.5	12.1
MAT Language[a]	114.1	9.6	98.6	10.9	97.5	11.3	107.2	9.0
Elementary Reading Proficiency[b]	234.7	14.6	212.6	12.2	208.7	28.0	228.0	19.7
Elementary Writing Proficiency[c]	5.9	1.3	5.1	1.2	4.6	1.2	5.6	1.5
Secondary Reading Proficiency[d]	238.0	19.0	215.0	20.0	217.7	31.5	223.6	26.9
Secondary Writing Proficiency[e]	6.1	0.9	5.2	0.7	5.5	1.3	5.3	0.9
L1 Cognitive Ability								
Otis-Lennon[a]	116.4	13.3	99.0	12.1	97.9	13.4	106.4	13.9
L2 Aptitude								
MLAT Spelling Clues[f]	14.2	4.7	8.8	4.5	8.9	5.8	7.8	5.1
MLAT Words in Sentences[g]	13.6	3.8	10.7	3.1	9.9	3.4	11.5	3.0
MLAT Paired Associates[h]	13.4	6.4	8.4	4.5	8.5	4.6	13.4	5.9
L2 Motivation[i]	0.26	1.1	−0.14	1.1	−0.19	0.67	0.02	0.82

(Continued)

Table 1.2 *Continued*

Testing measures	High-achieving (n = 49)		Low-achieving (n = 55)		LD (n = 30)		ADHD (n = 22)	
	M	SD	M	SD	M	SD	M	SD
L2 Literacy								
L2 Word Decoding[j]	28.9	5.8	21.4	6.4	18.9	8.4	26.9	5.3
L2 Spelling[k]	10.7	3.0	7.1	3.2	6.1	3.6	9.8	2.4

[a] Standard scores ($M = 100$, $SD = 15$).
[b] Scaled scores ($M = 211.0$, $SD = 17.3$, range 100–290).
[c] Raw scores ($M = 5.6$, $SD = 1.1$, range 0-8) (in 1.0 increments).
[d] Scaled scores ($M = 226.6$, $SD = 26.6$, range 72–290).
[e] Raw scores ($M = 5.5$, $SD = 0.9$, range 0–8) (in 0.5 increments).
[f] Raw scores (maximum possible score = 50).
[g] Raw scores (maximum possible score = 45).
[h] Raw Scores (maximum possible score = 24).
[i] z-Scores.
[j] Raw scores (maximum possible score = 40).
[k] Raw scores (maximum possible score = 20).

was conducted to determine which testing measures best discriminated the four groups of L2 learners, that is, high- and low-achieving, LD and ADHD. To find the variables that were good discriminators, a stepwise variable selection process is used. After the stepwise process has selected a set of discriminator variables, the discriminant analysis procedure creates a set of linear functions of those variables called canonical discriminant functions. The variable values for a case are substituted into these functions and the resulting functional values then determine group membership for that case.

The results of the analysis showed that six testing measures best discriminated the four groups: MAT Language, L2 Word Decoding, Secondary Writing Proficiency and the three MLAT subtests, that is, Spelling Clues, Words in Sentences and Paired Associates (Wilk's Lambda = 0.434, $F(18,416) = 7.94$, $p < 0.0001$).

Using these six testing measures, an additional discriminant analysis was conducted to determine the percentage of participants in each group classified correctly using cross-validation. In cross-validation, each participant in turn is classified based on the canonical discriminant function(s) generated from the other participants. This step eliminates bias from the classification procedure. Table 1.3 shows the percentage of participants classified correctly in each group. Results showed that the analysis correctly classified 71.4% of the high-achieving group, 74.6% of the low-achieving group, 20% of the LD group, and 40.9% of the ADHD group.

Table 1.3 Number and percent of students classified into high-achieving, low-achieving, LD and ADHD groups

Group	High-achieving	Low-achieving	LD	ADHD
High-achieving ($n = 49$)	71.4	16.3	4.1	8.2
Low-achieving ($n = 55$)	9.1	74.6	12.5	3.6
LD ($n = 30$)	13.3	66.7	20.0	0.0
ADHD ($n = 22$)	36.4	22.7	0.0	40.9

The total error rate was 0.42. With the exception of the LD group, this classification scheme was much better than chance alone, especially in the high- and low-achieving groups.

Because so few of the participants in the LD group were correctly classified (6/30 cases), a post hoc analysis was conducted to examine the groups into which the other LD students were 'reclassified'. Findings showed that the 24 students in the LD group who were incorrectly classified were reclassified as either high-achieving ($n = 4$) or low-achieving ($n = 20$). Because most of the LD participants (20/30) were reclassified as low-achieving, a Multiple Analysis of Variance (MANOVA) was conducted to determine whether the original 30 students in the LD group and the 55 students in the low-achieving group exhibited significant differences on the testing measures, that is, L1 and L2 literacy, L1 cognitive ability, L2 aptitude, L2 motivation. The results of the MANOVA showed no overall differences between the two groups.

Post hoc analysis was also conducted to examine the groups into which the ADHD students were 'reclassified'. Findings showed that the 12 students in the ADHD group who were incorrectly classified were reclassified as either high-achieving ($n = 7$) or low-achieving ($n = 5$).

Discussion

In this study we investigated which measures of L1 and L2 literacy, L1 cognitive ability, L2 aptitude and L2 motivation best determined membership in each of four groups of L2 learners: students identified as high-achieving, low-achieving, LD and ADHD. Our study showed that measures of L1 reading and writing, L2 word decoding and L2 aptitude on the MLAT were important discriminators among high- and low-achieving L2 learners and L2 learners classified as LD and ADHD. These findings are consistent with both Sparks and Ganschow's (1991) Linguistic Coding Differences Hypotheses and Cummins' (1984) Linguistic Interdependence Hypothesis, which propose that there are strong connections between L1 and L2 skills. Sparks and Ganschow have also conducted numerous studies which have found significant differences on measures of L1 literacy (reading, writing, spelling) and L2 aptitude (on the MLAT) between high- and low-achieving L2 learners (Ganschow & Sparks, 2001).

L1 literacy variables, that is, MAT Language, Secondary Writing Proficiency, were found to be important discriminators among the four groups of L2 learners. Both of these L1 tests measure linguistic communication skills including reading, writing, editing and composing. (On the MAT, a group-administered standardised achievement test, students must read the items before they provide a response.) One of the tests, the MAT Language, was administered to the participants when they were in the fourth grade, five years before they began to study Spanish. Even though the MAT was administered in elementary school, it was still an important discriminator between high- and low-achieving and also between high-achieving and LD L2 learners several years later. These findings highlight the importance of early success in L1 literacy for L2 achievement in high school.

In this study, the measure of L2 word decoding was an important discriminator among the four groups. This finding suggests that students' knowledge of the phonological (sound) and phonological/orthographic (sound and sound-symbol) systems in Spanish discriminates between high-achieving and low-achieving L2 learners and also between high-achieving L2 learners and students classified as learning disabled enrolled in L2 classes. These results support previous studies conducted by Sparks and colleagues in which L2 word decoding was found to be a good predictor of overall oral and written L2 proficiency (Sparks *et al.*, 1997c) and a recent study in which L2 word decoding skill was found to be a good predictor of L2 reading comprehension (Sparks *et al.*, 2008b).

In addition, the finding that L2 word decoding was an important discriminator among the four groups supports studies in the L1 and L2 literature as well as cross-linguistic research. In L1, researchers have shown that students who become skilled readers are those who can decode words accurately and fluently (Rayner *et al.*, 2001). Likewise, L2 researchers have found that L1 literacy and phonological processing skills are good predictors of L2 learning in both younger (Dufva & Voeten, 1999; Kahn-Horwitz *et al.*, 2005, 2006) and older L2 learners (Mesechyan & Hernandez, 2002; Sparks *et al.*, 1995, 2006). In a recent study Sparks *et al.* (2008b) also found that L1 word decoding skills in elementary school were strongly predictive of L2 word decoding skills several years later in high school. The findings in the present study are consistent with recent research which has shown that there is a relationship between L1 decoding and subsequent performance in L2 learning and also support Cummins' (1984) and Sparks and Ganschow's (1991, 1993a, 1995a) hypotheses about the strong connections between L1 and L2 learning.

The findings on L2 decoding skills are also important for L2 learners classified as LD. For years, findings have shown that students classified as LD generally have difficulties with the sound/symbol aspects of language and that these difficulties persist throughout their schooling (Rayner *et al.*, 2001; Snow *et al.*, 1998). Likewise, in the L2 literature, Sparks and colleagues have found that students classified as LD and others identified as at-risk for L2 learning perform significantly more poorly on both L1 and L2 phonological/orthographic measures than high-achieving L2 learners (Ganschow & Sparks, 2001). These findings have been demonstrated with both high school and college populations and suggest strongly that successful development of L1 decoding skills is important not only for L1 literacy but for L2 literacy and achievement as well.

The results of the discriminant analysis showed that the three subtests included on the Modern Language Aptitude Test (MLAT) Short Form were an important discriminator among the four groups. The MLAT Short Form measures L2 aptitude by tapping language-related skills in either a 'fake' L2 (Paired Associates) or in English (Words in Sentences, Spelling Clues). These three subtests measure several language-related skills including phonetic coding, grammar and vocabulary. The finding that the MLAT was an important group discriminator was not unexpected because it measures relevant linguistic skills used in learning languages (Skehan, 2002). In numerous studies, Sparks and his colleagues have found significant differences on the MLAT between good (high-achieving) and poor (low-achieving) L2 learners in both high school (Sparks & Ganschow, 1995b, 1996; Sparks *et al.*, 1992a, b) and college (Ganschow *et al.*, 1991).

Findings also showed that neither L1 cognitive ability (IQ) nor motivation for L2 learning were important discriminators among the four groups. The finding that students' IQ scores did not discriminate group membership was not surprising. Numerous studies since the 1960s have found that IQ generally is not a robust predictor of L2 achievement and proficiency (e.g. see Carroll, 1962; Gardner & Lambert, 1965; Sparks & Ganschow, 2001). In recent studies, IQ has not been found to distinguish groups of L2 learners or to predict L2 proficiency (e.g. Ganschow & Sparks, 2001; Sparks *et al.*, 2006). Although L2 motivation has been found to be correlated with L2 achievement, motivation did not discriminate among the four groups in the present study. This finding is consistent with the claims of researchers who have criticised studies involving motivation because the studies have failed to either measure or control for participants' levels of L1 or L2 skills (e.g. Au, 1988; Sparks, 1995; Sparks & Ganschow, 1991, 1995a).

One of the most important findings of this study is that the Discriminant Analysis procedure correctly classified only 20% of the students (6/30) in the LD group. Post-hoc analysis showed that most of the students in the LD group (20/30) were reclassified as low-achieving L2 learners. In addition, there were no significant overall differences between the LD and low-achieving groups on the testing measures used in this study. These findings show that students classified as LD and students classified as low-achieving enrolled in L2 classes exhibit similar skills on measures of L1 and L2 literacy, L2 aptitude and L1 cognitive ability as well as similar levels of motivation for L2 learning. These findings are consistent with a long line of studies which have shown that students classified as LD enrolled in high school L2 classes do not exhibit lower motivation for L2 learning or weaker L1 literacy skills, L2 aptitude and L1 cognitive ability than low-achieving (poor, at-risk) L2 learners (see reviews by Sparks, 2001, 2005, 2006b).

Moreover, four of the LD students who were misclassified were reclassified as high-achieving L2 learners. When their scores on the testing measures were examined, these four students exhibited average to above-average scores on the MAT Reading Standard Scores (SS = 111–131, or 77th–98th percentile) and the MAT Language (SS = 98–127, or 45th–96th percentile) subtests. On the state proficiency measure, these four students achieved above-average scores on both the fourth and ninth grade reading and writing tests. In several studies, Sparks and his colleagues have found that students classified as LD met none of the standard criteria for this classification, that is, IQ-achievement discrepancies, or below-average achievement scores in reading and writing (Sparks, 2001, 2005; Sparks *et al.*, 1999, 2003). Those findings and the results of the present study, showing that 80% of the LD students were incorrectly classified, suggest that some students classified as LD have L1 achievement skills and cognitive ability that are more similar to students not classified as LD.

The findings of the Discriminant Analysis procedure also showed that only 41% of ADHD students (9/22) were correctly classified. Of the 13 ADHD students who were incorrectly classified, eight were reclassified as high-achieving and five were reclassified as low-achieving. These findings show that, in some cases, students classified as ADHD do not exhibit significant differences on L1 and L2 literacy, L1 academic aptitude or L2 aptitude measures when compared to either high-achieving or low-achieving L2 learners. The findings suggest that L2 learners classified as ADHD may be a diverse group that exhibits a range of L1 and L2 literacy, L1 cognitive ability and L2 aptitude skills. This finding is similar to a recent study which found that college students classified as ADHD who had fulfilled a U.S. university's L2 requirement exhibited academic achievement skills and GPAs similar to the middle 50% of students at the university (Sparks *et al.*, 2004b).

Conclusions and Implications

There are limitations on generalising the findings of this study. For example, the small sample sizes in the LD and ADHD groups limit the power of the statistical analyses. Also, the use of informal, non-validated measures of L2 decoding, L2 spelling and L2 motivation was necessary because standardised instruments are unavailable. In addition the population of L2 learners in this study was not representative of a typical body of L2 learners because all of the students classified as LD and ADHD enrolled in the school's L2 classes were included rather than a random sample of students with these disabilities who may be enrolled in Spanish classes.

Nevertheless, there are several implications that can be drawn from this study for low-achieving students and students with disabilities beginning to study an L2 in high school. First, low-achieving L2 learners are best discriminated from high-achieving L2 learners by their different levels of language learning skills, both in L1 and L2, and by their L2 aptitude on the MLAT. Although cognitive ability (IQ) and motivation are important for learning in all subjects, language skills appear to play the most prominent role in discriminating high- and low-achieving L2 learners.

Second, students classified as ADHD are likely to have a 'diverse' profile of L1 and L2 achievement and L2 aptitude skills. In some cases, their language learning skills may be more similar to high-achieving L2 learners. Students classified as ADHD should not be considered as 'disabled' in relation to L2 learning; rather, they should enroll in the relevant courses and attempt to learn the language.

Third, there are no important language-related differences between L2 learners classified as low-achieving and as LD. Research findings over several years have shown that low-achieving L2 learners and students classified as LD exhibit similar language learning profiles. If a low-achieving learner or a student classified as LD exhibits problems in learning a L2, their problems are likely to be related to the same factor: overt or subtle language problems. In most cases, their L2 learning problems are due to weaker L1 skills, which result in weaker L2 aptitude and weaker L2 achievement and proficiency.

Finally, the findings raise questions once again about the lack of a valid definition or empirically-based diagnostic criteria for LD. In view of the increasing number of studies that have found no significant language learning differences between low-achieving and LD students in L2 classes, the authors suggest that educators revise their assumptions about students with L2 learning problems. In particular, educators should question the notions that: (1) there is a specific 'disability' for L2 learning (Sparks, 2006b); (2) students with above-average intelligence who have L2 learning problems must have a 'disability'; (3) only students classified as LD can have L2 learning problems; (4) students classified as LD cannot learn a L2; and (5) non-disabled students cannot have overt or subtle language learning problems. When teaching a student with L2 learning problems, L1 and L2 educators should not focus on a diagnosis or lack of diagnosis as disabled but on understanding the student's language learning differences and developing methods for teaching the language skills necessary for L2 learning.

Notes

1. In the United States, L2 study generally starts at the high school level, so Sparks *et al.*'s initial studies investigating the relationship between L1 and L2 were conducted with adolescent (high school) and adult (college) populations.
2. Students who are provided with an Individualised Educational Program (IEP) by the school district are those who meet the criteria for eligibility and have been classified as disabled under the Individuals with Disabilities Education Act (IDEA). An IEP provides the student with an 'appropriate education program' with special education services (e.g. special education class) and other related services (e.g. testing accommodations). Students who are provided with a 504 Plan by the school district are those who qualify for related services (e.g. testing accommodations) but not special education services under Section 504 of the Rehabilitation Act (deBettencourt, 2002).
3. In the large majority of cases, students' fourth grade MAT and state proficiency scores were used for this study. However, some participants had not been enrolled in this school district in fourth grade. In those cases, their sixth grade MAT and state proficiency scores were used.
4. The authors are indebted to Mrs Carol Ihlendorf for her gracious assistance and unflagging support during the completion of this study.

References

American Psychiatric Association (1994) *Diagnostic and Statistical Manual of Mental Disorders (DSM-IV)*. Washington, DC: American Psychiatric Association.
Au, S. (1988) A critical appraisal of Gardner's social-psychological theory of second language (L2) learning. *Language Learning* 38 (1), 75–100.
Carroll, J. (1962) The prediction of success in intensive foreign language training. In R. Glaser (ed.) *Training and Research in Education* (pp. 87–136). Pittsburgh, PA: University of Pittsburgh Press.
Carroll, J. (1990) Cognitive abilities in foreign language aptitude: Then and now. In T. Parry and C. Stansfield (eds) *Language Aptitude Reconsidered* (pp. 1–29). Englewood Cliffs, NJ: Prentice-Hall.
Carroll, J. and Sapon, S. (1959) *Modern Language Aptitude Test (MLAT): Manual*. San Antonio, TX: Psychological Corp. Republished by Second Language Testing, Inc.
Cisero, C. and Royer, J. (1995) The development of cross-language transfer of phonological awareness. *Contemporary Educational Psychology* 20 (3), 275–303.
Comeau, L., Cormier, P., Grandmaison, E. and Lacroix, D. (1999) A longitudinal study of phonological processing skills in children learning to read a second language. *Journal of Educational Psychology* 91 (1), 29–43.

Cummins, J. (1984) Implications of bilingual proficiency for the education of minority language students. In P. Allen, M. Swain and C. Brumfit (eds) *Language Issues and Education Policies: Exploring Canada's Multilingual Resources*. Oxford: Pergamon Press.

deBettencourt, L. (2002) Understanding the difference between IDEA and Section 504. *Teaching Exceptional Children* 34 (1), 16–23.

Dufva, M. and Voeten M. (1999) Native language literacy and phonological memory as prerequisites for learning English as a foreign language. *Applied Psycholinguistics* 20 (3), 329–348.

Ehrman, M. and Oxford, R. (1995) Cognition plus: Correlates of language learning success. *Modern Language Journal* 79 (1), 67–89.

Ganschow, L. and Sparks, R. (1995) Effects of direct instruction in Spanish phonology on the native language skills and foreign language aptitude of at-risk foreign language learners. *Journal of Learning Disabilities* 28 (2), 109–120.

Ganschow, L. and Sparks, R. (1996) Anxiety about foreign language learning among high school women. *Modern Language Journal* 80 (2), 199–212.

Ganschow, L. and Sparks, R. (2001) Learning difficulties and foreign language learning: a review of research and instruction. *Language Teaching* 34 (1), 79–98.

Ganschow, L., Sparks, R., Anderson, R., Javorsky, J., Skinner, S. and Patton, J. (1994) Differences in language performance among high, average, and low anxious college foreign language learners. *Modern Language Journal* 78 (1), 41–55.

Ganschow, L., Sparks, R., Javorsky, J., Pohlman, J. and Bishop-Marbury, A. (1991) Identifying native language difficulties among foreign language learners in college: A 'foreign' language learning disability? *Journal of Learning Disabilities* 24 (9), 530–541.

Gardner, R. (1985a) *Social Psychology and Second Language Learning: The Role of Attitudes and Motivation*. London: Arnold.

Gardner, R. (1985b) *The Attitude/Motivation Test Battery: Technical Report*. University of Western Ontario, London, Ontario, Canada.

Gardner, R. (1990) Attitudes, motivation, and personality as predictors of success in foreign language learning. In T. Parry and C. Stansfield (eds) *Language Aptitude Reconsidered* (pp. 179–221). Englewood Cliffs, NJ: Prentice-Hall.

Gardner, R. and Lambert, W. (1965) Language aptitude, intelligence, and second-language achievement. *Journal of Educational Psychology* 56 (4), 191–199.

Gardner, R., Tremblay, P. and Masgoret, A. (1997) Towards a full model of second-language learning: An empirical investigation. *Modern Language Journal* 81 (4), 344–362.

Gliksman, L., Gardner, R. and Smythe, P. (1982) The role of integrative motivation on students' participation in the French classroom. *Canadian Modern Language Review* 38 (4), 625–647.

Harcourt Assessment, Inc. (1992) *Metropolitan Achievement Test*. San Antonio, TX: Harcourt Assessment, Inc.

Harcourt Assessment, Inc. (1996) *Otis-Lennon School Ability Test*. San Antonio, TX: Harcourt Assessment, Inc.

Hulstijn, J. and Bossers, B. (1992) Individual differences in L2 proficiency as a function of L1 proficiency. *European Journal of Cognitive Psychology* 4 (4), 341–353.

Kahn-Horwitz, J., Shimron, J. and Sparks, R. (2005) Predicting foreign language reading achievement in elementary school students. *Reading and Writing: An Interdisciplinary Journal* 18 (6), 527–558.

Kahn-Horwitz, J., Shimron, J. and Sparks, R. (2006) Weak and strong novice readers of English as a foreign language: Effects of first language and socioeconomic status. *Annals of Dyslexia* 56 (1), 161–185.

Koda, K. (2005) *Insights into Second Language Reading: A Cross-Linguistic Approach.* Cambridge: Cambridge University Press.

Lindsey, K., Manis, F. and Bailey, C. (2003) Prediction of first-grade reading in Spanish-speaking English-language learners. *Journal of Educational Psychology* 95 (3), 482–494.

Masgoret, A. and Gardner, R. (2003) Attitudes, motivation, and second language learning: A meta-analysis of studies conducted by Gardner and associates. *Language Learning* 53 (1), 123–163.

McCollum, D. (2003) Investigating non-cognitive components of foreign language achievement. *Applied Language Learning* 13 (1), 19–32.

Meschyan, G. and Hernandez, A. (2002) Is native-language decoding skill related to second-language learning? *Journal of Educational Psychology* 94 (1), 14–22.

Pimsleur, P., Sundland, D. and McIntyre, R. (1964) Underachievement in foreign language learning. *International Review of Applied Linguistics* 2 (2), 113–150.

Rayner, K., Foorman, B., Perfetti, C., Pesetsky, D. and Seidenberg, M. (2001) How psychological science informs the teaching of reading. *Psychological Science in the Public Interest* 2 (1), 31–74.

Skehan, P. (1986) Where does language aptitude come from? In P. Meara (ed.) *Spoken Language* (pp. 95–113). London: Centre for Information on Language Teaching and Research.

Skehan, P. (2002) Theorizing and updating aptitude. In P. Robinson (ed.) *Individual Differences and Instructed Language Learning* (pp. 69–93). Amsterdam: John Benjamins.

Snow, C., Burns, M. and Griffin, P. (eds) (1998) *Preventing Reading Difficulties in Young Children.* Washington, DC: National Academic Press.

Sparks, R. (1995) Examining the linguistic coding differences hypothesis to explain individual differences in foreign language learning. *Annals of Dyslexia* 45, 187–214.

Sparks, R. (2001) Foreign language learning problems of students classified as learning disabled and non-learning disabled: Is there a difference? *Topics in Language Disorders* 21 (1), 38–54.

Sparks, R. (2005) Intelligence (IQ), learning disabilities, attention deficit hyperactivity disorder, and foreign language learning problems: A research update. *Association of Departments of Foreign Languages (ADFL) Bulletin* 36 (2), 43–50.

Sparks, R. (2006a) Learning styles—Making too many 'wrong mistakes': A response to Castro and Peck. *Foreign Language Annals* 39, 520–528.

Sparks, R. (2006b) Is there a 'disability' for learning a foreign language? *Journal of Learning Disabilities* 39 (6), 544–557.

Sparks, R. and Ganschow, L. (1991) Foreign language learning difficulties: Affective or native language aptitude differences? *Modern Language Journal* 75 (1), 3–16.

Sparks, R. and Ganschow, L. (1993a) Searching for the cognitive locus of foreign language learning problems: Linking first and second language learning. *Modern Language Journal* 77 (3), 289–302.

Sparks, R. and Ganschow, L. (1993b) The impact of native language learning problems on foreign language learning: Case study illustrations of the Linguistic Coding Deficit Hypothesis. *Modern Language Journal* 77 (1), 58–74.

Sparks, R. and Ganschow, L (1993c) The effect of a multisensory structured language approach on the native and foreign language aptitude skills of at-risk learners: A replication and follow-up study. *Annals of Dyslexia* 43, 194–216.

Sparks, R. and Ganschow, L. (1995a) A strong inference approach to causal factors in foreign language learning: a response to MacIntyre. *Modern Language Journal* 79 (2), 235–244.

Sparks, R. and Ganschow, L. (1995b) Parent perceptions in the screening for performance in foreign language courses. *Foreign Language Annals* 28 (3), 371–391.
Sparks, R. and Ganschow, L. (1996) Teachers' perceptions of students' foreign language academic skills and affective characteristics. *Journal of Educational Research* 89 (3), 172–185.
Sparks, R. and Ganschow, L. (2001) Aptitude for learning a foreign language. *Annual Review of Applied Linguistics* 21, 371–391.
Sparks, R. and Ganschow, L. (2007) Is the Foreign Language Classroom Anxiety Scale (FLCAS) measuring anxiety or language skills? *Foreign Language Annals* 40 (2), 260–287.
Sparks, R., Ganschow, L. and Pohlman, J. (1989) Linguistic coding deficits in foreign language learners. *Annals of Dyslexia* 39, 179–195.
Sparks, R., Ganschow, L., Javorsky, J., Pohlman, J. and Patton, J. (1992a) Test comparisons among students identified as high-risk, low-risk, and learning disabled in high school foreign language courses. *Modern Language Journal* 76 (2), 142–159.
Sparks, R., Ganschow, L., Javorsky, J., Pohlman, J. and Patton, J. (1992b) Identifying native language deficits in high- and low- risk foreign language learners in high school. *Foreign Language Annals* 25 (5), 403–418.
Sparks, R., Ganschow, L., Pohlman, J., Artzer, M. and Skinner, S. (1992c) The effects of a multisensory, structured language approach on the native and foreign language aptitude skills of high-risk foreign language learners. *Annals of Dyslexia* 42, 25–53.
Sparks, R., Ganschow, L. and Patton, J. (1995) Prediction of performance in first-year foreign language courses: Connections between native and foreign language learning. *Journal of Educational Psychology* 87 (4), 638–655.
Sparks, R., Ganschow, L., Artzer M. and Patton, J. (1997a) Foreign language proficiency of at-risk and not-at-risk foreign language learners over two years of foreign language instruction. *Journal of Learning Disabilities* 30 (1), 92–98.
Sparks, R., Ganschow, L., Artzer, M., Siebenhar, D. and Plageman, M. (1997b) Anxiety and proficiency in a foreign language. *Perceptual and Motor Skills* 85 (2), 559–562.
Sparks, R., Ganschow, L., Patton, J., Artzer, M., Siebenhar, D. and Plageman, M. (1997c) Prediction of foreign language proficiency. *Journal of Educational Psychology* 89 (3), 549–561.
Sparks, R., Artzer, M., Patton, J., Ganschow, L., Miller, K., Hordubay, D. and Walsh, G. (1998a) Benefits of multisensory language instruction in Spanish for at-risk learners: A comparison study of high school Spanish students. *Annals of Dyslexia* 48, 239–270.
Sparks, R., Ganschow, L., Artzer, M., Siebenhar, D., Plageman, M. and Patton, J. (1998b) Differences in native language skills, foreign language aptitude, and foreign language grades among high, average, and low proficiency learners: Two studies. *Language Testing* 15 (2), 181–216.
Sparks, R., Philips, L., Ganschow, L. and Javorsky, J. (1999) Comparison of students classified as learning disabled who petitioned for or fulfilled the college foreign language requirement. *Journal of Learning Disabilities* 32 (6), 553–565.
Sparks, R., Philips, L. and Javorsky J. (2003) Students classified as LD who petitioned for or fulfilled the college foreign language requirement – Are they different?: A replication study. *Journal of Learning Disabilities* 36 (4), 348–362.
Sparks, R., Ganschow, L., Artzer, M., Siebenhar, D. and Plageman, M. (2004a) Foreign language teachers' perceptions of students' academic skills, affective

characteristics, and proficiency: Replication and follow-up studies. *Foreign Language Annals* 37 (2), 263–278.

Sparks, R., Javorsky, J. and Philips, L. (2004b) College students classified with attention deficit hyperactivity disorder (ADHD) and the foreign language requirement. *Journal of Learning Disabilities* 37 (2), 169–178.

Sparks, R., Javorsky, J. and Philips, L. (2005) Comparison of the performance of college students classified as ADHD, LD, and LD/ADHD in foreign language courses. *Language Learning* 55 (1), 151–177.

Sparks, R., Patton, J., Ganschow, L., Humbach, N. and Javorsky, J. (2006) Native language predictors of foreign language proficiency and foreign language aptitude. *Annals of Dyslexia* 56 (1), 129–160.

Sparks, R., Humbach, N. and Javorsky, J. (2008a) Individual and longitudinal differences among high- and low-achieving, LD, and ADHD L2 learners. *Learning and Individual Differences* 18, 29–43.

Sparks, R., Patton, J., Ganschow, L., Humbach, N. and Javorsky, J. (2008b) Early L1 reading and spelling skills predict later L2 reading and spelling skills. *Journal of Educational Psychology* 100, 162–174.

Wolf, M. (ed.) (2001) *Dyslexia, Fluency, and the Brain*. Timonium, MD: York Press.

Appendix 1: Descriptions of L1 Literacy, L1 Cognitive Ability and L2 Aptitude Measures

Metropolitan Achievement Test (MAT) (Grade 4)

These tests are group-administered, multiple choice instruments that measure students' basic academic skills. The *Reading* subtest measures reading vocabulary and reading comprehension skills. The *Language* subtest measures language communication skills, including writing, editing, and composing.

Modern Language Aptitude Test, Short Form (MLAT)

This test measures L2 aptitude with a simulated format to provide an indication of the probable degree of success in L2 learning. The Short Form includes three subtests:

Part III – Spelling Clues: The student reads English words presented as abbreviated spellings (e.g. luv) and then chooses the one word (out of five choices) that corresponds most nearly in meaning (e.g. carry, exist, affection, wash, spy). The time limit for this subtest is five minutes.

Part IV – Words in Sentences: The student reads a key sentence in which a word is underlined, reads another sentence in which five words and phrases are marked as possible choices, and chooses the word or phrase in the second sentence that has the same grammatical function as the marked word or phrase in the key sentence. The time limit for this subtest is 15 minutes.

Part V – Paired Associates: The student studies and practices a list of nonsense words with assigned English meanings and chooses the correct word from a multiple choice set to match the nonsense word. The time limit for this subtest is four minutes.

Otis-Lennon School Ability Test

This test measures the thinking and reasoning abilities that are most relevant to school achievement and has two sections. The *Verbal* section consists of subtests that assess understanding of the nature of language and the ability to use complex thought processes that involve language. The *Nonverbal* section consists of subtests that assess quantitative reasoning: the ability to reason with geometric figures. The Verbal and Nonverbal scores are combined to yield a Total IQ score. The test is group-administered. The examinee must read the items without assistance before s/he can respond to them.

State Proficiency Tests (Grades 4 and 9)

These tests are group-administered instruments that measure students' basic academic skills. The *Reading* subtest measures the ability to read text and answer questions in a multiple choice format. The *Writing* subtest measures the ability to write an essay from prompts provided in the test and is scored holistically.

Appendix 2: L2 Motivation Survey

Directions: Indicate your opinion about each statement by circling the alternative below that best indicates the extent to which you agree or disagree with that statement.

Strongly Disagree   Moderately Disagree   Slightly Disagree   Neutral   Slightly Agree   Moderately Agree   Strongly Agree

(1) If I were visiting a foreign country, I would like to be able to speak the language of the people.
(2) Studying a foreign language can be important for me because I'll need it for my future career.
(3) It is important for Americans to learn foreign languages.
(4) Learning a foreign language is a waste of time.
(5) It embarrasses me to volunteer answers in my foreign language class.
(6) Studying a foreign language can be important for me because other people will respect me more if I have knowledge of a foreign language.
(7) I wish I could speak another language.
(8) When I leave school, I will give up the study of a foreign language entirely because I am not interested in it.
(9) Studying a foreign language can be important for me because it will allow me to meet and converse with more and varied people.
(10) I often wish I could read newspapers and magazines in another language.

(11) I really enjoy learning a foreign language.
(12) Studying a foreign language is an enjoyable experience.
(13) Studying a foreign language can be important for me because I think it will someday be useful in getting a good job.
(14) I love learning a foreign language.
(15) Studying a foreign language can be important for me because I will be able to participate more freely in the activities of other cultural groups.
(16) Foreign language is an important part of my school programme.
(17) I would really like to learn a lot of foreign languages.
(18) Studying a foreign language can be important for me because it will make me a more knowledgeable person.
(19) Learning a foreign language is really great.
(20) Studying a foreign language can be important for me because it will allow me to be more at ease with fellow citizens who speak that language.
(21) I hate foreign language class.
(22) If I planned to stay in another country, I would make a great effort to learn the language even though I could get along in English.
(23) I would rather spend my time on subjects other than foreign language.
(24) I think that learning a foreign language is dull.
(25) I would study a foreign language in school even if it were not required.
(26) I plan to learn as much foreign language as possible.
(27) I enjoy meeting and listening to people who speak other languages.

Appendix 3: Lists of Spanish Real Words, Pseudowords and Spelling Words

Real words	Pseudowords	Spelling words
anoche	loche	bien
enero	regua	arpa
isla	traceo	dulce
orilla	placeta	gafas
usted	sucrete	litro
mesa	popeta	maíz

señora	porrosca	pago
jefa	asurge	después
entretenimiento	hastilla	secreto
salón	movadiza	paisaje
inventado	vestuto	placita
mural	cantón	tranquilo
la amada	calahoria	mirando
agencia	meradario	debajo
filólogo	zebajo	horarios
repentinamente	pantaora	tagarote
antena	cebaduría	periódico
corriente	grallanado	felicidad
alto	llenosidad	zanahoria
preocupacíon	yagüe	abecedario

Chapter 2
Writing Abilities in First and Second Language Learners With and Without Reading Disabilities

KATHERINE NDLOVU and ESTHER GEVA

Introduction

Canada is a country that absorbs many immigrants each year, and most immigrants tend to settle in large urban centres. The present research was conducted in Toronto, Canada's largest metropolitan area, with a very diverse multilingual and multicultural population. In Toronto, 44% of the population of 4.5 million people was born outside of Canada, and 41% of the population has a native language other than English or French, Canada's two official languages (Statistics Canada Census, 2001). Due to an immigration policy that favours educated and skilled workers, Canada tends to receive a large number of families who had high social standings in their home counties. Of course, this is a generalised observation and it must be noted that Canada also accepts many refugee families. However, although parents in immigrant families may fall within lower income brackets while they adjust to life in Canada, they are often highly educated and tend to place great value on the academic achievement of their children.

Diverse school populations reflect the larger demographic context, with approximately half of the school-aged population in Toronto being ESL (English as a Second Language) speakers. ESL learners may have recently emigrated from non-English speaking countries, or may have been born in Canada but have a limited knowledge of English due to being raised with a different home language. In school, ESL students spend the majority of the day in regular classrooms while ESL instruction is provided on a withdrawal basis several times a week. Withdrawal ESL classes often involve students who speak a variety of first languages and are grouped by level of English language proficiency rather than by age. Students are eligible for this extra support for up to two years.

While researchers in recent years have begun focusing their efforts on understanding and facilitating ESL students' literacy development, particularly in regards to reading (August & Shanahan, 2006; Geva *et al.*, 2000; Lesaux & Siegel, 2003), much remains to be done in the domain of ESL writing development. Additionally, there is a dearth of empirical information available on children who are ESL speakers and have a Reading Disability (RD). It is surprising that writing has not received more attention within the field of reading disabilities, 'despite the fact that spelling, handwriting, and written composition difficulties are almost invariably involved' (Willows, 1998: 203). Hence, the present study focused on ESL-RD learners, with the aim of enabling researchers, professionals and educators to better understand and support writing development in this vulnerable population. As will be discussed in more detail later, it is particularly urgent to acquire empirical information on the literacy development of ESL students who have an RD given that there are problems related to both over-identification and under-identification of these students in schools. In addition to the difficulties related to the identification of ESL-RD students, appropriate approaches to intervention with this group of vulnerable learners are unclear.

ESL Literacy Development

Due to its deep orthography, English is a challenging language to learn to write. That is, it is a morphophonetic language and the spelling of words is not phonetically transparent (e.g. 'heal' and 'health' share the same root, and the root is preserved in the spelling of 'health', though the pronunciation of the 'heal' component in 'health' is altered). Yet, learning to write well in English, be it students' first (L1) or second language (L2), is an important stepping-stone for advancement in school and the workplace. In the academic context, writing is crucial for success in school exercises, assignments, essays and examinations. As a later life-skill, writing is a vehicle for human communication and expression. Writing is considered the most complex facet in the development of literacy. In native speakers, learning to write follows the development of oral language skills as well as the acquisition of basic reading skills. In fact, writing builds on many of the skills acquired from the process of learning to comprehend both oral language and text (Berninger *et al.*, 2002). However, for young ESL learners the acquisition of oral language and the knowledge of print occur simultaneously when the child enters school (Chall, 1996). As a result, the development of aspects of oral language proficiency and of literacy skills may progress at different rates for ESL students (Durgunoglu *et al.*, 1993; Geva *et al.*, 1997). A recent meta-analysis (Geva, 2006) concluded that for ESL students, underlying cognitive-linguistic processes (such as phonological awareness and speed of lexical access) are the most robust predictors for word recognition of ESL learners, and that indices of oral language proficiency typically explain only 3–4% of the unique variance on word recognition. The relationship between these cognitive-linguistic processes, word based skills and writing development in ESL and ESL-RD children has not been explored to date.

However, it is known that due to the multifaceted cognitive and linguistic demands of writing, it can be challenging for students (Bereiter, 1980; Scardamalia, 1981). Presumably, the challenge may be greater if children are ESL speakers, have an RD, or are both ESL-RD. Everyday oral language exchanges do not typically require the same degree of mastery and specificity with regards to academic and sophisticated vocabulary and syntax (Cummins, 1991; Olson, 1977). Additionally, most children seem to be able to use, decode and comprehend more advanced vocabulary and sentence structures when reading before they can use those same words and syntax in their written expression. Thus, based on the higher demands in areas such as vocabulary and syntax, it is possible that ESL children may continue to struggle with written expression after they have become adept at conversing and reading in English.

The fact that children with an RD may also have writing difficulties is suggested by research on EL1 (English as a first language) children (Willows, 1998). Both reading and writing seem to draw on similar underlying cognitive and linguistic processes, specifically related to factors such as phonological processing and orthographic knowledge (Berninger *et al.*, 2002). Both lower level and higher level reading and writing skills have been shown to be related (Berninger *et al.*, 2002). At the word level, difficulties with word identification are related to spelling problems. At the text level, poor reading comprehension seems to relate to difficulties with written composition. Whether these relationships between RD and writing difficulties are similar for ESL learners is not yet confirmed. Research on the characteristics of writing difficulties experienced by ESL, RD and ESL-RD children is necessary to enable more sensitive ways of assessing and identifying children whose writing development is at risk.

The Dilemma of Whether, When and How to Formally Assess ESL Learners

For the purposes of this discussion, a Reading Disability (RD) will be considered a subtype of a learning disability. Discerning which ESL learners have an RD is a process that has been subject to heated criticism and controversy (Limbos & Geva, 2001). In past years, the claim has been made that diagnoses of learning disabilities have been biased by socioeconomic, ethnic, linguistic and cultural factors, and that developmental and psychoeducational considerations pertaining to the attainment of adequate academic L2 language proficiency necessary for literacy skills and academic achievement have been ignored (Cummins, 1991). This is extremely problematic because, by its very definition, a learning disability *cannot* be attributable to social, cultural, economic or emotional factors (Learning Disabilities Association of Ontario, 2005). Rather, an RD stems from difficulties with fundamental underlying cognitive and linguistic processes. The quandary that arose as a result of this controversy was about how best to assess cognitive and linguistic functioning in ESL learners in a fair manner. An example of the way the dilemma manifested itself can be seen in the school-boards of Toronto where critics, who felt that ESL learners were over-represented in special education classes, pushed for the adoption of a policy whereby ESL learners would not be formally assessed by psychoeducational professionals until they had been in the English school system for five to seven years. This policy was well-intentioned and was adopted by many school boards in the region in order to allow the children time to acculturate and to develop their oral language proficiency. However, the consequences for ESL learners who actually did have a learning disability have been a lack of early identification and intervention, and hence long-term negative ramifications (Geva, 2000).

A recent study of teachers' ability to accurately identify young ESL learners (Grades 1–2) who may be at risk for reading failure highlighted the need for increased sensitivity (Limbos & Geva, 2001). Findings revealed that when teachers were asked to spontaneously nominate students who they thought were at-risk for reading disabilities, 9 out of 10 ESL learners who actually were RD would have fallen through the cracks. Although teachers were relatively accurate at identifying EL1 learners at risk for reading failure, they were less accurate for ESL learners. This may be because teachers, in an attempt to be sensitive, are reluctant to nominate immigrant or minority children for psychoeducational assessment. Alternatively, it may be due to an over-reliance on children's oral language proficiency as a means of 'red-flagging' problematic development.

As a result of the dilemma of whether to formally assess ESL learners, researchers have begun focusing on ways to address over-representation or under-representation of immigrant or minority children in special education. To this end, in recent years researchers have been studying developmental trajectories associated with language and literacy skills in normally developing L2 children, the role of underlying cognitive and linguistic processes associated with language and literacy development in L2 learners, and the presentation of learning deficits in some of these learners. As previously discussed, recent work has shown that cognitive-linguistic skills and literacy skills can develop independently of oral language proficiency in children's second language (Geva, 2006; Geva *et al.*, 2000). The finding that phonological awareness and word recognition skills develop and can be measured early on in ESL learners has important practical implications. It suggests that it is possible to assess children's phonological awareness and word recognition skills in their second language (L2) before their oral language proficiency matches that of their EL1 peers, and that problems in these areas are indicative of underlying difficulties, such as an RD, rather than language status (August & Shanahan, 2006; Geva *et al.*, 2000). The present study built on this information by using these two variables to determine and classify participants' status.

The research presented below examined what Juel's (1988) 'simple view' of writing development classifies as *lower level* (e.g. spelling, syntax) and *higher level* writing skills (e.g. ideation, organisation, creativity). It is thought that in order to achieve higher-level productions of text, the lower-level skills must be consolidated and fluent (Bereiter, 1980; Scardamalia, 1981). These writing skills were examined *out of context* (i.e. spelling words in a list, writing sentences in isolation) and *in context* (i.e. by looking at various components within a larger body of text, including spelling, sentence structure and overall story coherence). Writing skills were measured at the word level with a test of spelling, at the sentence level with a test of syntax, and at the text level with a test of story production. The specific characteristics of writing difficulties for ESL and ESL-RD children were documented.

Research Aims and Rationale

The present study is part of a larger longitudinal research endeavour that began in 1996 and tracked ESL learners' literacy development from Grades 1–6. The present study focused on children in Grade 5 (10–11 years old) because they are supposed to have made the transition from the stage of *learning to read and write*, to the stage of *reading and writing to learn* (Chall, 1996). In Grade 5 and onwards, children are required to write longer, more abstract and complex texts in order to meet curricular standards. At this important stage in children's writing development, individual differences due to language proficiency and learning capacity have the potential to produce profound long-term detrimental effects if sensitive identification and intervention does not occur (Berninger & Amtmann, 2003).

The present study had several objectives: (1) to examine the extent to which the writing abilities of ESL learners in upper elementary school resemble those of their EL1 peers; (2) to examine the extent to which having an RD affects children's writing abilities; (3) to examine the extent to which the development of writing abilities in ESL-RD children resembles that of EL1-RD children; and (4) to compare the profiles of upper elementary EL1, ESL, RD, non-RD, EL1-RD and ESL-RD learners in terms of various factors that are thought to contribute to writing ability, including cognitive processes, cognitive-linguistic processes, oral language proficiency and literacy skills.

In line with the above objectives three main hypotheses were examined:

Hypothesis 1. That EL1 learners would outperform ESL learners on measures of writing ability.

Hypothesis 2. That children who did not have a reading disability would outperform children who did have a reading disability on measures of writing ability.

Hypothesis 3. That EL1 learners who had a reading disability would outperform ESL learners who had a reading disability on measures of writing ability.

Method

Participants

The research was conducted following a cross-sequential longitudinal design, and involved three successive cohorts of students. The sample was drawn from 12 schools in three different school-boards within metropolitan Toronto. These schools were located in areas of predominantly low-to-middle socio-economic status. When the initial overall sample was recruited, children who had special disabilities (e.g. sensory impairment, autism) were excluded. Additionally, at the onset, it was required that children had been living in an English-speaking country for at least four months to ensure that they had some exposure to English language and literacy instruction. Due to the fact that most ESL students in the sample began school in Canada in English in Grade 1, it was presumed that English was the first language that they had learned to read and write in. The total sample for the present research included 273 Grade 5 children; only one child was eliminated from the overall sample due to the fact that he had not completed the target measure of written expression (i.e. Test of Written Language–III).

Of the total sample, 177 (65%) were ESL participants and 96 (35%) were EL1 participants. Information regarding children's first language was gathered from their school files, with appropriate informed parental consent, at the onset of the study. Classroom teachers were also interviewed, and they confirmed children's language status. Gender distribution in the sample was roughly equal: 126 (46%) of the children were females, 147 (54%) were males. The ages at the time of testing in Grade 5 ranged from 10 years, 0 months to 11 years, 8 months, with a mean age of 10 years, 9 months. The ESL students came from 10 different language groups; 70 spoke Punjabi, 59 Portuguese, 28 Tamil, six Urdu, four Hindi, three Cantonese, three Gujerati, two Mandarin, one Senegalese and one Russian. Because Canada is an immigration country, although the first language and home language of the EL1 students was English, they came from a variety of ethnic origins, including South-East Asian, European and Caribbean.

Instruments

Although 22 measures were administered to the Grade 5 children as part of the larger study, only eight of these will be examined in the present study. These tests were selected on the basis of theoretical considerations. In order to account for potential differences in children's non-verbal intelligence, the Raven's Standard Progressive Matrices test was administered. Two measures of students' cognitive-linguistic processing skills that are known to be good predictors of literacy development in L1 and L2 learners were used: phonological awareness (modelled on the Rosner Test of Auditory Analysis), and rapid automatised naming (RAN). One aspect of oral language proficiency, receptive vocabulary (Peabody Picture Vocabulary Test – Revised), was used in order to assess whether the EL1 and ESL groups differed in the breadth of their knowledge of English words. In terms of literacy assessment, a measure of reading at the word level was used as a basic indicator of reading skill (Wide Range Achievement Test 3 – Reading subtest). Writing abilities, the main variables of interest, were assessed at the word level using a measure of spelling (Wide Range Achievement Test 3 – Spelling subtest), at the sentence level (Test of Written Language III – Sentence combining subtest), and at the text level (Test of Written Language III – Story subtest). Raw scores from all measures were used for analysis due to the fact that standardisation samples are not typically representative of ESL students. Additional information about the measures is found below.

Non-verbal reasoning

A test of nonverbal intelligence, the Raven's Standard Progressive Matrices (from here on: RAVEN) (Raven et al., 1983) was used to evaluate children's non-verbal reasoning ability. It is known for reducing the effects of variables such as oral language proficiency, primary language and cultural background and is thus considered to be a test of intelligence that is relatively free of bias towards ESL learners. During the test children are shown an incomplete illustration of a matrix and then asked to choose the correct pattern from a set of five or six that will complete the matrix. Children point to or say the number corresponding to the missing piece.

Phonological awareness

A test of phonological awareness (PA), modelled on the Rosner Test of Auditory Analysis Skills (TAAS) (Rosner & Simon, 1971), was developed to determine students' ability to identify and manipulate the sounds within words. In order to minimise the effect of vocabulary knowledge, only high frequency words (e.g. sunshine, picnic, leg) were included as the initial stimuli and target responses in this task. The order of items reflects developmental trends and task demands increase gradually. The test begins with elision items that require children to delete a morpheme in compound words (e.g. say 'sunshine', now say it again but do not say 'shine'). The following items require children to delete a phoneme from one-syllable words (e.g. say 'hand', now say it again but do not say /h/). The last set of items is the most challenging as it requires children to delete single phonemes in consonant blends (e.g. say 'left', now say it again but don't say /f/).

Rapid automatised naming

This continuous naming task measures the speed and accuracy of children's retrieval of letter-names. It was taken from a Rapid Automatisation Naming Test (RAN) (Denckla & Rudel, 1976). To determine eligibility for the test, children are asked to read a series of five high frequency English letters. Provided they read those letters correctly, children are then presented with a series of 50 letters (each of the original five is repeated 10 times in a random order) and asked to say the letter names aloud as quickly and accurately as possible. The examiner records miscues and uses a handheld stopwatch to measure the time in seconds taken to complete the task. The amount of time that a child takes to name all 50 letters is taken as the total raw score.

Receptive vocabulary

A test of verbal comprehension, the Peabody Picture Vocabulary Test-Revised (PPVT-R) (Dunn & Dunn, 1981), was used to assess children's oral language proficiency. The PPVT-R is a standardised test that requires a child to select one of four pictures that best depicts a target word read aloud by the examiner (e.g. to point to a picture of a 'kayak' on a page depicting four different types of boats). It consists of 175 items, including nouns, verbs and adjectives. The PPVT-R is considered to be a valid and reliable test of receptive vocabulary (reliability coefficients range from 0.52 to 0.90).

Word-level reading

A test of word recognition, the Reading subtest on the Wide Range Achievement Test Third Edition (WRAT 3-R) (Wilkinson, 1993), was used to determine children's ability to identify and decode age-appropriate words. Children read single words in English orally from a list that gradually increases in difficulty. The test consists of 42 monosyllabic and polysyllabic words (including nouns, verbs, adjectives and prepositions). The WRAT-3 is considered to be a valid and reliable test (reliability coefficients range from 0.85 to 0.95).

Spelling

A test of spelling was taken from the Wide Range Achievement Test Third Edition (WRAT 3–S; Wilkinson, 1993, Spelling subtest). It was used to measure children's ability to accurately spell English words. The test consists of a list of 40 monosyllabic and polysyllabic words that increase in complexity and obscurity as the test progresses. The examiner dictates the target word to the student, then uses it in a sentence and finally repeats the word. The WRAT–3 is considered to be a valid and reliable test (reliability coefficients range from 0.85 to 0.95).

Written syntax

The Sentence Combining subtest from the Test of Written Language Third Edition (TOWL-III) (Hammill & Larsen, 1996) was used to evaluate syntactic skills in writing. Children are required to read and then combine several short sentences into one longer, more complex, grammatically correct sentence that retains the meaning of the original sentences (e.g. 'The dog is black' and 'The dog is large' could become 'The large dog is black' or 'The black dog is large'). The test taps into children's ability to use English grammar (e.g. knowledge of conjunctions, correct subject-verb agreements, appropriate verb tense, ability to produce grammatically correct compound sentences) in their writing. Spelling, punctuation and capitalisation errors are *not* penalised. A list of correct answers is provided in the TOWL–III scoring manual. Any response that departs from the examples in a significant way, or that is 'awkward or confusing' is deemed incorrect. Each answer is given a score of either 1 or 0, and there are 20 items on the test that increase in length and complexity of the stimulus sentences and target outcomes. Scoring was conducted by two trained research assistants who double-scored a random selection of 20% of the tests; reliability correlations between the two scorers was very high ($r = 0.98$). Sentence Combining is a complex task because it taps into both language proficiency (i.e. knowledge of English grammar) as well literacy skills (i.e. the ability to generate one's answers under somewhat controlled conditions). The TOWL III is considered to be a valid and reliable test (internal consistency, test–retest reliability with alternate forms, and inter-scorer reliability coefficients approximate 0.80–0.90 for different ages).

Story composition

A test of higher-level writing ability, the TOWL–III Story Composition (Hammill & Larsen, 1996; Spontaneous writing format, Form B) was the dependent measure of main interest. The test is designed to be used with children aged 7–18 years. In this test the child is shown a complex picture stimulus depicting an evocative, interesting scene and then given 15 minutes to write a story based on the picture. The story is scored using three subtests. The first is entitled *Contextual conventions* and refers to the ability to utilise the basic mechanics of writing in context (i.e. capitalisation, punctuation, spelling). It consists of 12 items that examine the appropriate use of capital letters, various types of punctuation (e.g. quotation marks, commas, apostrophes, question marks) and spelling. A holistic rating system is used for most items (e.g. wherein $0 =$ poor, $1 =$ average, $2 =$ good) and a total of 18 points are available. In addition to the global rating indices offered in the TOWL–III manual, the frequencies corresponding to the number of punctuation, capitalisation, and spelling errors were recorded for each child as supplemental information (e.g. if a child made 17 spelling errors that figure would be recorded in addition to the global rating score of '0' in order to increase the test's sensitivity).

The second subtest is entitled *Contextual language* and examines higher-level aspects of writing in context (e.g. grammar, vocabulary, verb usage). It consists of 14 items that target the quality of sentence structure (e.g. presence of run-on sentences, compound and complex sentences), the components of sentences (e.g. introductory phrases, conjunctions), and the quality of writing (e.g. subject–verb agreements, complexity of vocabulary used). A total of 31 points are available. Supplementary information was included in addition to the global rating scores offered by the test developers for: the percentages of T-units (i.e. Thought-units: independent complete clauses containing a subject and object, as well as any connected dependent clauses) within (1) badly constructed, (2) simple and (3) complex or compound sentences; the number of correctly spelled words with seven or more letters; and the number of correctly spelled words with three or more syllables.

The third subtest for scoring students' stories is entitled *Story Construction*. In this subtest the examiner considers the overall coherency and quality of the story. The plot and sequence of the story are marked for logical and smooth progression. The story beginning and ending are considered. The quality of the prose, character development, use of emotion, and action are also scored on rating scales wherein more points are awarded for better use of the target devices. A total of 21 points are available.

Scoring of the TOWL–III Story Composition was conducted by two graduate students. Reliability coding was conducted for each of the three subtests (Contextual Conventions, Contextual Language and Story Construction) due to the complexity of the scoring system and the element of subjectivity on some items. A supplemental set of guidelines with additional details was constructed by the scorers to aid in obtaining reliability and to decrease ambiguity for difficult items. The first rater scored all 273 stories. A randomised sample of 20% of the stories was selected to be double-scored by the second marker. Consistency between the two raters was calculated with intra-class correlation coefficients using a two-way random model. A high degree reliability of was achieved ($r = 0.92$, Cronbach's $\alpha = 0.96$) for the Contextual Conventions subtest. For the Contextual Language subtest, a high degree of reliability was also achieved ($r = 0.87$, Cronbach's $\alpha = 0.93$). However, for the Story Construction subtest, reliability scoring was less consistent due to the subjective nature of the items ($r = 0.68$; Cronbach's $\alpha = 0.81$). The difficulty of scoring subjective aspects of writing has been acknowledged by other researchers in the field (e.g. Weigle, 2002). Consequently, results from the Story Construction subtest need to be interpreted with some caution.

Procedures

Participants were recruited via a letter that was sent home with all students and contained detailed information about the process and goals of the research project. A consent form was included that could be signed and returned by parents. At the beginning of testing sessions, verbal assent was obtained by asking children whether they would like to participate. All testing was conducted by fully-trained graduate students and research assistants in the children's schools. Participants were tested individually or in groups, depending on the measure, in a quiet place in the school. In Grade 5, children were withdrawn from their classes on four separate occasions for testing sessions that lasted approximately 30 minutes.

Results

The results section is divided into four main sections; the first presents the way that students' classification as ESL learners was confirmed, the second details the manner in which students were objectively classified as having a RD, the third presents the group comparisons on cognitive, linguistic and literacy measures, and the fourth section presents results pertaining to the three main hypotheses in relation to children's story-writing.

Classification of students as ESL learners

An independent samples t-test revealed that there were significant differences in age between the EL1 and ESL participants ($t(1,271) = 3.37$, $p < 0.01$), with the EL1 participants being on average two months older than the ESL participants. Due to the age difference, age was used as a covariate when comparing L1 and L2 groups. In order to determine whether the ESL classification remained valid in Grade 5, a comparison of normally developing (i.e. without RD) students was conducted using vocabulary as the dependent variable. An ANCOVA, using language group (EL1 or ESL) as the independent variable, revealed a significant difference between ESL-non-RD and EL1-non-RD students ($F(1,245) = 27.12$, $p < 0.001$) such that the ESL-non-RD students had lower scores on the test of receptive vocabulary. A subsequent ANCOVA revealed that there were no significant differences between ESL-RD and EL1-RD students on the vocabulary test ($F(1,22) = 0.001$, ns).

Classification of students as reading disabled

As there are no standardised screening measures to detect RD in ESL children and independent information from teachers would likely not be reliable (Limbos & Geva, 2001), it was necessary to use an empirical method to identify RD students. The results from the tests of phonological awareness and word-level reading were used to determine which subjects met criteria for having a RD. All children who scored more than one standard deviation below the mean on *both* tests of phonological awareness and word identification were classified as being RD. This stringent and systematic methodology was designed to isolate students who were significantly behind their ESL and EL1 peers. Other studies have shown that RD is a dimensional rather than a categorical state. As with other procedures based on cut-offs it is necessary to acknowledge that the reading difficulties of students identified as RD may vary in terms of severity. The chosen classification method yielded a sample of 25 students. This number constituted 9.16% of the participants.

Of the 25 students with reading disabilities, eight were EL1 (32%) and 17 (68%) were ESL. These proportions corresponded closely to those in the overall sample. Additionally, the proportions of ESL students from various first language groups were proportionately represented (eight were Portuguese, seven were Punjabi, one was Hindi, one was Tamil). In the RD sample, 15 (60%) were male and 10 (40%) were female, similar to the overall group. The average age was 10 years, 8 months; an independent samples t-test indicated that there were no significant differences in age between the RD and non-RD groups ($t(1,271) = 0.28$, ns). Additionally, there were no significant differences in age between ESL-RD and EL1-RD students ($t(1,271) = 1.29$, ns).

Group differences on cognitive, linguistic and literacy measures

Due to the difference between the language groups with respect to age, age was covaried in the univariate and multivariate analyses. Language group (ESL or EL1) and reading disability status (RD or non-RD) were the independent variables, resulting in a 2 × 2 structure for all of the subsequent ANCOVAs and MANCOVAs. Bonferroni correction was applied to adjust the alpha level for multiple analyses. See Table 2.1 for a summary of the descriptive statistics and results from comparisons of performance on non-verbal reasoning ability, cognitive-linguistic, oral language proficiency and literacy measures.

An ANCOVA revealed that there were no significant differences in terms of non-verbal reasoning ability between ESL-EL1 learners ($F(1,271) = 0.41$, ns) or RD–non-RD children ($F(1,271) = 1.65$, ns). In addition to there being no significant main effects, there was no significant interaction between ESL-EL1 and RD–non-RD groups ($F(1,271) = 0.00$, ns).

A MANCOVA was conducted to examine group differences on other cognitive, linguistic and literacy measures, including phonological awareness, rapid automatised naming and word recognition. There were no significant ESL-EL1 differences on these variables, that is, on their phonological

Table 2.1 Performance on cognitive, linguistic and literacy measures

		ESL			EL1			RD	
		Non-RD (n = 160)	RD (n = 17)	Total (n = 177)	Non-RD (n = 88)	RD (n = 8)	Total (n = 96)	Non-RD (n = 248)	RD (n = 25)
Non-verbal cognitive skills RAVEN	M SD	34.15 8.51	31.53 8.04	33.90 8.48	35.66 9.18	33.25 8.53	35.45 9.12	34.68*** 8.76	32.08*** 8.06
Cognitive-linguistic skills PA	M SD	21.09 3.90	9.53 2.24	19.98 5.09	20.01 4.85	9.63 3.07	19.15 5.53	20.71*** 4.29	9.56*** 2.47
RAN	M SD	21.59 4.35	29.65 8.09	22.37 5.36	23.56 9.00	27.63 4.34	23.90 8.77	22.29*** 6.45	29.00*** 7.08
Oral language skills Vocabulary	M SD	101.65 14.81	91.24 15.28	100.65*** 15.13	112.14 13.24	92.50 13.36	110.50*** 14.26	105.37*** 15.11	91.64*** 14.43
Literacy skills Reading	M SD	37.83 5.04	26.65 2.69	36.75 5.88	37.65 4.90	26.38 2.33	36.71 5.67	37.76*** 4.98	26.56*** 2.53
Lower-level writing skills Spelling	M SD	32.66 4.88	23.29 2.39	31.76 5.45	31.50 4.60	23.25 2.38	30.81 5.01	32.25*** 4.81	23.28*** 2.34
Sentence combining	M SD	4.30 3.60	2.53 1.88	4.13 3.51	4.09 3.53	2.19 0.83	3.95 3.48	4.23* 3.57	2.42* 1.93

Note: RAVEN = Ravens' Progressive Matrices; PA = phonological awareness; RAN = rapid automatised letter naming; PPVT = Peabody Picture Vocabulary Test – Revised; WRAT-Reading = Wide Range Achievement Test – 3rd edition, Reading subtest; WRAT-Spelling = Wide Range Achievement Test – 3rd edition, Spelling subtest; TOWL-III Sentence Combining = Test of Written Language – 3rd edition, Sentence Combining subtest.
*$p < 0.05$. **$p < 0.01$. ***$p < 0.001$.

awareness scores ($F(1,268) = 0.65$, ns), rapid automatised naming scores ($F(1,268) = 0.09$, ns), or word identification scores ($F(1,268) = 0.18$, ns). However, there were significant differences between the RD–non-RD groups on all of these variables, that is, the RD group had significantly lower phonological awareness scores ($F(1,268) = 140.84, p < 0.001$), slower rapid automatised naming scores ($F(1,268) = 17.73, p < 0.001$), and lower word identification scores ($F(1,268) = 107.74, p < 0.001$). It is important to note that having below average phonological awareness and word identification scores were the criteria used to select the RD group, and so it was expected that these scores be significantly lower for the RD sample. There were no significant interactions between language groups and RD groups for any of the variables, that is, phonological awareness scores ($F(1,268) = 0.34$, ns), rapid automatised naming scores ($F(1,268) = 1.74$, ns), or word identification scores ($F(1,268) = 0.01$, ns).

A MANCOVA was conducted to examine group differences on word spelling and sentence combining. There were no significant differences between ESL and EL1 groups for either spelling ($F(1,264) = 0.73$, ns) or syntax ($F(1,264) = 0.27$, ns). There were significant differences between RD and non-RD groups on both spelling ($F(1,264) = 67.94, p < 0.001$) and syntax ($F(1,264) = 5.21, p < 0.05$) such that the non-RD group outperformed the RD group. There were no significant language group by RD group interactions on either spelling ($F(1,264) = 0.10$, ns) or syntax ($F(1,264) = 0.01$, ns).

Group differences in writing measures

Table 2.2 summarises the results of group comparisons on the Story Composition measure. The number of words that children wrote in their stories was compared using an ANCOVA. There were no significant effects for language (ESL-EL1) group ($F(1,268) = 1.72$, ns), RD group ($F(1,268) = 0.12$, ns), or for the language group by reading disability group interaction ($F(1,268) = 0.80$, ns).

In order to examine the quality of writing in context, analyses involving various clusters of specific writing skills were conducted. Firstly, a MANCOVA with the three story subtests was conducted. There were no significant differences between ESL and EL1 groups on the Contextual Conventions ($F(1,268) = 0.47$, ns), Contextual Language ($F(1,268) = 3.83$, $p = 0.05$), or Story Construction ($F(1,268) = 1.92$, ns) subtests. Of note is the fact that the ESL-EL1 group difference is approaching significance at the $p < 0.05$ level for the Contextual Language subtest in favour of the ESL students. There were significant differences between RD and non-RD students on the Contextual Conventions ($F(1,268) = 13.50, p < 0.001$), Contextual Language ($F(1,268) = 40.50, p < 0.001$), and Story Construction ($F(1,268) = 30.62, p < 0.001$) subtests such that the non-RD students

Table 2.2 Writing abilities as measured by performance on the story writing task

TOWL–III story composition		ESL			EL1			RD	
		Non-RD (n = 160)	RD (n = 17)	Total (n = 177)	Non-RD (n = 88)	RD (n = 8)	Total (n = 96)	Non-RD (n = 248)	RD (n = 25)
Contextual conventions	M	6.68	2.88	6.31	5.27	3.63	5.14	6.18***	3.12***
	SE	3.48	1.83	3.54	3.29	2.00	3.22	3.47	1.88
	%ile	63rd	25th	50th	37th	37th	37th	50th	25th
	SS	11	8	10	9	9	9	10	8
Punctuation and capitalisation errors	M	4.94	7.67	5.20	5.05	5.62	5.10	4.98	7.01
	SE	4.69	4.16	4.70	3.62	3.42	3.59	4.33	3.99
Spelling errors per 100 words	M	6.63	17.84	7.71	8.23	15.84	8.86	7.20***	17.20***
	SE	5.99	10.78	7.34	5.94	9.49	6.59	6.00	10.23
Contextual language	M	16.59	10.47	16.00	14.80	9.00	14.31	15.95***	10.00***
	SE	4.35	3.30	4.62	4.07	3.30	4.31	4.33	3.30
	%ile	84th	37th	75th	63rd	25th	63rd	75th	37th
	SS	13	9	12	11	8	11	12	9
Correctly spelled words ≥7 letters	M	9.73	2.76	9.06	7.02	2.62	6.66	8.76***	2.72***
	SE	5.27	2.68	5.48	5.08	1.77	5.04	5.35	2.39

Table 2.2 Continued

TOWL–III story composition		ESL			EL1			RD	
		Non-RD (n = 160)	RD (n = 17)	Total (n = 177)	Non-RD (n = 88)	RD (n = 8)	Total (n = 96)	Non-RD (n = 248)	RD (n = 25)
Badly constructed sentences	M SE	42.05 33.59	77.34 26.02	45.44 34.49	45.19 32.36	84.79 24.99	48.49 33.56	43.16*** 33.12	79.72*** 25.41
% Simple sentences	M SE	24.08 18.83	11.46 13.44	22.87 18.73	21.42 19.11	9.41 17.35	20.42 19.18	23.14** 18.94	10.80** 14.46
% Compound and complex sentences	M SE	34.28 24.67	11.20 15.74	32.06 24.88	33.40 21.69	5.79 12.83	31.10 22.40	33.97*** 23.62	9.47*** 14.83
Story construction	M SE %ile SS	12.85 2.88 75th 12	9.00 3.41 50th 10	12.48 3.14 63rd 11	12.06 3.30 63rd 11	8.25 4.27 37th 9	11.74 3.53 63rd 11	12.57*** 3.06 75th 12	8.76*** 3.63 50th 9
Total score for three story subtests	M SE	36.11 9.46	22.35 7.90	34.79 10.15	32.13 9.48	20.88 8.22	31.19 9.85	34.70*** 9.64	21.88*** 7.86
Word count	M SE	164.76 54.22	149.00 45.06	163.25 53.50	142.09 51.40	149.50 80.27	142.71 53.84	156.71 54.23	149.16 56.86

**$p < 0.01$. ***$p < 0.001$.

outperformed the RD students. There were no significant interactions between language and RD groups on the Contextual Conventions ($F(1,268) = 1.96$, ns), Contextual Language ($F(1,268) = 0.02$, ns), or Story Construction ($F(1,268) = 0.00$, ns) subtests. Percentiles, based on average group performance scores, were taken from the TOWL–III scoring manual and are listed in Table 2.2. The pattern of percentiles reflected the trend of the aforementioned MANCOVA results. They indicated that non-RD ESL and EL1 students consistently scored in the normal range, higher than ESL-RD and EL1-RD students.

Given that there were no significant differences between ESL and EL1 groups on any of the three subtests, subsequent analyses focused on the writing quality of RD students. In order to examine differences between groups on lower level writing skills in context, a MANCOVA with the number of punctuation and capitalisation errors per 100 words, the number of spelling mistakes per 100 words, and the total number of non-duplicated correctly spelled long words (i.e. with seven or more letters) as dependent variables was conducted. Although the trend of results shows that RD children made an average of two more punctuation and capitalisation errors per 100 words than non-RD children, the degree of difference between RD–non-RD children on this item did not reach significance ($F(1,268) = 2.90$, $p = 0.09$). There were significant differences between RD and non-RD students on the spelling measures; RD students made an average of 10 more spelling mistakes per 100 words ($F(1,268) = 42.37$, $p < 0.001$), and spelled fewer long words correctly ($F(1,268) = 25.56, p < 0.001$). As expected, based on previous results, there was no significant main effect for language group ($F(1,268) = 1.78$, ns), nor a significant language group by RD group interaction ($F(1,268) = 0.77$, ns).

In order to examine students' syntactic or grammatical skill when writing in context, a MANCOVA with the percentage of T-units found in badly constructed, simple, and compound or complex sentences as the dependent variables was conducted. RD children had significantly more badly constructed sentences ($F(1,268) = 26.32$, $p < 0.001$), significantly fewer simple sentences ($F(1,268) = 8.69, p < 0.01$), and significantly fewer compound and complex sentences ($F(1,268) = 24.09$, $p < 0.001$). Again, there was no significant main effect for language group ($F(1,268) = 0.34$, ns), nor a significant language group by RD group interaction ($F(1,268) = 0.09$, ns).

Finally, to examine students' higher level skills when writing in context, a MANCOVA was conducted with the quality of students' plot, sequencing, and prose in the story as the dependent variables. RD students had significantly more difficulty than non-RD students in creating a coherent plot ($F(1,268) = 27.32$, $p < 0.001$), a smooth, logical sequence of events ($F(1,268) = 30.19, p < 0.001$), and in using effective prose ($F(1,268) = 27.62$, $p < 0.001$). There was no significant main effect for language group

($F(1,268) = 0.48$, ns), nor a significant language group by RD group interaction ($F(1,268) = 0.42$, ns).

Discussion

The present study examined the writing skills of upper elementary school children, with a particular interest in the development of children who were ESL speakers as well as children with reading disabilities (RD). It was hypothesised that EL1 learners would outperform ESL learners on a task that evaluates the ability to write a story, given that writing represents one of the most complex aspects of literacy development (Hypothesis 1). However, contrary to expectations, the ESL learners did as well as the EL1 learners on the measure of written expression. This result is encouraging because it indicates that after approximately 4.5 years of receiving instruction in English and learning to read and write in English at a very young age, ESL learners are able to match their EL1 peers who attend the same schools and to develop their writing abilities well.

It was also expected that children with poor phonological awareness and word-level reading difficulties would also have difficulties writing. As assumed in Hypothesis 2, these children with RD performed more poorly on the test of written expression than children without RD, indicating that there may be similar underlying linguistic and cognitive deficits affecting the development of both reading *and* writing. Finally, it was hypothesised that being ESL speakers and therefore having poorer oral language proficiency would exacerbate difficulties that ESL-RD children experienced in the area of writing (Hypothesis 3). However this hypothesis was not supported; ESL learners with RD did not perform more poorly than EL1 learners with RD. There were no significant differences in the cognitive, linguistic or academic profiles of the two groups of children (ESL-RD and EL1-RD). It seems that the more powerful factor when considering risk for writing failure is RD status; language status (L1–L2) does not exacerbate difficulties resulting from underlying linguistic and cognitive processing deficits.

The writing skills and the general profile of ESL learners

The results of this study indicate that after several years of attending school in English, ESL learners are able to achieve age- and grade-appropriate writing abilities; the mean scores for ESL-non-RD students were all above the 50th percentile as based on standardised norms. Although normally developing ESL students continued to lag behind their EL1 counterparts in terms of their oral language proficiency (i.e. vocabulary growth), they performed equally well on all measures of writing abilities. This observation held on measures of lower level writing skills that require relatively little higher level planning and that place fewer demands on content generation and the coordination of multiple skills (i.e. spelling and syntax). Additionally, when generating a story, ESL learners matched EL1 learners in terms of the mechanics of writing such as punctuation, spelling, capitalisation, as well as on higher order aspects of writing such as generating appropriate sentence structures and monitoring for grammatical appropriateness and complexity. This was also the case when the quality of writing was judged on the basis of the overall organisation and flow of the compositions. In fact, the ESL students showed a slight advantage on certain aspects of the story writing that measured factors such as the generation of grammatically correct sentences. The reasons for a potential bilingual advantage in terms of writing ability are not clear, but may be related to extraneous factors that were not included in this study such as parental education, home literacy environment, and socio-economic status. Regardless, the ESL learners were able to master lower and higher level writing skills as well as to express themselves in writing both in and out of context as competently as their EL1 peers (see story samples in Figure 2.1a and b).

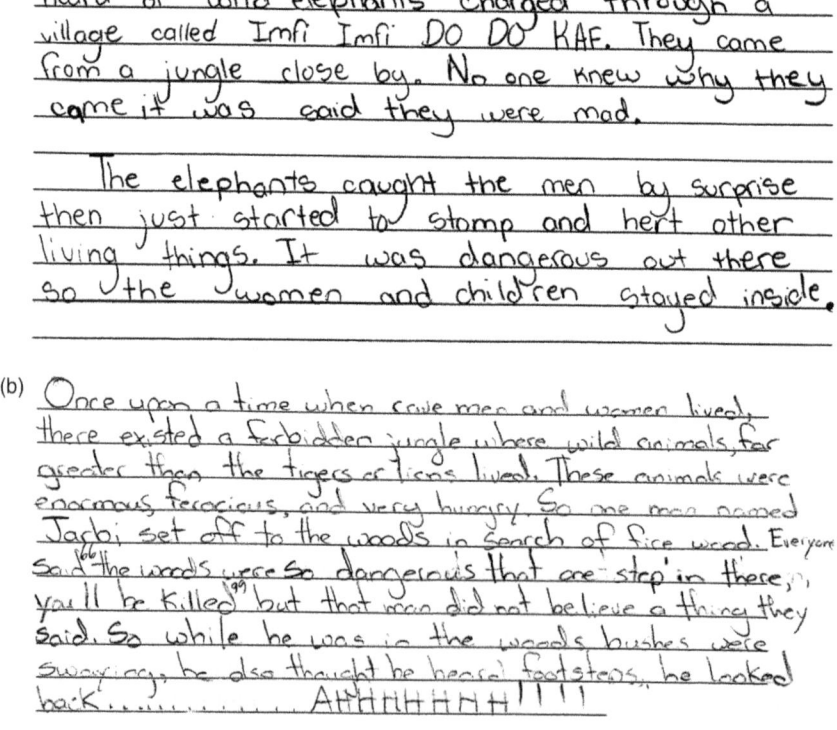

Figure 2.1 (a) Excerpt from a story written by an EL1-non-RD student (b) Excerpt from a story written by an ESL-non-RD student

Other researchers have found similar results when investigating the early development of reading skills of bilingual children without reading disabilities. For example, in another Canadian study, Lesaux and Siegel (2003) found that ESL learners who had attended school in English since kindergarten attained similar scores on a variety of reading measures to their EL1 peers. Findings such as these strengthen the notion that, with appropriate instruction, ESL learners are able to develop strong reading and writing skills in English after a few years of schooling in an English speaking environment and exposure to balanced literacy programmes.

In this study the profiles of ESL and EL1 students were similar not only on writing tasks, but also on other cognitive, linguistic and literacy components that underlie writing ability. In particular, there were no L1–L2 group differences in the phonological awareness, speed of rapid automatised naming or word-recognition skills of normally developing ESL and EL1 learners. As expected, L1 and L2 students scored similarly on a test of non-verbal intelligence.

The writing skills and the general profile of RD learners

This study confirms that RD children who have deficits in the areas of phonological awareness and word recognition have a significant amount of difficulty with writing as well. Although it has long been assumed that both reading and writing draw on similar cognitive and linguistic skills and hence impairments in certain key functions affect both processes, there has been little empirical data recorded on the matter.

In the current study RD children, regardless of their language status, had difficulty with most aspects of writing. To begin with, they struggled with spelling and written syntax in and out of context. In other words, they had difficulty with spelling and the monitoring of syntax when the task required them to generate a story-text, as well as when spelling and syntax were targeted in isolation and were not embedded in a more complex task. When writing a story, children with RD struggled with the mechanics of writing, including punctuation, capitalisation, spelling, with higher level aspects of writing such as sentence structure constraints and the generation and coordination of vocabulary, as well as with aspects of the overall structure of their compositions including the ability to compose stories with interesting plots and story lines.

Interestingly, differences between the RD and non-RD groups were due to the quality, rather than the quantity, of their story writing. In other words, although children with RD wrote as many words on average as children without RD, they made more than twice as many spelling errors, spelled far fewer multi-syllabic words correctly, and the vast majority of their sentences were either fragments, run-ons, or other badly constructed sentences. As can be seen in the excerpts of stories written by students with RD (see story samples in Figure 2.2a and b), poor spelling and

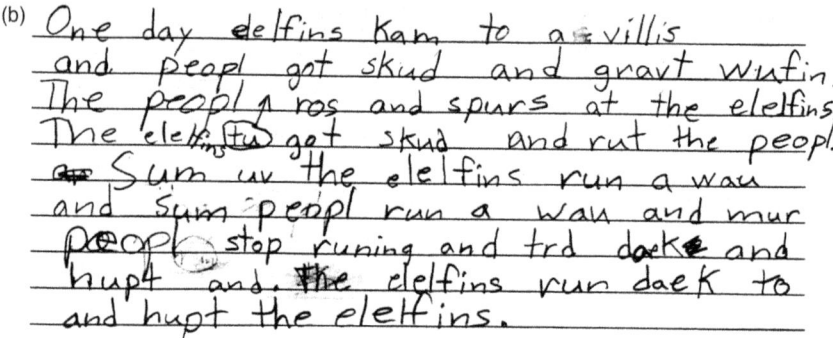

Figure 2.2 (a) Excerpt from a story written by an EL1-RD student; (b) excerpt from a story written by an ESL-RD student

sentence-structure was a significant and pervasive problem and contributed to the stories being difficult to comprehend. The finding that RD students spelled almost three times fewer multi-syllabic words correctly may be attributed to two complementary factors. First, this may be due to their profound spelling difficulties and the trouble they have in segmenting words into syllables and phonemes while monitoring for corresponding orthographic patterns. At the same time, this difficulty may also reflect poorer vocabulary knowledge, as it is possible that due to their reading difficulties they are less exposed to longer and more sophisticated words. These two explanations are not mutually exclusive in that the RD children may be unwilling to attempt to use multi-syllabic words in their writing because they are unsure of the spelling or meaning of those words. RD students also had difficulty producing well-written simple, compound and complex sentences, the quality of their prose was poor, and their stories lacked coherent plots and smooth sequencing of events. In summary,

RD children performed significantly below their non-RD peers on measures of lower and higher level writing skills both in and out of context.

There were no differences in non-verbal intelligence between RD and non-RD students, indicating that it is underlying cognitive-linguistic and literacy skills rather than non-verbal cognitive ability that distinguish RD students from their normally developing peers. RD students had impoverished receptive vocabularies and slower rapid automatised naming ability. The repercussions of having a smaller vocabulary was seen in their written productions as both EL1-RD and ESL-RD children wrote fewer long words and used more immature, vague words in their stories (see story samples in Figure 2.2a and b). By the time students have reached Grade 5, the majority of new vocabulary is acquired through reading. However, for RD students who read less than their normally developing peers, the rate at which their vocabulary grows is significantly slower, a phenomenon related to the Matthew effect by which the poor readers become poorer over time (Stanovich, 1986). Thus, the implications of having a small vocabulary include difficulties with both recognising words when reading text, as well as with producing words when attempting to write detailed, interesting, age-appropriate texts.

When analysing the task demands of producing text in writing, the reasons as to why writing is such an exceedingly complex task and furthermore why it is particularly demanding for RD children become clear (for a useful volume of writing research see MacArthur *et al.*, 2006). When writing, students must tap into their ability to process phonological and orthographic information quickly and accurately in order to spell words, access syntactic knowledge in order to sequence the words into grammatically correct sentences, attend to punctuation and capitalisation conventions, bear in mind the conventions of paragraph-structures in order to put sentences into a logical sequence, and organise paragraphs in such a way as to create a comprehensible plot in the larger body of text. Coordinating these various tasks simultaneously is very taxing on students' cognitive capacity, working- and short-term memory and executive functioning skills (Levine & Reed, 1999). Writing requires the ability to sustain attention, retain and manipulate a large amount of information, plan ahead and organise information. Students must coordinate subskills of writing such as spelling, punctuation and capitalisation while retaining the content and message that they wish to convey. Additionally, there are visual-motor integration demands involved in the physical aspects of handwriting that add further complexity to the process of writing. When considering the cognitive demands and the degree of coordination of systems that is required in order to produce text in conjunction with the knowledge that many of the subskills required for writing are not automatic for RD students and the fact that they process textual information more slowly, it becomes apparent why RD students have such severe difficulty in writing.

ESL-RD students cognitive, linguistic and academic profiles

The present research found that RD children who were L2 speakers of English were not at increased risk for writing failure when compared to their L1 peers with reading disabilities. There were no differences on any aspects of lower or higher level writing skills in or out of context between ESL-RD and EL1-RD students. In fact, there were no significant differences between ESL-RD and EL1-RD Grade 5 students in terms of other measures of their cognitive, linguistic or academic profiles. This pattern of results is comparable to those of other recent studies which found that poor decoders had very similar word-level reading skills whether English was their first or second language (da Fontoura & Siegel, 1995; Geva & Yaghoub-Zadeh, 2006; Geva et al., 2000; Lesaux & Siegel, 2003; Lipka et al., 2005; Wade-Woolley & Siegel, 1997).

Interestingly, there were no differences in receptive vocabulary, an aspect of oral language proficiency, between ESL-RD and EL1-RD students either. The finding that EL1-RD students had equally impoverished vocabularies as ESL-RD students is unexpected and striking given the fact that normally developing ESL students had significantly poorer vocabularies than their EL1 peers. The difference between L1 children with and without RD may be related to the previously discussed Matthew effect (Stanovich, 1986). The result is a cause for concern, however, future research with larger samples of EL1-RD students is necessary in order to confirm the trend of results and to elucidate the mechanisms underlying vocabulary growth in RD children. In sum, similar processing deficiencies in the areas of phonological processing and poor vocabulary typify the profiles of L1 and L2 students with RD in the present study, manifesting themselves in similar academic difficulties in the area of writing.

Conclusion and Implications

The present study supports the validity of using below average word identification and phonological awareness as a means of identifying both ESL and EL1 students who are at-risk for reading *and* writing disabilities. The method of selecting those students who were significantly below average in both of these areas yielded a percentage of the population that is predicted by both researchers and clinicians (approximately 10%; International Dyslexia Association, 2000). Furthermore, the proportions of first language groups in the RD sample were representative of those in the overall sample, indicating that this method of identification neither over-identifies nor under-identifies ESL students. This is a key finding, as the debate over whether too many or too few ESL students are identified as being learning disabled and receive appropriate special education support is one with a long and heated history (Limbos & Geva, 2001).

Diagnosing RD in L2 learners is complex and problematic (Geva & Wade-Woolley, 2004). There is currently no standardised battery of RD screening measures that is appropriate for L2 learners who come from diverse linguistic and educational backgrounds. Indeed, it may not be possible to develop such batteries. For this reason it is important to clarify the conditions under which L1–L2 differences are less likely to be a sufficient explanation for academic failure. Clearly, developing objective and timely ways to ascertain risk in L2 students is an important step in ensuring early and appropriate identification. The current results should give educators and professionals conducting psychoeducational assessments or informal screening more confidence in their ability to identify ESL students who also have learning disabilities because it suggests that similar methods and constructs should be used for both ESL and EL1 students. It appears that measuring the underlying cognitive-linguistic processes of phonological awareness and rapid automatised naming along with the academic indicators of poor word identification and spelling are equally good indicators of risk for reading and writing failure for ESL students as they are for EL1 students. Poor vocabulary may be an additional sign of risk for RD and writing difficulties for both L1 and L2 students at this age and would become evident in an assessment of children's oral language proficiency.

When examining writing more specifically, it seems that in the process of identifying a student with RD the 'red flags' in their writing include poor spelling, poor sentence structure, and an overall sense of disorganisation. The evidence of a poor vocabulary manifests itself in writing lacking words that add detail, spark interest and convey maturity. Of note is the finding that length of story writing was not an indicator of RD status in the current sample because RD students wrote the same amount of words as other students on average. Bearing in mind these 'red-flags', it follows that in terms of intervention, *regardless* of their language status as ESL or EL1, students identified as RD need intensive support to develop the basic building blocks of writing (e.g. spelling) and editing skills to check for grammatical and mechanical mistakes, as well as a template or strategy to provide structure to their writing (e.g. explicit instruction on how to construct coherent paragraphs) thereby targeting the development of both their lower and higher level writing skills (Berninger & Amtmann, 2003; Danoff *et al.*, 1993; James *et al.*, 2001). RD students also need specialised intervention targeting their underlying linguistic difficulties, that is, exercises to develop their phonological processing skills by improving their phonological awareness and the automaticity of letter-sound connections, as well as instruction to enlarge their lexicon thus giving them easier access to a greater range of vocabulary and enabling them to enrich their writing using more complex and sophisticated words.

The current study provides a snapshot of written expression abilities in elementary school aged children because all participants came from a single grade. Differences between ESL and EL1 students in terms of their writing ability may have existed in earlier grades but have dissipated by Grade 5. Investigating the development of ESL and RD students over time is necessary in order to learn more about early warning signs for risk of writing difficulties as well as the typical prognosis. It should be possible to identify RD students and provide appropriate and timely intervention for spelling, punctuation, capitalisation and grammar before children reach Grade 5. Other researchers should attempt to replicate the current means of identifying RD students, using different tasks that measure the same variables with different samples of children.

With appropriate and early instruction in English, ESL students are able to attain well-developed writing skills by the time they reach the later grades in elementary school. However, students with RD struggle with most aspects of writing and therefore require sensitive identification and intervention before they progress on to middle school. Both ESL and EL1 students with RD have similar profiles and as a result they can be assessed in similar ways, with particular emphasis on their phonological processing and word identification skills. By implication, intervention methods that are successful with EL1-RD students should also be implemented with ESL-RD students.

Acknowledgements

The research reported on in this chapter was partially funded by grants to the second author from the Social Sciences and Humanities Research Council of Canada, The Ontario Ministry of Education, and the University of Toronto.

References

August, D. and Shanahan, T. (eds) (2006) *Developing Literacy in Second-Language Learners: Report of the National Literacy Panel on Language-Minority Children and Youth*. Mahwah, NJ: Lawrence Erlbaum.

Bereiter, C. (1980) Development in writing. In L.W. Gregg and E.R. Steinberg (eds) *Cognitive Processes in Writing* (pp. 763–796). Hillsdale, NJ: Lawrence Erlbaum.

Berninger, V.W. and Amtmann, D. (2003) Preventing written expression disabilities through early and continuing assessment and intervention for handwriting and/or spelling problems: Research into practice. In H.L. Swanson, K.R. Harris and S. Graham (eds) *Handbook of Learning Disabilities* (pp. 345–363). New York: Guilford Press.

Berninger, V.W., Abbott, R.D., Abbott, S.P., Graham, S. and Richards, T. (2002) Writing and reading: Connections between language by hand and language by eye. *Journal of Learning Disabilities. Special Issue: The Language of Written Language* 35 (1), 39–56.

Chall, J.S. (1996) *Learning to Read: The Great Debate* (3rd edn). Fort Worth: Harcourt Brace College.
Cummins, J. (1991) Conversational and academic language proficiency in bilingual contexts. In J.H. Hulstijn and J.F. Matter (eds) *Reading in Two Languages* (pp. 75–89). Amsterdam: International Association of Applied Linguistics.
da Fontoura, H.A. and Siegel, L.S. (1995) Reading, syntactic, and working memory skills of bilingual Portuguese-English Canadian children. *Reading and Writing* 7 (1), 139–153.
Danoff, B., Harris, K.R. and Graham, S. (1993) Incorporating strategy instruction within the writing process in the regular classroom: Effects on the writing of students with and without learning disabilities. *Journal of Reading Behavior* 25 (3), 295–322.
Denckla, M.B. and Rudel, R.G. (1976) Rapid 'automatized' naming (R.A.N.): Dyslexia differentiated from other learning disabilities. *Neuropsychologia* 14 (4), 471–479.
Dunn, L. and Dunn, L. (1981) *Peabody Picture Vocabulary Test – Revised*. Circle Pines, MN: American Guidance Service.
Durgunoglu, A.Y., Nagy, W.E. and Hancin-Bhatt, B.J. (1993) Cross-language transfer of phonological awareness. *Journal of Educational Psychology* 85 (3), 453–465.
Geva, E. (2000) Issues in the assessment of reading disabilities in L2 children – beliefs and research evidence. *Dyslexia* 6, 13–28.
Geva, E. (2006) Second-language oral proficiency and second-language literacy. In D. August and T. Shanahan (eds) *Developing Literacy in Second-Language Learners: Report of the National Literacy Panel on Language-Minority Children and Youth* (pp. 123–139). Mahwah, NJ: Lawrence Erlbaum.
Geva, E., Wade-Woolley, L. and Shany, M. (1997) Development of reading efficiency in first and second language. *Scientific Studies of Reading* 1 (2), 119–144.
Geva, E. and Wade-Woolley, L. (2004) Issues in the assessment of reading disability in second language children. In I. Smythe, J. Everatt, and R. Salter (eds) *International Book of Dyslexia: A Cross-Language Comparison and Practice Guide* (pp. 195–206). Chichester, UK: John Wiley.
Geva, E., Yaghoub-Zadeh, Z. and Schuster, B. (2000) Understanding individual differences in word recognition skills of ESL children. *Annals of Dyslexia* 50, 123–154.
Geva, E. and Yaghoub-Zadeh, Z. (2006) Reading efficiency in native English-speaking and English-as-a-second-language children: The role of oral proficiency and underlying cognitive-linguistic processes. *Scientific Studies of Reading* 10 (1), 31–57.
Hammill, D.D. and Larsen, S.C. (1996) *Test of Written Language* (3rd edn). Austin, Texas: Pro Ed.
International Dyslexia Association. (2000) Dyslexia basics fact sheet. On WWW at http://www.interdys.org/servlet/compose?section_id=5&page_id=79. Accessed 17.07.06.
James, L.A., Abbott, M. and Greenwood, C.R. (2001) How Adam became a writer: Winning writing strategies for low-achieving students. *Teaching Exceptional Children* 33, 30–37.
Juel, C. (1988) Learning to read and write: A longitudinal study of 54 children from first through fourth grades. *Journal of Educational Psychology* 80 (4), 437–447.
Learning Disabilities Association of Ontario (2005) Definition of learning disabilities. On WWW at http://www.ldao.ca/resources/education/pei/assessment/index.php. Accessed 26.04.05.

Lesaux, N.K. and Siegel, L.S. (2003) The development of reading in children who speak English as a second language. *Developmental Psychology* 39 (6), 1005–1019.

Levine, M.D. and Reed, M. (1999) *Developmental Variation and Learning Disorders* (2nd edn). Cambridge, MA: Education Publishing Services.

Limbos, M. and Geva, E. (2001) Accuracy of teacher assessments of second-language students at risk for reading disability. *Journal of Learning Disabilities* 34 (2), 136–151.

Lipka, O., Siegel, L.S. and Vukovic, R. (2005) The literacy skills of English language learners in Canada. *Learning Disabilities Research & Practice* 20 (1), 39–49.

MacArthur, C.A., Graham, S. and Fitzgerald, J. (2006) *Handbook of Writing Research*. New York: Guilford Press.

Olson, D.R. (1977) From utterance to text: The bias of language in speech and writing. *Harvard Educational Review* 47 (3), 257–281.

Raven, J.C., Court, J.H. and Raven, J. (1983) *Manual for Raven's Progressive Matrices and Vocabulary Scales*. London: H.K. Lewis & Co.

Rosner, J. and Simon, D.P. (1971) The auditory analysis test: An initial report. *Journal of Learning Disabilities* 4 (7), 384–392.

Scardamalia, M. (1981) How children cope with the cognitive demands of writing. In C.H. Fredericksen and J.F. Dominic (eds) *Writing: The Nature, Development and Teaching of Written Communication. Vol. 2: Writing: Process, Development, and Communication* (pp. 81–104). Hillsdale, NJ: Lawrence Erlbaum.

Stanovich, K.E. (1986) Matthew effects in reading: Some consequences of individual differences in the acquisition of literacy. *Reading Research Quarterly* 21 (4), 360–406.

Statistics Canada Census (2001) On WWW at http://www12.statcan.ca/english/census01/home/index.cfm. Accessed 20.07.06.

Wade-Woolley, L. and Siegel, L.S. (1997) The spelling performance of ESL and native speakers of English as a function of reading skills. *Reading and Writing: An Interdisciplinary Journal* 9 (5–6), 387–406.

Weigle, S.C. (2002) *Assessing Writing*. Cambridge: Cambridge University Press.

Wilkinson, G.S. (1993) *Wide Range Achievement Test –Three*. Wilmington, DE: Wide Range.

Willows, D.M. (1998) Visual processes in learning disabilities. In B.Y.L. Wong (ed.) *Learning about Learning Disabilities* (pp. 163–193). San Diego, CA: Academic Press.

Chapter 3
Second Language Assessment in Dyslexia: Principles and Practice

TURID HELLAND

Introduction

Differentiating between typical and atypical second language (L2) development is a challenging task which confronts many foreign language educators. Assistance is often sparse, as the L2 teacher is usually an expert on typical L2 development but more rarely on special needs teaching, and, conversely, the special needs teacher is an expert on special needs teaching in the first language (L1) but seldom has expertise in L2 teaching. Even for teachers who happen to hold both kinds of expertise, differentiating between typical and atypical L2 development is difficult. In the present paper the term dyslexia is used to refer to a constitutional impairment affecting basic academic skills, in accordance with The British Dyslexia Association's (1998) definition. A cross-cultural study of dyslexia suggests that there is a universal neuro-cognitive basis for the condition, and that differences in reading performance among dyslexics of different countries should be seen in correspondence with different orthographies (Paulesu *et al.*, 2001).

The phoneme/grapheme conversion in a shallow orthography is a one-to-one relationship, or nearly so. In English, with its deep orthography, this relationship is far more complex, although regularities can be found. Identical phonemes may have several graphemic representations, such as, for instance, the initial phonemes in cake/quake/character/kill, the vowel in thought/taught and the final phonemes in witch/which. The complexity of grapheme/phoneme correspondence in English is, of course, a specific challenge for all students and teachers of English both as L1 and L2, but it is usually overcome by the typical learner through training. It is important for the L2 teacher to have knowledge of the learner's L1. If students have problems with phonology and grammatical structures in L1, there is a greater chance that they will have problems with L2 acquisition (Sparks *et al.*, 1989, 2006).

The relationship between oral and written language is a long-debated question. Some researchers hold that they are two separate systems, while others have argued that writing is not language, but rather a way of recording language by means of visible marks (Bloomfield, 1933). Different cultures have developed different writing systems. Most European orthographies use the Latin alphabet, but languages differ greatly as to phoneme/grapheme correspondence. Cultural and historic contingencies can explain why some orthographies are transparent/shallow, in the sense that the mapping of phonemes onto graphemes is close, while others are deep, meaning that the mapping of phonemes onto graphemes is distant. Italian orthography, for example, is categorised as transparent, while Norwegian is categorised as semi-transparent and English as deep orthography (Elley, 1992). The Italian alphabet comprises 21 letters and the mapping of print to sound is fairly regular (Job et al., 2006). The Norwegian alphabet has 29 letters comprising 40 phonemes, with approximately 35 graphemes (Hagtvet et al., 2006), whereas English has 26 letters comprising about 40 phonemes, but which are actually represented by more than 500 graphemes (Elley, 1992).

Reading and Spelling Difficulties of Dyslexic Norwegian L1 Learners

There is a consensus that dyslexia is a specific learning disability of constitutional origin, but definitions vary as to the inclusion of comorbidities. One definition says that dyslexia is characterised by difficulties with reading and spelling due to an unexpected deficit within the phonological system. Secondary effects are problems with reading comprehension, reduced reading experience, reduced vocabulary and reduced learning capacity (Lyon, 1995; Lyon et al., 2003). The British Dyslexia Association (1998) uses a broader definition, stating that dyslexia is a constitutional impairment with impaired reading, spelling and written language as its hallmarks, but that its basis is a complex neurological impairment also affecting oral language, numeracy, notational skills, motor functions and organisational skills. The latter definition corresponds to the experience of many clinicians.

Dyslexia in Norwegian subjects has been described in accordance with different traditions. In a functional analytic tradition, dyslexia is categorised into auditory, visual and mixed audio/visual subtypes (Gjessing, 1977, 1986). Symptoms of auditory dyslexia are impaired auditory discrimination and memory skills. At an early stage, similar phonemes are confused, and this later develops into problems with phonetic analyses and syntheses. Examples of this subtype of errors are vowel and consonant confusions (k/t, m/n, y/u, æ/ø, i/j), sequential errors (far/*fra, sol/*slo), and abbreviations (elektriker/*ektike, såpeboble/*soble), which can be observed both in reading and spelling. Reading is characterised by phonological errors, slow reading and omissions. Visual dyslexia is characterised by exaggerated phonetic spelling of irregular words, where silent letters are omitted (h in hjem/*jem, d in god/*go) or overcompensated for (blå/*blåd, jakt/*hjakt). Reading is typically slow, and whole-word reading is especially problematic. Audio/visual dyslexia is typically a mixture of the other two subtypes. Two dominant symptoms seen in all three subtypes are double consonants following a short vowel (dobbel/ *dobel), and compound words, typically written and pronounced as one word (politistasjon/*politi stasjon).

From a process analytic perspective, dyslexia is defined as an impairment within the phonological system, and the learners' word decoding strategy may be either phonological or orthographic. The errors described above can be categorised according to which strategy the subject uses (Høien & Lundberg, 1997). Since Norwegian has a fairly regular orthography, the child can learn to read and write through a phonemic approach. Qualitative analyses have shown that children who struggled to learn reading and spelling read accurately but slowly (Hagtvet et al., 2006). However, the symptoms of dyslexia vary not only with age and training, but also with patterns of neuro-cognitive assets and deficits associated with the condition.

Testing English as L2 in Norwegian Dyslexic Pupils

In the Norwegian school system English is a compulsory subject from Grade 1 onwards. It is tested in one of the main written exams at the end of Grade 10 and is also compulsory in vocational training. Norwegian students attained top scores on an international rating of English as L2, which may also be due to extensive use of English in the mass media (Alabau et al., 2002). Thus, the implicit learning of English as L2 outside school is fairly high in Norway. Usually, dyslexic pupils do not achieve the same high standards (DITT, 2001). For this reason, it would be desirable to have a basis for evaluating and creating intervention programmes in English as L2 for Norwegian dyslexic pupils. As no assessment tools were found for this purpose, either in Norwegian or in any of the other Scandinavian languages, our research group (Kaasa et al., 2004) designed a test to assess this group of children.

As described earlier, English and Norwegian have many linguistic features in common, but some typological traits within syntax, morphology and phonology diverge. However, the main challenge in the transition from L1 Norwegian to L2 English is in English orthography. This difficulty affects spelling, reading and text comprehension. As for the oral part of learning L2 English, linguistic competence in L1 will play a role, affecting sentence comprehension, syntax learning, inflections and conjugations, vocabulary and/or meta-knowledge in L2. In the next section of this chapter we first introduce the principles we wanted to apply in constructing a test battery of L2 in dyslexia. Then we describe the test instrument, and third, we briefly review the results from the tests of 20 dyslexic 12-year-olds and 20 matched controls using the same test battery. In the last section a new analysis of single word spelling will be presented.

When designing the test battery, we were guided by the following principles: an L2 test has to integrate knowledge of several essential components: contrasts between L1 and L2 with regard to language typology and orthography, typical symptoms of dyslexia in L1, typical symptoms of dyslexia in L2, essential components of a language test, and essential components of a dyslexia test. In addition, it has to demonstrate both assets and deficits in the skills being tested, and it has to meet standards of reliability and validity (Smythe & Everatt, 2000).

The first component concerns contrastive linguistics. In L1 learning, language typology does not affect how the child acquires the language. However, L2 learning depends on when the language is learned, how it is learned and how it differs from L1 (Pienemann *et al.*, 2005; Valdés & Figueroa, 1994). Thus, the target group has to be reflected in the test.

The second component is knowledge of typical symptoms of dyslexia (Beaton, 2004). A dyslexia diagnosis should be based on assessment at symptomatic, cognitive, biological, and environmental levels (Morton & Frith, 1995), preferably executed in L1. If this basis has been established, it suffices for an L2 test to be linguistic only and assesses problems at the symptomatic level. An L2 test should be divided into two main parts: one for oral communication, and one for written communication. As for oral communication, it should be acknowledged that L1 acquisition is mainly based on an auditory perceptual process which starts as soon as the child is exposed to language (Kuhl, 2004). The speech sounds are stored in perceptual categories typical for the first language, which can make it difficult to perceive different sound categories in another language (Kazanina *et al.*, 2006). Specific language impairment (SLI) is often seen in dyslexia (Bishop & Snowling, 2004), and since one of the typical symptoms of SLI is poor auditory language processing, L2 learning may be especially difficult for this group of students, and this difficulty manifests itself in L2 comprehension, vocabulary and speech processing problems.

The third component is expected symptoms of dyslexia in L2, where typical transfer problems are taken into account (Hua & Dodd, 2006). This means that both listening comprehension and oral production should be assessed. The written part should consist of writing, reading and translation of age-adjusted texts. As pointed out earlier, the discrepancy in English phoneme/grapheme correspondence is large and is especially challenging for dyslexics. Clinical experience indicates that dyslexics have a tendency to deal with this in two ways, either by spending more time, or by responding hurriedly, with no time for reflection. Thus, at least some of the tasks should be time-limited. Few mistakes, but slow processing (i.e. few words read or written per minute), or many mistakes and many words, can both be characteristic of a dyslexic profile.

The fourth component is that task demands have to be adjusted to the typical benchmarks of dyslexia. Since impaired working memory is a typical trait in dyslexia, the language tasks and instructions should be relatively short to avoid interference by memory problems. In addition, care needs to be taken over vocabulary selection. For instance, if comprehension and production of syntactic structure is the main object of a task, one should try to make sure that the vocabulary used in the task consists of high frequency words for the age group, and could be supported by pictures. Clinical experience shows that it is often hard to make dyslexic children talk or write in their L2. The tester should bear in mind that for children with language problems learning an L2 is often associated with feelings of failure (Piechurska-Kuciel, this volume; Ridsdale, 2004). They very often try to hide their shortcomings. Thus the testing should always start by making the child comfortable in the situation, perhaps with an introductory talk on L2 learning in dyslexia, the pupil's own experiences, and what help is offered. Then the test should start with less demanding tasks, gradually increasing in difficulty. This principle should be applied in the construction of each subtest and as well as in the sequence of the subtests. In most cases comprehension tasks should be a good starting point. As for spoken language, model sentences and elicitation tasks have proved to be efficient both in making the pupils talk and in testing specific linguistic areas (Thornton, 1996). To assess oral production skills and functional language use, questions about daily life and picture-based story telling can be used. In addition, the test should not be exhausting; it should have face validity, and should be balanced, meaning that it is as important to assess what the subjects have mastered as what they have not mastered.

The fifth component concerns age-related norms of oral and literacy skills. Typically, a reading battery in L1 dyslexia assessment consists of word reading (non-words and real words), scored for time and errors, and text reading (oral and silent) with comprehension check, while a writing battery consists of single word dictation, sentence dictation and free writing/story writing (Carlsten, 1982; Geva & Ndlovu, this volume; Klinkenberg & Skaar, 2001). These elements should also feature in an L2 test. If possible, reading and spelling tests should be comparable, as a divergence between these skills is a good indicator of the L2 literacy competence.

The sixth component is that the test should provide valid indicators of the subject's 'zone of proximal development', or the zone between an individual's independent and guided performance (Vygotsky, 1962). One way of doing this is to compare related issues such as comprehension scores and production scores, or spelling scores and reading scores.

The English 2 Dyslexia Test

With these principles in mind, our research group devised a pen and paper-based English L2 test for Norwegian dyslexic pupils in Grades 6 and 7. The test has subsequently been developed into a computer-based version (Kaasa et al., 2004). These grades were chosen because L2 English is predominantly taught only as an oral subject, with no written exams, until Grade 8. From then on it is defined as a written subject with formal exams. One of our main intentions was that the nature of L2 problems should be identified as early as possible, and we found that Grades 6 and 7 represent a crossroads where the pupils already have some L2 competence, but where their next step will be into far more formal training emphasising written work. The test was to form a basis for intervention programmes at the point where L2 English becomes a far more complex subject in itself with a higher academic impact factor than earlier.

The 'English 2 Dyslexia Test' is divided into two parts: oral and written. Each part has three subtests. Its main scoring principles are quantitative, resulting in a graphic profile of the test results. The more recent computer-based version offers and encourages a qualitative evaluation procedure for some of the subtests.

The first subtest is *Comprehension*, which is made up of fifteen sentences with five different syntactic structures: declarative, interrogative, negative, inversion and passive, with three sentences of each category in random order. The participant is asked to point to a picture corresponding to the spoken sentence. The scoring is one point for each correct sentence, with a maximum of 15 points. The test is scored automatically by the computer program.

The second oral subtest is *Model sentences*, and it requires sentence comprehension and production. The participant is presented with a picture accompanied by a spoken sentence. Then a picture analogous to the first one is presented, and the students are asked to produce an analogous sentence to the one they just heard. Again, there are fifteen sentences, five of each syntactic structure appearing three times, as in the comprehension task. The responses are tape-recorded and each correct response receives one point, again giving a maximum score of 15 points, evaluated by the test leader. This simple scoring offers the opportunity to compare comprehension to production. In addition, the tester is encouraged to score the responses by categories of errors: syntactic, morphological, and phonological.

The third oral subtest is *Oral production and functional language use*. The main goal of this test is to make the participant use his or her own words and way of speaking. Therefore, the performance of the participant has to be evaluated by the tester in a subjective way. First, the students participate in a dialogue based on eight sentences, where they are asked to talk about issues in daily life, such as age, school and hobbies. The dialogue is tape-recorded, and each response-utterance is scored as communicative/not communicative, as evaluated by the tester. There is also a time score, allowing for a calculation of words per minute. Second, the participants are asked to study a picture story made up of four pictures for half a minute and then to retell the story. The story is tape-recorded, and the response is evaluated picture by picture by the tester as communicative/not communicative. The task is also timed, allowing for a calculation of words per minute.

The written part consists of *single word dictation, sentence reading* and *sentence translation*. The core of all three tests is a set of 22 words chosen according to three criteria: they are high-frequency, they have appeared many times in the pupils' textbooks, and they comprise essential differences between Norwegian and English orthography. The same 22 words appear in all three tasks in sentences, and only these words are to be scored. Thus performance in spelling, reading and translation can be compared. The maximum score is 22 points for each test, scored as correct/incorrect for the spelling and translation tests, and as communicative/not communicative for the reading test. Finally, as an extra writing test, the more able pupils may be asked to write a story using the pictures from the *Oral production and functional language use* subtest.

A preliminary version of the test battery described above was first tried out in a small-scale pilot study by two experienced speech therapists. This led to the exclusion of some redundant test items, and resulted in 15 items for each of the two first oral tests, and 22 items for each of the literacy tests. The revised version was then administered to 40 pupils. Participants were 20 dyslexic pupils and 20 controls, half of them from Grade 6 and half from Grade 7 matched on age and gender. They came from six different state schools from around the city of Bergen and participated voluntarily with the consent of parents and schools. The project was approved in advance by the Norwegian Social Science Data Service and the National Committees for Regional Research Ethics in Norway. According to school records, none of the participants had any syndromes, gross neurological deficits or sight or hearing loss, or were mentally retarded. The dyslexic participants had all been previously diagnosed as dyslexic by professionals, and received adapted teaching, mainly in class. The control participants had not received any special needs education.

Results from the testing have been published elsewhere (Helland & Kaasa, 2005; Kaasa, 2001) and will only be reported briefly here. All subtests discriminated significantly between the control group and the dyslexia group. Split-half reliability test of both the verbal and the written tasks were between 0.80 and 0.90.

If we are to design good intervention programmes, we need to see whether there is variation within the dyslexia group. Since we had earlier found that language comprehension differentiates between dyslexics in L1 (Helland, 2002), and since a significant correlation was seen between the L1 and L2 comprehension scores ($r = 0.55$), we used the median score of the L2 comprehension subtest in the dyslexia group to split the group in two, with 10 dyslexic participants in each group.

These were very small groups, and the statistical analyses should therefore be seen as highly tentative. The subgroups were labelled C+ and C−: the C stands for 'L2 comprehension', the + (plus) for 'at or above the median score' and the − (minus) for 'below the median score'. As the one-way analyses of variance and the subsequent Tukey HSD (Honestly Significant Differences) t-tests revealed, differences between the control group and the C− subgroup were significant across all measures. There were no significant differences between the control group and the C+ subgroup on the oral subtests, but the differences were significant on the three literacy subtests (spelling, reading and translation). The two dyslexia subgroups differed significantly on all subtests except for the spelling subtest, which was generally very low in both dyslexia subgroups. This is shown in Figure 3.1. The discrepancy between spelling, on the one hand, and reading and translation on the other, was largest in the C+ subgroup.

In sum the 'English 2 Dyslexia Test' proved able to differentiate between dyslexic and non-dyslexic pupils, and it differentiated between subtypes of dyslexia. It assessed oral and written skills by traditional principles of language and dyslexia assessment, and by principles of contrastive grammar. This indicated that the test was reliable and valid. Both the pupils and the testers seemed to like the test. One of the weakest performers put it this way after the testing session: 'I had no idea that I knew so much English!', which was an indication that the test had met one of its main goals, namely to make each subject show what they had really mastered. Our general impression was that pupils who otherwise experienced failure in L2 classes were given an opportunity to show some hidden sides of their L2 competence, in spite of low scores. In the Norwegian school system, where an L2 test specifically designed for dyslexics was non-existent before, this test seemed to fill a gap.

In compensatory teaching of dyslexic learners, the individual profiles shown in the test scores can be used to define the pupils' nearest zone of proximal development. As in the 'English 2 Dyslexia Test' orthography emerged as the most difficult part of the test, we wanted to find out more about Norwegian pupils' typical L2 English spelling skills at the point when they have been taught English for some time, without any demands on written performance, but are at the starting point of having to write L2 English as part of their school curriculum. This motivated us to continue

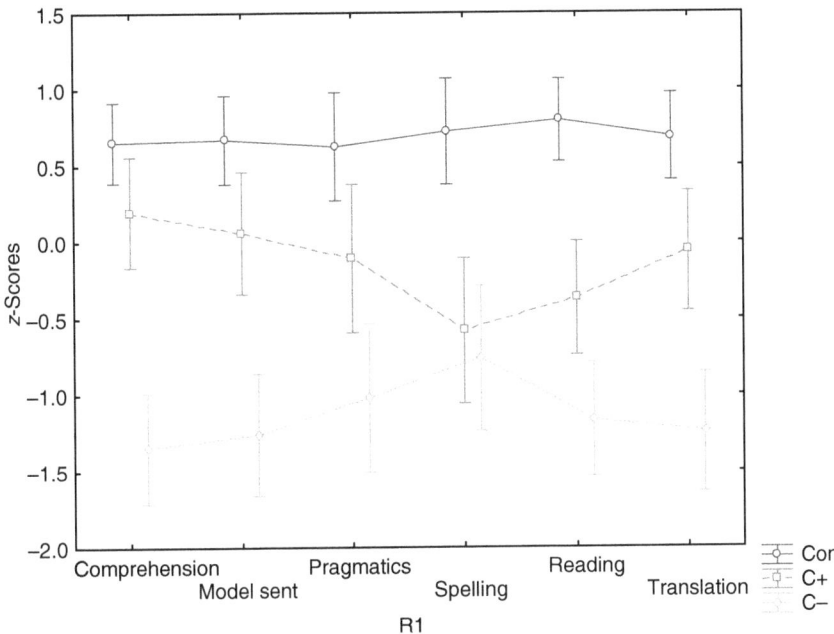

Figure 3.1 z-Scores from the English 2 Dyslexia Test (Helland & Kaasa, 2005). Con: control group; C+: dyslexia subgroup with no comprehension problems; C−: dyslexia subgroup with comprehension problems

our research with a deeper analysis of our participants' spelling performance, which is the topic of the next part of the paper.

Research Aims and Rationale

In the 'English 2 Dyslexia Test' described above, the three subtests of literacy, spelling, reading and translation are easily comparable since the same 22 words are used in all three tasks. But only the reading and the translation tasks showed significant differences between the two dyslexia subgroups, while both subgroups scored significantly lower on the spelling subtest (Helland & Kaasa, 2005). This is shown in Figure 3.2.

However, by simply dichotomising right/wrong spelling, as we did in our first study, some additional information distinguishing between the two dyslexia subgroups might have been overlooked. Performing a closer analysis of dyslexic Norwegians' L2 English spelling can be difficult, because at first glance their spelling may seem chaotic and unsystematic. We therefore selected four aspects for our new analyses: (1) how the

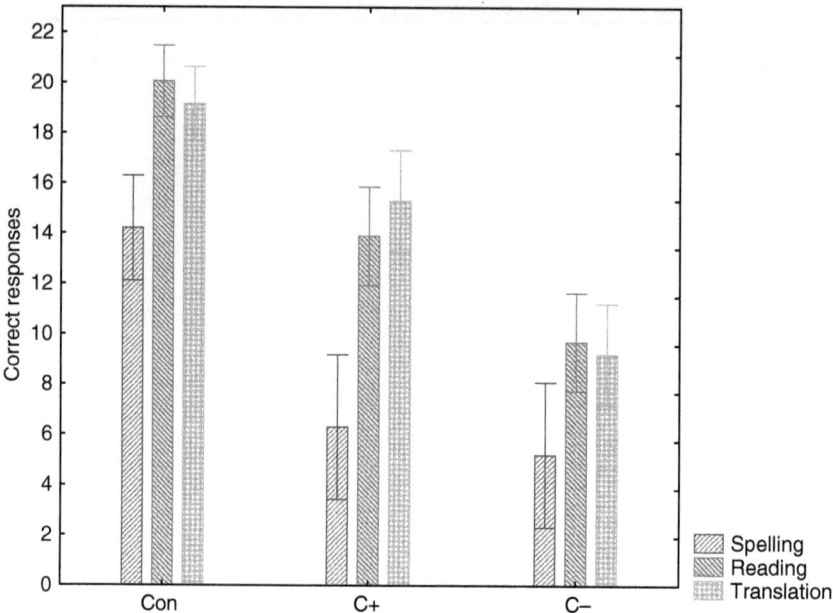

Figure 3.2 Spelling, reading and translation scores of 22 high-frequency English words (abbreviations as in Fig. 3.1)

spelling scores corresponded with the reading and translation scores; (2) how the richness of graphemes in English was dealt with; (3) what possible transfer of Norwegian orthography into English spelling could be observed; and (4) how unfamiliar phonemes were spelled. The richness of English graphemes was described earlier in this chapter. As for transfer from Norwegian orthographic conventions to English, the three extra letters of the Norwegian alphabet, æ, ø and å, may be indicators of transfer, if used. Their phonemes are represented in English: 'æ' corresponds approximately to /æ/ as in *man*, 'ø' approximately to /ɜ/ as in *bird*, and 'å' approximately to /ɔ/ as in *bought* or /ʌ/ as in *such*. As for unfamiliar phonemes, English has some phonemes that Norwegian does not possess, spelled as 'th' (/ð/ as in *this* and /θ/ as in *think*), and 'w' (/w/ as in *water*). These are high-frequency phonemes in English but are often mispronounced by Norwegian learners of English. Also, 'v' (/v/, as in *love*) is often misspelled as 'w' and mispronounced as /w/, probably due to an overgeneralisation. There are other phonemes, too, that differ, but to a minor degree, as they may be found in Norwegian dialects. It was hypothesised that more errors in these selected categories (graphemes, Norwegian letters, unfamiliar phonemes, overgeneralisation) would be seen in the

Dyslexia group compared to the Control group, and that more errors would be seen in the C− subgroup compared to the C+ subgroup.

Method

Instruments

As mentioned earlier, the 22 words selected for the dictation, reading and translation tasks were identical but presented in different sentences in the three tasks. Each word, with one exception (*beautiful*), was a one-syllable word but consisted of three graphemes or more. None of the words were transparent according to Norwegian orthographic conventions, but they were all high-frequency and were selected from ordinary Norwegian textbooks of English. Words can be divided into two basic classes: (1) lexical or open class words, meaning they can be inflected; and (2) function or closed class words, meaning they have no or only minor inflections (Hasselgård et al., 1998; van Gelderen, 2005). These are not sharply distinct categories but rather form a continuum. Typically, lexical words carry intonational stress, while function words are generally unstressed. This means that lexical words are more easily recognised and learned than function words. Categorised at the word level there were 13 content words and nine function words (see Table 3.1) in the spelling subtest.

For single word analyses each word was split into its graphemes, as can be seen in Table 3.1. Thus the word *should* (three graphemes, sh-ou-ld; six letters) was expected to be more difficult than the word *cat* (three graphemes, c-a-t, three letters). One of the words (*boy*), had an /ɔ/-phoneme (Norwegian equivalent spelling 'å'), three words (*girl, much, just*) had an /3/-phoneme or an /ʌ/-phoneme (Norwegian equivalent spelling 'ø'), and the vowel in three words (*cat, many, than*) will frequently be perceived as an /æ/-phoneme by Norwegians (Norwegian equivalent spelling 'æ'). The 'th' grapheme is represented in three words (*mouth, then, than*), and the 'w' in two words (*when* and *what*), with an extra challenge in the word *very*, where overgeneralisation from English may lead to overuse of the 'w' ('wery').

Analyses

A general remark about the data analyses in this study is that the samples, and especially the subsamples, were very small. Therefore, the analyses, the results and the discussion should be considered as highly tentative.

First, the spelling, reading and translation scores were correlated, and then analysed in a repeated measures ANOVA with a Group (3: Control, C+, C−) by literacy scores (3: spelling, reading, translation) design. Significant effects were followed up by a Tukey HSD subtest.

Table 3.1 The spelling test. Words, word level and graphemes

Dictated words	Word level	Graphemes								Max score
		1	2	3	4	5	6	7	8	
(1) boy	Content word	b	oy							2
(2) girl	Content word	g	i	rl						3
(3) school	Content word	s	ch	oo	l					4
(4) child	Content word	ch	i	l	d					4
(5) cat	Content word	c	a	t						3
(6) name	Content word	n	a	m(e)						3
(7) very	Function word	v	e	r	y					4
(8) should	Function word	sh	ou	ld						3
(9) nose	Content word	n	o	s(e)						3
(10) mouth	Content word	m	ou	th						3
(11) much	Function word	m	u	ch						3
(12) when	Function word	wh	e	n						3
(13) could	Function word	c	ou	ld						3
(14) just	Function word	j	u	s	t					4
(15) beautiful	Content word	b	e	au	t	i	f	u	l	8
(16) many	Content word	m	a	n	y					4
(17) then	Function word	th	e	n						3
(18) what	Function word	wh	a	t						3
(19) house	Content word	h	ou	S(e)						3
(20) little	Content word	l	i	tt	l					4
(21) than	Function word	th	a	n						3
(22) high	Content word	h	igh							2
Total										75

Each word was given a score corresponding to its total number of graphemes. This is shown in Table 3.1. One point was given for each grapheme that was correctly spelled. Thus, for example, *school* was split into four graphemes, s-ch-oo-l, giving a maximum score of 4 points. If the subject spelled the word 's-k-u-l' (which is typically in line with the shallow Norwegian orthography), only two graphemes were correct, yielding 2 points. The highest attainable total score on the 22 words was 75 points. The scores for each word and their total scores were analysed by one-way ANOVA, using the Control group and the two Dyslexia subgroups C+ and C− as independent variables and each single word and the total score as dependent variables. Significant differences were followed up by a Tukey HSD test.

The frequencies of the Norwegian letters 'æ', 'ø' and 'å', and errors of the 'th'-, 'w'-graphemes and 'v' (in 'very') were registered and analysed in four 2 × 2 Chi-square tests with a Group number by Frequency of error design. Groups were identified as Control by Dyslexia, and subgroup C+ by subgroup C−. Errors were numbers of Norwegian letters on the one hand, and wrong spelling of unfamiliar phonemes on the other.

To be able to compare the scores of each word and to also have an overview of which words were especially easy or especially hard to spell, the 'correctness' of each response was expressed as a percentage, on the basis of the number of graphemes in the target word. Thus 'skul' for *school*, with two out of four graphemes correct, is 50% correct, while 'kuld' for *could* is 33.33% correct.

Results

The scores on the spelling subtest correlated significantly with the reading and translation subtests ($r = 0.804$, $p < 0.001$ and $r = 0.790$, $p < 0.001$ respectively). The repeated measures ANOVA showed significant effects of Group: $F(2,36) = 35.848$, $p < 0.001$, of literacy scores: $F(2,72) = 76.031$, $p < 0.001$, and of interaction: $F(4,37) = 3.469$, $p = 0.01$. The post-hoc Tukey HSD test showed that the effect of Group was due to higher scores in Control versus C+ (<0.001) and C− (<0.001), and to C+ versus C− ($p = 0.02$); the effect of Literacy scores was lower scores in spelling versus reading and translation ($p < 0.001$ for both); and the effect of interaction was mainly due to the spelling scores in C+ being significantly lower than all scores in Control ($p < 0.01$), and to C− having significantly lower spelling scores than all other scores ($p < 0.01$) except the spelling scores in C+.

The one-way ANOVA for each of the 22 words and the total score are shown in Table 3.2. As can be seen, there were significant between-group differences in the scores of 16 words. Of these 16 words, the post-hoc test showed that the difference was between the Control group on the one hand and the two subgroups on the other hand, in seven words (*nose, mouth, much, could, beautiful, house, than*; four content words, three function words) and in the total score. An additional difference was seen between the Control group and the C− subgroup (with no difference between the

Table 3.2 The spelling test. The control group and the subgroups (C+, C−)

Words (max score)	Control	SD	C+	SD	C−	SD	F(df = 37)	Post hoc
boy (2)	2.00	0.00	1.80	0.42	1.80	0.42	2.31	ns
girl (3)	2.95	0.22	2.80	0.42	2.40	0.84	4.18*	Con>C−**
school (4)	3.50	0.83	2.60	1.17	2.20	1.14	6.45**	Con>C−**
child (4)	3.15	1.18	2.60	1.07	2.40	1.17	1.65	ns
cat (3)	2.95	0.22	2.80	0.42	2.40	0.97	3.42	Con>C−*
name (3)	2.90	0.45	2.50	0.53	2.10	0.74	7.26**	Con>C−***
very (4)	3.75	0.44	3.50	0.53	2.70	0.82	11.12**	Con>C−*** C+>C−**
should (3)	1.43	1.12	0.70	0.63	0.65	0.82	3.13	ns
nose (3)	2.90	0.31	2.20	0.63	2.20	0.63	10.07**	Con>C+** Con>C−**
mouth (3)	2.00	0.86	1.00	0.00	1.00	0.47	11.56**	Con>C+*** Con>C−***
much (3)	1.75	0.79	1.10	0.57	1.00	0.00	6.25**	Con>C+** Con>C−**
when (3)	2.60	0.75	2.20	0.79	2.10	0.74	1.80	ns
could (3)	1.58	0.91	0.75	0.54	0.75	0.68	5.62**	Con>C+** Con>C−**
just (4)	2.60	1.54	2.50	0.71	1.70	1.34	1.61	ns
beautiful (8)	6.15	1.57	4.90	0.74	4.60	0.97	6.19**	Con>C+** Con>C−**
many (4)	3.75	0.44	3.40	0.70	2.50	1.18	9.36**	Con>C−*** C+>C−**
then (3)	2.80	0.41	2.40	0.70	2.10	0.57	6.12**	Con>C−***
what (3)	2.45	0.69	2.20	0.79	1.90	0.88	1.76	ns
house (3)	2.90	0.31	2.40	0.70	2.40	0.52	5.37**	Con>C+** Con>C−**
little (4)	3.60	0.82	2.60	0.52	3.00	0.82	6.28**	Con>C+***
than (3)	2.15	0.75	1.20	0.63	1.20	0.63	9.40**	Con>C+*** Con>C−***
high (2)	1.55	0.51	1.10	0.32	0.90	0.57	6.81**	Con>C−***
sum (75)	61.40	8.60	49.25	6.58	44.00	10.98	14.91**	Con>C+*** Con>C−***

*$p < 0.05$. **$p < 0.01$. ***$p < 0.001$.

Control group and the C+ subgroup) in six words (*girl, school, cat, name, then, high*; five content words, one function word), and a difference between all groups (Control >C+>C−) was seen in two words (*very, many*; one content word, one function word). One word (*little*; content word) showed a significantly lower score in C+ versus Control. The six words which did not reach significance were *boy, child, when, just, what* (two content words, three function words) with *should* (function word) at the borderline.

The frequencies of use of the Norwegian letters 'æ', 'ø', 'æ' and the misspellings of the graphemes 'th', 'w' and 'v' are shown in Table 3.3. As can be seen, none of the Norwegian letters 'æ', 'ø', 'æ' were used in the Control group, while they were used six times in the Dyslexia group. For instance, *girl* was spelled 'gøl' by four subjects in the C− subgroup, and only once in the C+ subgroup. Both the Control group and the Dyslexia group made many errors involving 'th' and 'w', but twice as many 'th'-mistakes and three times as many 'w' mistakes were seen in the Dyslexia group compared to the Control group. The 'th'- and 'v'-errors were evenly distributed among the two dyslexia subgroups, while the 'w'-errors in the C+ subgroup were comparable to the 'w' errors in the Control group, and twice as many 'w'-errors were seen in the C− subgroup as in the C+ subgroup. The 'th' grapheme was often misspelled as 't', 'd', or 'w'. The error frequencies are shown in Table 3.3. The Chi square test showed a significant difference between the Control group and the Dyslexia group as regards the use of Norwegian letters and unfamiliar graphemes ($\chi^2 = 5.31$, $p = 0.02$ and $\chi^2 = 5.14$, $p = 0.02$, respectively), with no significant difference between the subgroups.

Figure 3.3 shows the percentage of correct morphemes in each of the words and the sum score. As can be seen, the groups exhibit a similar pattern,

Table 3.3 Norwegian letters and unfamiliar phonemes

Norwegian letters	Control n = 20	Dyslexia n = 20	Dyslexia subgroup C+ n = 10	Dyslexia subgroup C− n = 10
æ	0	0	0	0
ø	0	5	1	4
å	0	1	0	1
Unfamiliar phonemes				
th (/ð//θ/)	20	41	22	19
w (/w/)	7	22	7	15
v (in 'very')	5	4	2	2

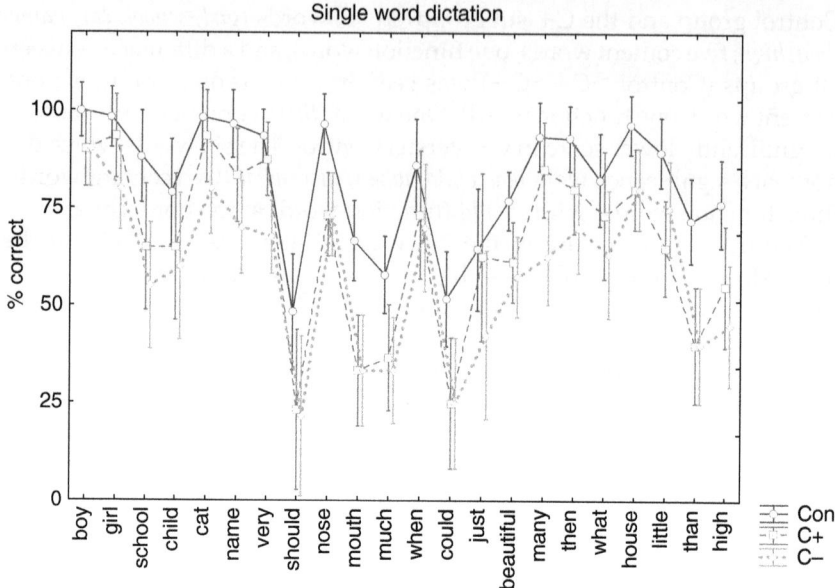

Figure 3.3 Scores for each word in the spelling test (abbreviations as in Fig. 3.1)

where *should, mouth, much, could, than* (one content word, four function words) seem to be particularly difficult to spell for the Dyslexia group.

Discussion

In this study we assessed dyslexic Norwegian pupils' L2 English spelling skills at the point when they were starting formal L2 spelling training in school, after four to five years of informal, predominantly oral training. To do this, we compared their spelling skills to their skills in reading and translation, analysed how they handled the complexity of grapheme/morphemes correspondence in English, looked for possible transfer of Norwegian letters not found in the English alphabet and investigated how unfamiliar phonemes were dealt with, and, finally, made a comparison across word scores to see which words were easier and which were more difficult. We hypothesised that the Control group as a whole would score significantly higher than the Dyslexia group, but that some variation would be seen within the Dyslexia group according to their comprehension scores. As a whole, the analyses confirmed these hypotheses and revealed subgroup differences in spelling that were not seen in the earlier analyses.

The Control group had an overall literacy score that was significantly higher than the scores of the two dyslexia subgroups. However, the scores on the spelling subtest were significantly lower than reading and translation scores. The group scored 61.5 points out of a maximum of 75 on the spelling subtest, which was significantly higher than the scores of the two dyslexia subgroups. From Figure 3.2 one can see that particularly difficult words were *should, much, could*, which have more graphemes than phonemes and are all function words. None of the three Norwegian letters were used in this group, but there were some problems with the unfamiliar grapheme 'th'. The 'w' grapheme and 'v' in *very* seemed to cause minor problems.

The C+ subgroup showed the same within-group pattern of literacy as the Control group, with significantly lower scores on the spelling subtest compared with the reading and translation subtests. As for the word by grapheme analyses, the sum score was 49.25 out of the possible 75 points on the spelling task. The errors were miscellaneous, but *should, mouth, much, could* and *than* were particularly difficult. This subgroup scored significantly lower than the Control group on seven of the 22 words (*nose, mouth, much, could, beautiful, house, than*; four content words, three function words). There was almost no use of Norwegian letters, but there were twice as many errors involving the unfamiliar grapheme 'th' compared to the Control group, with no difference as to the 'w' grapheme and to the 'v' in *very*. Figure 3.3 shows that this subgroup had a percent score in between the two other groups.

The C− subgroup also showed a within-group pattern similar to the other two groups, with significantly lower results on the spelling subtest compared with the other two subtests. The reading and translation scores in this group were also significantly lower than in the Control group. On the word by grapheme analyses, the sum score was of 44 out of the possible 75 points. Again, the errors were miscellaneous, with low scores on approximately the same words as the C+ subgroup, but with the word *high* added to the list. Well-known nouns (*girl, school, cat, name*, all content words) had significantly more errors in this group compared to the other two groups. This subgroup also scored significantly lower than the Control group on sixteen of the 22 words and lower than the C+ subgroup on two words (*very, many*; function words). There was some use of Norwegian letters, there were twice as many errors with the unfamiliar grapheme 'th' compared to the Control group, but similar to the C+ subgroup, and twice as many errors involving the grapheme 'w' and the 'v' in *very* compared to both the Control group and the C+ subgroup. Figure 3.3 shows that this subgroup had the lowest scores across all words compared to the other two groups.

In all, the groups differed, and there was a gradual differentiation, with the Control group having fewest errors, the C+ subgroup in the middle, and the C− achieving the lowest scores. As mentioned earlier, the gap between the spelling scores and the reading and translation scores can be an indicator of where the pupils' nearest zone of proximal development may lie. The most important inference to be drawn from the literacy patterns of the three groups is that they understand more written words than they can spell correctly, and this discrepancy may be a marker for potential learning. The C+ subgroup did as well as the Control group in reading and translation performance, indicating that they can master many of the same tasks in class. The overall low literacy scores in the C− subgroup, however, indicate that this subgroup will have difficulty in following regular class teaching.

Content words are easier than function words, and the error scores increased in accordance with the word level. The errors seen in the Control group were mainly at the function word level, while there were several more errors at the content word level in the C+ and C− subgroups, with most errors in the latter subgroup. If the two dyslexia subgroups are to follow the same developmental spelling pattern as the Control group, central content words should be overlearned before the pupils focus on function words.

The spelling of the phonemes /θ/ and /ð/ seemed to be difficult for both the Control group and the Dyslexia group. Interestingly, it is reported that these phonemes are among the last phonemes children with L1 English learn (Dodd *et al.*, 2006), which may indicate a more universal problem. Also, it is reported that the /w/ is one of the phonemes children with L1 English learn to say very early (Dodd *et al.*, 2006). To convert this phoneme into the grapheme 'w' did not seem particularly difficult for the Control group or the C+ subgroup, but was very problematic for the C− subgroup. One may speculate that this indicates a profound phonological impairment in C−, pointing to the necessity of more specific training on L2 English phonemes for this subgroup in comparison with the other two groups.

The three words *boy, girl* and *cat* that gained the highest scores in the Dyslexia group, have a closer grapheme/phoneme correspondence than many of the other words. They have a high content value, not only because they are content words, but also because they are among the first English words a Norwegian child learns. The importance of overlearning in dyslexia has been described by others (Schneider & Crombie, 2003) and may explain why these three words seemed particularly easy to spell. Also, the close grapheme/phoneme correspondence is in line with Norwegian orthographic conventions, which should facilitate learning. This may also explain why the longest word in the spelling task, *beautiful*, was not among the lowest scored words: it contains only two grapheme pitfalls, namely the second and third graphemes (e and a), and the other six graphemes are single letters with a high degree of correspondence to their phonemes.

Thus, analysing the spelling subtest this way revealed some of the expected differences between the two dyslexia subgroups. Since phonological processing impairment is a core problem in dyslexia, any analysis of spelling performance in L2 in dyslexia is especially difficult. There is a strong chance that L2 phonemes, familiar and unfamiliar, may not be perceived correctly, with a multitude of errors as possible outcomes. Alternatively, to make things even more complicated, there will always be uncertainty connected to the written graphemes of the dyslexic speller, as it is hard to know if they were what s/he intended to write, or not. This is especially important to reflect upon, since the subgroup with low scores on L2 comprehension may have an underlying specific language impairment as they had low scores on L1 comprehension as well. According to recent research on bilingualism, transfer from one language to another is highly sensitive to the developmental state of the learners' language (Pieneman et al., 2005). Therefore it is important for the L2 educator to have some knowledge of the pupil's history of language development.

The spelling problems in both dyslexic subgroups in this study were prominent and overlapping. All in all, this indicates how difficult the spelling of L2 English is for Norwegian dyslexic pupils, irrespective of their level of oral language comprehension and production. This suggests a need for a tolerant attitude towards spelling mistakes in L2 English in dyslexia. The primary focus should rather be on functional language use and on other aspects of written language than spelling. For instance, morphology, syntax and semantics can be evaluated separately from orthography. Even though school curricula emphasise both oral and written L2 competence, evaluation and grading are often based on written products, among other things because written products are easier to evaluate on a comparative or normative basis, and spelling is easier to evaluate than vocabulary, syntax and semantics. This is disadvantageous to dyslexic students, as they may easily be graded as very low achievers if no other L2 linguistic areas are evaluated. In the present study, reading and comprehension (as assessed both by oral and written tasks) proved easier than spelling for both dyslexic groups, as did functional skills for the C+ subgroup. This subgroup should function well in regular L2 activities in class, with some extra spelling support. The C− subgroup had significantly lower scores than the other two groups overall, and one may question whether participation in regular class activities in L2 English is the most expedient way of teaching for this subgroup.

Interestingly, the spelling profiles of the Control and Dyslexia groups followed a parallel pattern, indicating that their learning processes are similar, but with slower progress in the Dyslexia group compared to the Control group. From studies of dyslexic spelling in L1 Norwegian (Hagtvet & Lyster, 2003), one would expect that this tendency would be maintained, but that the distance between the two groups would increase.

This is often, quite wrongly, taken as proof that special needs teaching has no effect. Rather, in special needs education the learning effect should be evaluated by continual individual pre- and post-testing. By definition a learning impairment is something that makes certain aspects of learning more difficult than expected, and therefore comparisons with typical development are unfair.

Conclusion

The present chapter falls into two parts, one focusing on principles to be used in L2 testing in dyslexia and how these principles were operationalised in an L2 test, and one in which functional spelling was analysed in detail, since this seemed to be the most difficult area for dyslexic learners of English as L2.

In Norway dyslexic pupils are allowed certain extra rights at exams. These include more time, oral reading assistance, and the use of computers and spell-check programs. Also, in very special cases, written exams can be replaced by oral exams. As in many other European countries, English is taught as L2 from an early age. But as yet, there is little systematic understanding of how Norwegian dyslexic subjects learn English as L2, or of how they could be taught most efficiently. In the Norwegian school system, using assessment principles such as the ones presented here could be a useful starting point. The same principles could be applied to other languages as L2 besides English, which should have some potential for research on L2 acquisition in dyslexia across cultures. Since English as L2 is taught from the first grade in Norway, age-adjusted screening tests designed for dyslexic pupils for the whole school range should be advocated. There are studies addressing the question of whether intervention in L1 may enhance L2 as well (Linan-Thompson *et al.*, 2006). There are, however, no studies from Norwegian schools on this. Intervention is usually given by subject or curriculum: pupils get support restricted to L1 (Norwegian) and perhaps mathematics.

We named our test the 'English 2 Dyslexia Test', using the number 2 for two reasons: English as L2, and as a homonym for 'too', with the implied meaning 'English too, don't forget!' Being a part of the globalised world is as important for dyslexic individuals as it is for everyone else. We see the effects of globalisation in education, professional life, social life and leisure. For this reason alone, not to mention others, the tendency to overlook or ignore the value of L2 learning in dyslexia should be resisted. We should realise that there is a positive interaction between L1 and L2 acquisition, not a mutual inhibition. This means that we should strive to learn more about how dyslexic learners can take advantage of this interaction. From a broader perspective, there is a fascinating potential for comparative international research on L2 learning in dyslexia.

The procedure described here requires L2 teaching competence, competence in language impairment testing and in cognitive psychology. Integrating these fields should allow for insightful intervention. However, these are resource-consuming processes, and they can easily be sidelined in a school system that is usually short of resources. Moreover, few tests are designed for this purpose, and intervention is too often based on clinical judgement. In a busy school setting with limited resources L2 teaching in dyslexia may be overlooked, given little priority or simply rejected. In non-English cultures, L1 is given priority over English as L2. Nevertheless, thorough testing, intervention and follow-up can pay in the next round by generating good outcomes.

The key idea is that no one should be left out of education: it is for all. The issue of access to the globalised world is fortunately gaining more and more attention in dyslexia practice and research, and this paper points to some ways of ensuring this access. It is hoped that, with increasing amounts of research in this field, assessment procedures will become more standardised and efficient, will require fewer resources, and will also contribute to constantly improving intervention programmes.

Acknowledgement

I wish to thank my colleague, speech and language therapist Randi Kaasa, for data collection and valuable comments.

References

Alabau, I., Bonnet, G., Bot, K., Bramsbye, J., Dauphin, L., Erickson, G., Etelälahti, A., Evers, R., Hesse, H-G., Ibsen, E., Kühnbach, O., Lagergren, T., Levasseur, J., Nielsen, K., de Quay, P. and Tuokko, E. (2002) The assessment of pupils' skills in English in eight European countries. A European project. On WWW at http://cisad.adc.education.fr/reva. Accessed 08.07.06.

Beaton, A.B. (2004) *Dyslexia, Reading and the Brain*. New York: Psychology Press.

Bishop, D.V.M. and Snowling, M. (2004) Developmental dyslexia and specific language impairment: Same or different? *Psychological Bulletin* 130 (6), 858–886.

Bloomfield, L. (1933) *Language*. New York: Holt.

Carlsten, C.T. (1982) *Norsk rettskrivings- og leseprøver* [*Norwegian Spelling and Reading Tests*]. Oslo, Norway: Universitetsforlaget.

DITT (2001) *Language Shock – Dyslexia Across Cultures*. Brussels: BBC Educational Productions.

Dodd, B., Holm, A., Hua, Z., Crosbie, S. and Broomfield, J. (2006) English phonology: Acquisition and disorder. In Z. Hua and B. Dodd (eds) *Phonological Development and Disorders in Children. A Multilingual Perspective* (pp. 25–55). Clevedon: Multilingual Matters.

Elley, W.B. (1992) How in the world do students read? IEA-study of reading literacy. Unpublished manuscript, Hamburg.

Gjessing, H-J. (1977) *Lese- og skrivevansker. Dyslexi* [*Reading and writing impairments. Dyslexia*]. Bergen: Universitetsforlaget.

Gjessing, H-J. (1986) Function analysis as a way of subgrouping the reading disabled: Clinical and statistical analyses. *Scandinavian Journal of Educational Research* 30 (2), 95–106.

Hagtvet, B.E., Helland, T. and Lyster, S.A.H. (2006) Literacy acquisition in Norwegian. In R.M. Joshi and P.G. Aaron (eds) *Handbook of Orthography and Literacy* (pp. 15–30). Mahwah, NJ: Lawrence Erlbaum.

Hagtvet, B.E. and Lyster, S.A.H. (2003) The spelling errors of Norwegian good and poor decoders: A developmental cross-linguistic perspective. In N. Goulandris (ed.) *Dyslexia in Different Languages: Cross Linguistic Comparison.* (pp. 181–207). London: Whurr.

Hasselgård, H., Johansson, S. and Lysvåg, P. (1998) *English Grammar: Theory and Use.* Oslo: Universitetetsforlaget.

Helland, T. (2002) Neuro-cognitive functions in dyslexia. Variations according to language comprehension and mathematics skills. Unpublished doctoral thesis, University of Oslo.

Helland, T. and Kaasa, R. (2005) Dyslexia in English as a second language. *Dyslexia* 11 (1), 41–60.

Hua, Z. and Dodd, B. (2006) A multilingual perspective on phonological development and disorder. In Z. Hua and B. Dodd (eds) *Phonological Development and Disorders in Children. A Multilingual Perspective* (pp. 3 – 14). Clevedon: Multilingual Matters.

Høien, T. and Lundberg, I. (1997) *Dysleksi. Fra teori til praksis [Dyslexia. From Theory to Paxis].* Oslo: Gyldendal.

Job, R., Peresotti, F. and Mulatti, C. (2006) The acquisition of literacy in Italian. In M. Joshi and P.G. Aaron (eds) *Handbook of Orthography and Literacy* (pp. 105–119). Mahwah: Lawrence Erlbaum.

Kaasa, R. (2001) Lese- og skrivevansker og tilegnelse av engelsk. Undersøkelse på en gruppe 6. og 7. klassinger [Reading and reading difficulties and learning English. Assessment of a group of 6th and 7th graders]. Unpublished master thesis, University of Bergen.

Kaasa, R., Sanne, S. and Helland, T. (2004) *The English 2 Dyslexia Test.* Bergen: University of Bergen.

Kazanina, N., Phillips, C. and Idsardi, W. (2006) The influence of meaning on the perception of speech sounds. *PNAS* 103 (30), 11381–11386.

Klinkenberg, J.E. and Skaar, E. (2001) *STAS. Standardisert test i avkoding og staving [Standardised Test in Decoding and Spelling].* Hønefoss: Pedagogisk-psykologisk tjeneste.

Kuhl, P.K. (2004) Early language acquisition: Cracking the speech code. *Nature Reviews. Neuroscience* 5 (11), 831–843.

Linan-Thompson, S., Vaughn, S., Prater, K. and Cirino, P. T. (2006) The response to intervention of English language learners at risk of reading problems. *Journal of Learning Disabilities* 39 (5), 390–398.

Lyon, G.R. (1995) Towards a definition of dyslexia. *Annals of Dyslexia* 45, 3–27.

Lyon, G.R., Shaywitz, S.E. and Shaywitz, B.A. (2003) A definition of dyslexia. Defining dyslexia, comorbidity, teachers' knowledge of language and reading. *Annals of Dyslexia* 53, 1–14.

Morton, J. and Frith, U. (1995) Causal modeling: A structural approach to developmental psychopathology. In D.J.C. Dante Cicchetti (ed.) *Developmental Psychopathology, Vol. 1: Theory and Methods. Wiley Series on Personality Processes* (pp. 357–390). New York: John Wiley & Sons.

Paulesu, E., Démonet, J-F., Fazio, F., McCrory, E., Chanoine, V., Brunswick, N., Cappa, S.F., Cossu, G., Habib, M., Frith, C.D. *et al.* (2001) Dyslexia: Cultural diversity and biological unity. *Science* 291 (5511), 2165–2167.

Pienemann, M., Di Biase, B., Kawaguchi, S. and Håkansson, G. (2005) Process constraints on L1 transfer. In J.F. Kroll and A.M.B. De Groot (eds) *Handbook of Bilingualism. Psycholinguistic Approaches* (pp. 128–153). Oxford: Oxford University Press.

Ridsdale, J. (2004) Dyslexia and self-esteem. In M. Turner and J. Rack (eds) *The Study of Dyslexia* (pp. 249–279). New York: Kluwer Academic Press.

Schneider, E. and Crombie, M. (2003) *Dyslexia and Foreign Language Learning*. London: David Fulton.

Smythe, I., and Everatt, J. (2000) Dyslexia diagnosis in different languages. In P. Lindsay and G. Reid (eds) *Multilingualism, Literacy and Dyslexia* (pp. 12–21). London: David Fulton.

Sparks, R., Ganschow, L. and Pohlman, J. (1989) Linguisitic coding deficits in foreign language learners. *Annals of Dyslexia* 39, 179–195.

Sparks, R., Patton, J., Ganschow, L., Humbach, N. and Javorsky, J. (2006) Native language predictors of foreign language proficiency and foreign language aptitude. *Annals of Dyslexia* 56, 126–160.

The British Dyslexia Association (1998) *The British Dyslexia Association Handbook*. Reading: British Dyslexia Association.

Thornton, R. (1996) Elicited production. In D. McDaniel, C. McKee and H.S. Cairns (eds) *Methods of Assessing Children's Syntax* (pp. 77–102). Cambridge MA: MIT Press.

Valdés, G. and Figueroa, R.A. (1994) *Bilingualism and Testing: A Special Case of Bias*. Norwood, NJ: Ablex.

van Gelderen, E. (2005) Sample entry: Function words. In P. Strazny (ed.) *Encyclopedia of Linguistics* (Vol. 2). New York: Fitzroy Dearborn.

Vygotsky, L.S. (1962) *Thought and Language*. Cambridge, MA: MIT Press.

Chapter 4
Input, Processing and Output Anxiety in Students with Symptoms of Developmental Dyslexia

EWA PIECHURSKA-KUCIEL

Introduction

This chapter presents and discusses the results of empirical research on anxiety observed at the three stages of foreign language processing (i.e. input, processing and output) in secondary school students with symptoms of developmental dyslexia. First the characteristics of dyslexic students as foreign language learners are presented, followed by an outline of the concept of anxiety and its relevance in foreign/second language acquisition (SLA). A presentation and discussion of the results of the study follows, and the pedagogical implications and recommendations for future research and language instruction are addressed.

In Poland students with *developmental dyslexia* are included in mainstream education. They are considered to be individuals with special educational needs (SEN), who are supported by a special five-level therapeutic aid system: (1) parental assistance under the supervision of the tutor; (2) correction and compensation team; (3) individual therapy; (4) therapeutic classes; and (5) stationary therapeutic wards (Bogdanowicz, 2003).

Students begin to learn a foreign language in the third grade of primary school (at the age of 10; in 2008 they will start in the first grade – at the age of 7), and in secondary school another obligatory foreign language is introduced. Only the diagnosis of deep dyslexia authorises the student not to take a second foreign language course. Consequently, the student is obliged to study at least one foreign language regardless of the severity of his/her dyslexia. According to the regulations of the Ministry of Education and Sport, teachers must accommodate their demands to the needs and abilities of dyslexic students. There are also other provisions towards ensuring equal rights for dyslexics in mainstream schools, such as reducing stylistic and orthographic requirements or assigning more time in exams (Bogdanowicz, 2005).

Developmental dyslexia has a potentially negative influence on academic achievement (Reynolds *et al.*, 1996), especially foreign language acquisition (Schneider, 1999), causing difficulties with orthographic/ phonological, syntactic-grammatical and semantic processing (Schneider & Crombie, 2003). In addition, dyslexia is often the cause of social and affective problems such as low self-esteem, self-concept and self-confidence, a dependent personality, in conjunction with higher than average anxiety, emotional insecurity and depression (McNulty, 2003). Adult dyslexics also complain about shame, frustration and loneliness (Orenstein, 2000). They experience feelings of inferiority, stress and aggression, together with difficulties in expressing emotions (Hellendoorn & Ruijssenaars, 2000). Apart from all this, they suffer from serious social problems that have a tendency to be related to social immaturity, including social isolation, peer rejection or social inadequacy, which can especially be observed in adolescence (Martínez & Semrud-Clikeman, 2004).

Anxiety, a serious affective consequence of developmental dyslexia (Gindrich, 2002), has been found to influence human cognitive processes at their specific stages, from perception to retrieval (Terry & Burns, 2001). Hence, it is to be expected that foreign language acquisition in students affected by developmental dyslexia will be shaped by anxiety.

Cognitive and Affective Characteristics of Dyslexic Language Learners

Due to differences in internal cognitive processing which result from different experiences, memory and processing patterns, learners may respond in different ways to the same input information and training. Students affected by developmental dyslexia suffer from language processing deficits that lead to 'an impairment in the representation and manipulation of phonemes' (Fisher & DeFries, 2002: 767).

In some cases, these learning difficulties can be compensated for during first language (L1) acquisition. Still, learning a foreign language (FL) usually becomes a task that is too demanding, even for dyslexics skilled in mastering the intricacies of their L1 (Sparks *et al.*, 1998). The reason is that the compensatory strategies of dyslexic students may succeed in masking linguistic coding deficits in the mother tongue but are not effective when the learner is faced with a new linguistic coding system (Sparks & Ganschow, 1991). New print symbol–sound relationships and a new way of thinking present a particular challenge that such students are unable to overcome due to their specific language deficits (Schneider & Crombie, 2003).

To explain the cause of dyslexics' problems with mastering a foreign language, the Linguistic Coding Differences Hypothesis was proposed, according to which 'the primary causal factors in successful or unsuccessful FL learning are linguistic; that is, students who exhibit FL learning problems have overt or subtle L1 deficiences that affect their learning of a foreign language' (Ganschow et al., 1998: 248–249). It follows that general language skills affect the acquisition of the foreign language (Sparks & Ganschow, 1991). Skills in native language components provide the basic foundation for foreign language learning (Spolsky, 1989), which means that native and foreign language learning are interrelated, as they reflect basic language functions (Ganschow & Sparks, 1995).

Moreover, language deficits are believed to constitute a cause for affective differences, such as anxiety or low motivation (Sparks & Ganschow, 1993a). According to Sparks and Ganschow (1993b: 290), 'subtle or overt difficulties in an individual's understanding of or inability to use the language codes are a likely cause of FL learning difficulties, whereas affective differences are a likely consequence of these language learning difficulties'. Due to constitutional reasons, dyslexic foreign language learners may suffer from high language anxiety levels that may prevail throughout the whole language learning process (Ganschow et al., 1998). In this view, affective disturbances are treated as 'symptoms – behavioural manifestations – of a deeper problem' (Sparks & Ganschow, 1991: 6), such as developmental dyslexia.

Anxiety and the Process of Foreign Language Acquisition

Anxiety is one of the affective factors whose negative impact on the learning process is most pervasive (Oxford, 1999), even in unimpaired individuals. It is usually defined as 'a sense of discomfort and worry regarding an undefined threat' (Friedman & Bendas-Jacob, 1997: 1035). According to one of the simplest anxiety models (Liebert & Morris, 1967), anxiety consists of two distinctive components: *worry* (a cognitive concern about the individual's performance) and *emotionality* (emotional reactions occurring in response to stress). Worry leads to the wasting of energy that should be used for the task and memory activation, and instead is diverted to fruitless concerns about one's imaginary helplessness or inertia. With its effect on performance and self-deprecatory thoughts (Hopdapp & Benson, 1997), worry impairs academic performance (Minor & Gold, 1985). Emotionality, on the other hand, causes somatic reactions, such as high blood pressure, sweating palms or forearm tension (Scovel, 1991).

In traditional psychological approaches, anxiety is divided into *state* and *trait* anxiety. The *state* type denotes subjective and conscious feelings of apprehension and tension accompanied by stimulation or activation of the autonomous nervous system (Spielberger, 1966). *Trait anxiety* is connected with the general vulnerability of an individual and is conceptualised as a relatively stable personality characteristic (Eysenck, 1979).

To complement the existing typology, another type of anxiety has been introduced, that is, *situation-specific*, a form of trait anxiety (Keogh & French, 2001). It defines the likelihood of becoming anxious in particular situations, such as test taking or public speaking (MacIntyre, 1999). In the context of the foreign language classroom, this type of anxiety is called *language anxiety* (MacIntyre & Gardner, 1991c). It is usually defined as 'a distinct complex of self-perceptions, beliefs, feelings, and behaviours arising from the uniqueness of the language learning process' in the classroom (Horwitz *et al.*, 1986: 128).

The negative effects of language anxiety can be observed in many spheres of student functioning – social, personal, academic and cognitive (MacIntyre, 1999). *Social* effects of language anxiety shape the individual's relationships with the society, and consist of the learner's unwillingness to communicate in the foreign language classroom (MacIntyre & Gardner, 1991a) or in natural settings (MacIntyre & Charos, 1995). The *personal* effects of language anxiety comprise the deterioration of the individual's self-image, ego, goals and interests. From the point of view of this perspective, language anxiety in the learner may lead to self-deprecating or worrisome thoughts (Price, 1991; Young, 1991), overwhelming fear (Horwitz & Young, 1991), and physiological reactions. *Academic* effects are observable in education and are manifested in a negative correlation between language anxiety and course grades (MacIntyre & Gardner, 1994a) and proficiency tests (Young, 1986). Anxious students are found either to avoid studying and skip classes, or to over-study in order to increase their confidence and thus reduce their level of anxiety (Oxford, 1999). *Cognitive* effects of language anxiety refer to information processing and knowledge application. They mostly encompass interference with students' cognitive performance in language processing (Tobias & Everson, 1997).

Language anxiety is claimed to be a unique experience that plays a significant causal role in individual differences in the FL acquisition process (MacIntyre & Gardner, 1991c). Such an assertion stands in contrast to Sparks and Ganschow's claim that anxiety in foreign language learning, like any other affective variable, is the effect of differences in general language skills (e.g. Sparks *et al.*, 1998). In response to the above, MacIntyre (1995, 1999) and Horwitz (2000) argue that anxiety is a complex variable that can be both a *cause* and a *consequence* of poor language learning because 'some people are anxious about language learning *independent* of processing deficits and [...] such anxiety reactions can interfere with language learning' (Horwitz, 2000: 256).

The analysis of general cognitive processes involved in language acquisition is based on the information processing model borrowed from studies on language and communication (Rice, 1999). The processes are claimed to involve the following stages: *input* (when the new material is first approached), *central processing* or *throughput* (when the existing knowledge and the new material are connected) and *output* (when the acquired material is demonstrated) (Manolopoulou-Sergi, 2004). This three-stage model was adapted by Tobias (1985) to show the functioning of test anxiety in cognitive processing. The model was applied to display the activation of language anxiety at the different stages of language processing to locate 'the source of performance problems' (MacIntyre & Gardner, 1994b: 3).

According to the model described above, language processing takes place in three consecutive stages. At the input stage, when learners are presented with new linguistic items, anxiety may act as a filter that hinders the intake of information. It causes attention deficits and poor initial information processing, so individuals with higher anxiety may easily get distracted from the task as they divide time 'between the processing of emotion-related and task-related cognition' (MacIntyre & Gardner, 1989: 255). The interplay of these two aspects of cognition makes highly anxious students slower and less accurate because worry limits the capacity system needed for temporary storage and information manipulation essential for complex cognitive tasks. Anxious students may often ask for repetition or may have to reread material even in their mother tongue in order to compensate for the lacking or incomplete input (Bailey *et al.*, 2000).

At the processing stage, anxiety may influence the speed and accuracy of learning as worry and intrusive thoughts compete with the cognitive task in progress and limit processing resources of working memory (Eysenck & Calvo, 1992). As a result, lower cognitive efficiency can be observed in the form of a decline in accuracy. In this way, task-relevant processing can exploit fewer cognitive resources, giving way to lower efficiency. The student's ability to understand messages is reduced, as well as the ability to learn new vocabulary items in the foreign language (MacIntyre & Gardner, 1994a).

The third stage of information processing is the *output stage*. Here anxiety 'encompasses the worry experienced when students are required to demonstrate their ability to produce previously learned material' (Onwuegbuzie, *et al.*, 2000: 90). At this stage, anxiety interferes with the retrieval of items from memory, leading to the learner's inability to recall a necessary item, though it may be obvious that they know many more items than they are able to produce (MacIntyre & Gardner, 1991b). Moreover, cognitive processing at this stage is also affected by processing problems encountered at the preceding stages. Highly anxious students are found to use different types of grammatical constructions (Kleinmann in Horwitz *et al.*, 1991). They also attempt fewer interpretive and more concrete messages (Steinberg & Horwitz, 1986) and avoid producing complicated and personal utterances in the foreign language (Horwitz *et al.*, 1986). The visual representation of the relationship

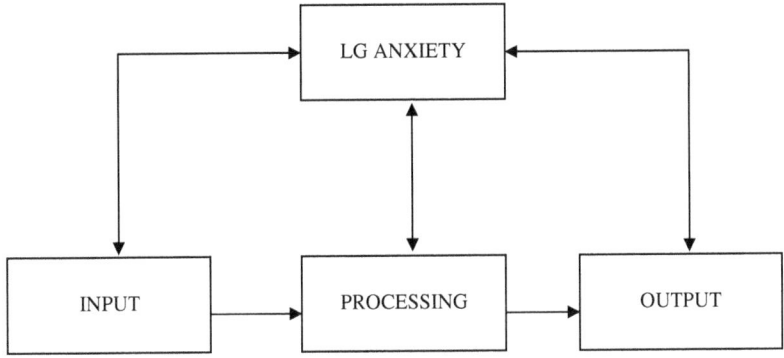

Figure 4.1 Anxiety and stages of language processing

between anxiety and different stages of cognitive processing is shown in Figure 4.1.

The model shows how the activation of foreign language anxiety affects cognitive processes. The two-way arrows between anxiety and the stages of cognitive processing show how anxiety, which is present at each stage, induces increased anxiety at consecutive stages. It is called the 'down-spiralling effect' of increasing anxiety at the prospect of worsening cognitive processes (Arnold & Brown, 1999: 9). First, at the input stage the learner is afraid that she/he will not be able to gather all the necessary information, which gives rise to anxiety. At the next stage, with anxiety rising, the learner has problems organising information, and thus any processing problems that are further encountered increase the experienced anxiety. Finally, performance problems at the output stage lead to higher levels of anxiety about language production.

Research Aims and Rationale

The primary purpose of the present research was to investigate foreign language anxiety that occurs at the three stages of language processing in secondary school students with and without dyslexia symptoms. This study fills a gap in current research on specific anxiety in foreign language processing in developmental dyslexia, which has – to date – remained unexplored.

Developmental dyslexia is correlated with numerous negative effects, such as poor working memory, low self-esteem, or slow speed of information processing (Crombie, 2000). A high-anxiety learner may suffer from a variety of language anxiety effects, but a dyslexic student is even more prone to affective disorders (Gindrich, 2002). It is expected that developmental dyslexia may be a significant reason for experiencing high foreign language anxiety levels. As a consequence, students with developmental dyslexia symptoms might experience serious processing problems and higher levels of foreign language anxiety. Accordingly, the main hypothesis formulated for the purpose of this study was: the foreign language anxiety levels of students with symptoms of developmental dyslexia at the three stages of foreign language processing are higher than those of their unimpaired peers (Hypothesis 1).

It is claimed that the three stages of foreign language processing are interrelated (MacIntyre & Gardner, 1994a, b; Tobias, 1985), which means that difficulties at any stage lead to more problems during the following stages. Therefore the stage that can display the strongest signs of language processing problems for a student with developmental dyslexia symptoms is the output stage, because it is the result of all the cognitive work performed during the preceding stages. Moreover, the threat evoked by the necessity to perform in the foreign language may enhance anxiety due to automaticity problems (Crombie, 2000) and difficulties with word finding and naming, as well as mimicking speech sounds (Sparks & Ganschow, 1991). Dyslexics, with their low self-esteem, are likely candidates for apprehension resulting from their expectations of yet another failure in front of their teachers and peers. Consequently, anxiety appearing at this stage may the affective consequence of developmental dyslexia, but it may also be due to processing problems specific for this stage and cumulating difficulties with processing at the previous stages. Thus the next hypothesis for this study was: the output stage is the most anxiety-breeding for students with developmental dyslexia symptoms (Hypothesis 2).

It is also worth observing the application of the model of foreign language anxiety development advocated by MacIntyre and Gardner (1989) in relation to foreign language processing by dyslexics. It proposes that foreign language anxiety has a dynamic character. At the beginning of the language learning process, a foreign language student encounters instances of state anxiety. After a string of repeated episodes of state anxiety in a foreign language classroom, anxiety 'solidifies into situation-specific anxiety' (MacIntyre & Gardner, 1991b: 272) that may be identified as a situation-specific trait affecting the quality of the SLA process. With language proficiency growing and more positive experiences encountered in the SLA process, foreign language anxiety has a tendency to decrease.

The inclusion policy in Poland advocates accommodating students with developmental dyslexia in mainstream education, offering them fairer chances for development. The standard language instruction, however, does not recognise the needs of dyslexic students. Hence, it can be expected that affective problems caused by developmental dyslexia are likely to persist throughout the students' secondary school career. If this is the case, the model of anxiety development proposed by MacIntyre and

Gardner (1989) may not be confirmed longitudinally. Accordingly, the last hypothesis set for this study was: foreign language anxiety levels in students with developmental dyslexia symptoms do not show a decreasing tendency throughout the length of their secondary school studies (Hypothesis 3).

Method

Participants

The participants of the study were 393 students coming from 17 classes (natural groups) of the six three-grade secondary grammar schools in Opole, located in south-western Poland. This type of school accommodates students aged 16–18, which corresponds to grades 10–12 in the American K-12 educational system; in other educational contexts such schools may also be called high schools or senior schools. The sample comprised 266 girls and 127 boys. At the beginning of the study, when they entered secondary school education, their average age was 16.7 with a minimum of 15 and maximum of 18. They all attended English classes as the second compulsory foreign language (three to five hours a week), and German or French was their primary compulsory foreign language. The classes were chosen at random, on condition that English was not the priority language: its lower-stakes status was expected to correlate with lower tension.

On the basis of the Revised Adult Dyslexia Checklist results (Vinegrad, 1994), the sample was divided into three groups: the lower quartile (≤ 22) formed a group of 142 students (103 girls and 39 boys) with no developmental dyslexia symptoms (ND), the upper quartile (≥ 26) was a group of 105 students (63 girls and 42 boys) with dyslexic symptoms (D). The remaining group of students (middle quartiles) was excluded from further analysis.

Instruments

The first instrument used was the 20-item Revised Adult Dyslexia Checklist (Vinegrad, 1994). It was designed to assess symptoms of developmental dyslexia in different areas in larger populations and to give a preliminary indication of whether problems are dyslexia-related. It was translated into Polish by Bogdanowicz and Krasowicz (1996), with *yes* and *no* answers ($\alpha = 0.73$). The maximum number of points was 40 and minimum 20. Sample items were: 'Is your spelling poor?' and 'When you say a long word, do you sometimes find it difficult to get all the sounds in the right order?'

The other instrument used in the study was a questionnaire consisting of several scales measuring anxiety at the three stages of language processing. First of all, it included the Input Anxiety Scale developed by MacIntyre and Gardner (1994a). The level of input anxiety depends on the student's ability to attend to, concentrate on, and encode external stimuli. Sample items in the scale included statements such as: 'I get upset when I read in English because I must read things again and again' or 'I am not bothered by someone speaking quickly in English.' Its reliability was assessed in terms of the Cronbach's alpha coefficient ($\alpha = 0.71$).

The Processing Anxiety Scale (MacIntyre & Gardner, 1994a) measures apprehension when performing cognitive operations. The amount of processing anxiety depends on the complexity of the information, demands on memory, and the organizational level of the presented material. This scale comprises sample items such as: 'I am anxious with English because, no matter how hard I try, I have trouble understanding it' and 'I do not worry when I hear new or unfamiliar words, I am confident that I can understand them'. Its reliability was slightly lower ($\alpha = 0.62$).

The Output Anxiety Scale (MacIntyre & Gardner, 1994a) measures anxiety when the ability to use previously learned material must be demonstrated. High anxiety at this stage might hinder the ability to use productive skills, like speaking or writing in the foreign language. Sample items in the scale were: 'I may know the proper English expression but when I am nervous it just won't come out' and 'I get upset when I know how to communicate something in English but I just cannot verbalize it' ($\alpha = 0.83$).

Each above-mentioned scale, translated into Polish, consisted of six 4-point Likert-format items ranging from 1 – *I totally disagree* to 4 – *I totally agree*. All positive items were key-reversed so that a high score on the scale represented a high anxiety level. The maximum number of points on each scale was 24 and the minimum 6.

Procedures

The design of the study was longitudinal (lasting three years) with three measures taken at different points in time (time-series). It was also differential (Graziano & Raulin, 1993) because it focused on the comparison of two groups of participants: students with and without symptoms of developmental dyslexia on the dependent variable, that is, language anxiety.

The data collection procedure took place in three phases over the length of secondary school education. The anxiety measurements were taken: in December 2002 when the participants were in their first year, December 2003 in their second year and January 2005 in their third and final year. The students were asked to complete the same questionnaire each time. The Revised Adult Dyslexia Checklist (Vinegrad, 1994) was administered in Year 2. The participants were asked to give sincere answers without taking excessive time to think.

The data were computed by means of the STATISTICA programme, with the main operations being descriptive statistics: means and standard deviation (SD) and t-tests for independent and paired-samples.

Results

Students in both groups experienced the highest levels of anxiety in Year 1. The scores of the group with symptoms of developmental dyslexia (D) on the Input, Processing and Output Anxiety Scales were 15.49, 15.15 and 14.89 on the three scales out of the maximum 24 points. The average of this scale for the group with no developmental symptoms of dyslexia (ND) was 15.4, 14.42 and 15.6.

In Year 2 all the anxiety results fell in both groups. In the D group measurement on the Input Anxiety Scale was 14.2. On the Processing Anxiety Scale they scored 13.42 and 14.69 on the Output Anxiety Scale. The ND group results were: 12.32, 11.76 and 12.64.

In Year 3 not all scores continued to drop. They were 13.69, 13.21 and 14.2 respectively for the D group and 12.2, 12.41, 12.52 for the ND group. The main results are presented in Table 4.1.

As far as the Input Anxiety scale is concerned, in the case of the D group a significant decrease was noted after the first year of secondary school, and the level of input anxiety remained stable towards its end. A similar trend was observed in the ND group, but the decrease was much more pronounced.

The scores obtained on the Processing Anxiety Scale followed a similar path of development in both groups: a significant drop after the first year, and no change in the last measurement. Again, the decrease in the ND group was bigger.

The Output Anxiety Scale results showed a similar pattern, but only in the ND group: a notable drop after the first year followed by constancy. In the case of the D group the scores remained stable throughout secondary school (see Table 4.2 for within-group comparisons).

When taking into consideration comparisons between groups, it must be noted that in Year 1 the levels of Input and Output Anxiety in both groups were similarly high except for the Processing Anxiety results, which were significantly higher in the D group. In Year 2 a significant and regular disparity between the group results could be observed. The last measurement showed a continuing discrepancy, with the qualifier that both groups experienced similarly high Processing Anxiety (see Table 4.3 for between-group comparisons).

The main results are displayed in Figure 4.2. It can be seen that all the anxiety results in both groups decreased in the course of the research, but the decline was less pronounced around the end of secondary school education. It is also visible that the D group's scores, though similar at the

Table 4.1 Summary of descriptive statistics

	Input anxiety				Processing anxiety				Output anxiety			
	D		ND		D		ND		D		ND	
	Mean	*SD*	*Mean*	*SD*	*Mean*	*SD*	*Mean*	*SD*	*Mean*	*SD*	*Mean*	*SD*
Year 1	15.49	1.94	15.40	1.84	15.15	2.11	14.42	2.24	14.89	1.92	15.60	1.81
Year 2	14.2	3.55	12.32	3.31	13.42	3.33	11.76	3.00	14.69	3.99	12.64	3.43
Year 3	13.69	3.39	12.20	3.25	13.21	3.06	12.42	3.02	14.20	3.84	12.52	3.69

Table 4.2 Comparison of anxiety at stages of language processing in students with (D) and in students without developmental dyslexia symptoms (ND)

		t	
		D	ND
Input anxiety	Year 1 × Year 2	3.0*	9.68**
	Year 2 × Year 3	1.85	0.53
Processing anxiety	Year 1 × Year 2	4.88*	8.43**
	Year 2 × Year 3	0.83	−0.76
Output anxiety	Year 1 × Year 2	0.45	7.64**
	Year 2 × Year 3	1.72	0.47

*$p < 0.05$. **$p < 0.001$.

Table 4.3 Comparison of anxiety at stages of language processing between students with (D) and without developmental dyslexia symptoms (ND)

		t
Year 1	Input anxiety	0.39
	Processing anxiety	2.59*
	Output anxiety	−0.67
Year 2	Input anxiety	4.26**
	Processing anxiety	4.09**
	Output anxiety	4.34**
Year 3	Input anxiety	3.5*
	Processing anxiety	0.96
	Output anxiety	3.47*

*$p < 0.05$. **$p < 0.001$.

initial phase, did not decrease as dynamically as the ND group's scores throughout the length of the study. It also appears that the output stage is most anxiety-breeding in students with symptoms of dyslexia.

Discussion

The main hypothesis formulated for the purpose of the research focused on the interplay between developmental dyslexia symptoms and anxiety experienced during the three stages of language processing,

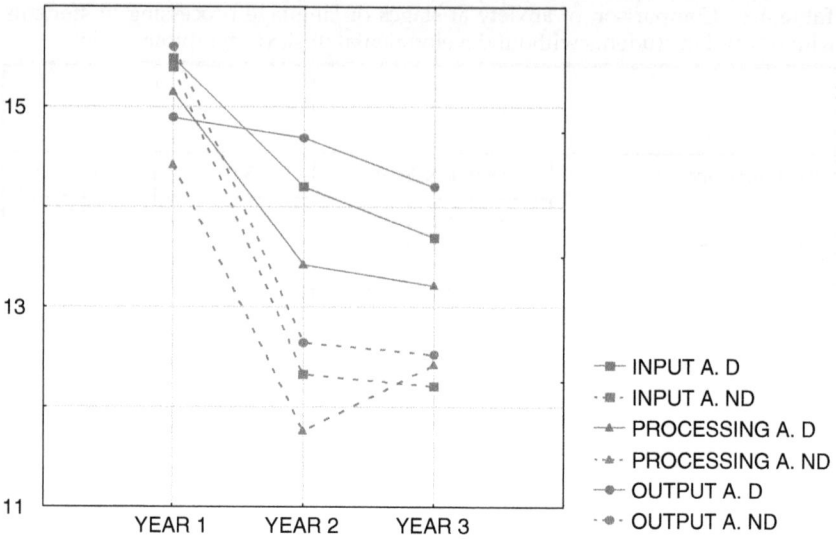

Figure 4.2 Input, processing and output anxiety in students with (D) and without developmental dyslexia symptoms (ND)

saying: the language anxiety levels of students with symptoms of developmental dyslexia at the three stages of language processing are higher than those of their unimpaired peers. The results of the study only partially support the hypothesis. The figures show generally higher levels of anxiety in students with developmental dyslexia symptoms, with the exception of the measurements taken in the first year of secondary school study. The findings appear to support related studies in the literature on dyslexia, where individuals with learning disabilities were found to be more anxious than students with no apparent learning disabilities (Riddick *et al.*, 1999).

Nevertheless, the intensity of anxiety in students with symptoms of dyslexia and with no signs of learning disability was equally high at the input and output stages at the beginning of their secondary school education. This finding can be attributed to the fact that in Year 1 all the students found themselves in a new learning environment. They had recently experienced a transition from a different school type (junior high school or, in other educational contexts, middle school), which was likely to cause feelings of worry and anxiety (Pappamihiel, 2001). This is especially relevant for adolescents who have a tendency to be sensitive to emotional disturbances; though older adolescents, such as the participants of the present study, mostly complain about academic issues as salient stressors (Williams & McGillicuddy-De Lisi, 2000). The school transition creates a need to cope with novel expectations and challenges, to which higher anxiety is a likely response.

Moreover, all the participants began the English course at elementary level, which means that real and false beginners were placed in the same language classes, irrespective of their previous experience with the foreign language. That almost certainly caused additional stress for those inexperienced with English, as well as those who had already had negative experiences with foreign language learning, which is a common case of dyslexic students with a long history of failures in acquiring a foreign language (Schneider & Crombie, 2003). The comparable level of anxiety in both students with and without symptoms of developmental dyslexia shows that all the students reacted similarly to challenges encountered at stages of input and output.

At the beginning of their secondary school studies, students with developmental dyslexia symptoms suffered from significantly higher levels of anxiety at the processing stage. The abilities required at this stage appeared to have a critical influence on their anxiety level; especially the students' relatively slow processing mechanisms that required more concentration and time (Schneider & Crombie, 2003), and the deficiencies of memory systems (Jeffries & Everatt, 2004). In their next year, when they were already familiar with the school, teachers and classroom routines, the discrepancy between anxiety levels in dyslexia symptomatic and asymptomatic students was more notable on all levels of language processing. While anxiety in students without developmental dyslexia symptoms dropped significantly, students with symptoms of developmental dyslexia reacted to FL learning challenges with higher levels of negative emotions, such as anxiety. The finding seems to corroborate the position taken by Ganschow and Sparks (e.g. Sparks *et al.*, 1998), according to whom negative affective states of students with learning deficits originate in differences in language mechanisms.

In Hypothesis 2, it was supposed that the output stage would be the most anxiety-breeding for students with developmental dyslexia symptoms. The results support this hypothesis in Years 2 and 3 but not in Year 1, the beginning of secondary school education. In this year anxiety was similarly high in all students, which may be attributed to the novelty of the language learning situation.

Nevertheless, in the course of their language studies the level of anxiety at the output stage did not decrease in students with developmental dyslexia symptoms even by the end of their secondary school studies. There may be several reasons for this finding. First of all, anxiety might be evoked by deficits in language processing, which might also be identified at any other stage. Second, there might be cumulative effects of processing problems encountered at previous stages. Third, the need for an active use of the language, directly connected with the foreign language acquisition process, can be assumed to evoke feelings of apprehension and doubt.

The specificity of the output stage lies in the active role of a learner as a foreign language user. Here dyslexics' problems with communication, especially oral communication (Ganschow et al., 1991), seem to play a vital role. Anxiety related to language production can be attributed to the uniqueness of the language learning experience viewed from the perspective of oral interpersonal communication. The student's limited linguistic repertoire threatens self-perception of genuineness, a peril common to all unskilled language learners, causing evident anxiety reactions.

The self-image of a student with developmental dyslexia symptoms is already shattered by the affective consequences of developmental dyslexia. In response to their own desperate yet futile attempts to convey coherent messages in the foreign language, certainly frustration with their own inability to meet the expectations of others, as well as their own, is further evoked. For a dyslexic, the process of foreign language acquisition is most often a long path of failures, and consequently low self-esteem and a growing belief in his or her own inadequacy (Schneider & Crombie, 2003). Such beliefs, together with low self-worth and mounting fear of negative evaluation, result in increasing levels of anxiety connected with the student's fear of losing face and showing their incompetence, which do not disappear in spite of growing abilities in the foreign language.

The output stage is the last in the processing sequence and bears signs of any problems encountered during the previous stages (input and processing). Obviously, linguistic deficits may not allow for effective cognitive processing while attending to input and organising it. Consequently, problems at the output stage are likely to arise due to input and processing difficulties, giving way to performance problems. Altogether, the output stage seems to be especially challenging for a student with developmental dyslexia, with its increased demand on cognitive, affective and social skills, requiring the use of a whole array of techniques not usually deployed in other subjects.

The last hypothesis focused on time effects of anxiety measurements. It stated that language anxiety levels in students with developmental dyslexia symptoms do not show a decreasing tendency throughout the length of their secondary school studies (Hypothesis 3). The findings of the study allow for partial corroboration of the hypothesis. In the case of students without dyslexia symptoms, the following pattern of the dynamics of the anxiety decrease can be observed: a significant fall towards the middle year (Year 2) in comparison to Year 1, and a final plateau between the middle and last years. The anxiety measurements in students with developmental dyslexia symptoms globally follow a similar pattern, with the exception of output anxiety, whose measurements remain permanently high throughout their secondary school experience.

Nevertheless, this global decreasing tendency allows for the optimistic conclusion that students with learning deficits are able to identify more favourable experiences in their language learning process and encounter positive emotions connected with growing proficiency, which enables them to manage their anxiety, in spite of traditional language instruction. This finding can also be attributed to the process of experience growth directly connected with time in traditional face-to-face learning, where the learning outcome is expected to be a function of time (Hwang *et al.* 2004). It may then be presumed that after a year of secondary school studies, the participants became accustomed to the challenges of their learning environment, and their familiariaty with secondary school demands allowed them to develop more effective anxiety management.

Towards the end of secondary school education, the anxiety levels of the study participants did not continue to decrease. This finding can be explained by the fact that in five months' time the students would be facing their final matriculation exams in various subjects, which constituted an influential stressor. In such a situation, preparations taken for these exams with their washback effect may have considerably influenced the experience of anxiety in the school environment.

Still, it must be pointed out that all of the mean anxiety results in both groups of students – with and without dyslexia symptoms – are not very high judging by the maximum number of points on each scale. Hence, it may be concluded that Polish secondary school students generally experience moderate levels of input, processing and output anxiety. This result can be ascribed to several factors. The specificity of English as a foreign language should be taken into consideration. The standing of this language in Poland in comparison to other foreign languages is quite high. Young Polish people are aware of the role of English as the *lingua franca* of Europe and the rest of the world. To be able to find a good job, they know they need to have a working knowledge of English, which pushes them to study the language at school as an obligatory subject, and is a strong motivational factor for developing their language experience. In addition, many students nowadays have opportunities to travel abroad for holidays, so the prospect of being able to communicate is a strong drive in studying English. Moreover, the contemporary, locally dominant approach to teaching English is also an important variable whose role should be taken into consideration. Communicative Language Teaching (CLT) stresses the importance of real communication, meaningful tasks and meaningful language (Richards & Rodgers, 1986). Although it has been claimed that this approach is extremely anxiety-breeding (Arnold & Brown, 1999), for a dyslexic student it may actually be quite beneficial because accuracy is not a priority. In CLT, the key focus is on the development of speaking and listening skills. The skill of reading, so problematic for a dyslexic, is developed at the level of the context and not of single words, and writing on lower levels is limited to pursuing real-life purposes (note or letter writing).

This research shows that students with dyslexic symptoms generally suffer from greater anxiety than students without symptoms of developmental dyslexia, which – in the case of the former – has cumulative effects. First, there is anxiety caused by language deficits (trait anxiety). Then there is also anxiety that is situation-specific, that is, the type of anxiety caused by the uniqueness of language learning. In dyslexics, these two types of anxiety interact to create an additional anxiety value, which could explain higher anxiety levels in dyslexia symptomatics. The results of the present study tend to corroborate findings of previous research on affective consequences of dyslexia (e.g. Sparks & Ganschow, 1996). Accordingly, it may be presumed that there are strong affective consequences of developmental dyslexia, which may appear as high anxiety levels experienced by the student with symptoms of developmental dyslexia throughout the course of language study. Figure 4.3 shows a tentative model of the relationship between developmental dyslexia and anxiety, based on the results of the present study, as well as extensive research by Sparks and Ganschow (see Ganschow & Sparks, 2000).

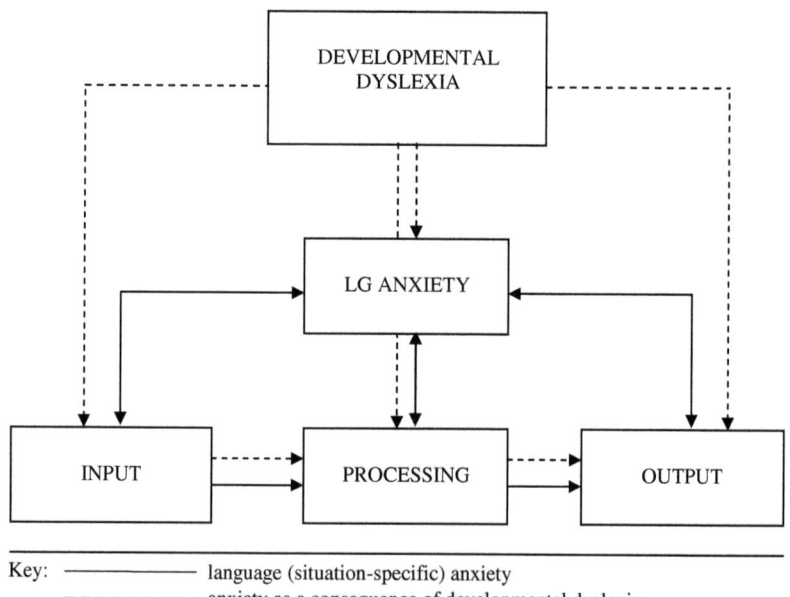

Key: ——————— language (situation-specific) anxiety
- - - - - - - - anxiety as a consequence of developmental dyslexia

Figure 4.3 Effects of developmental dyslexia on language anxiety at stages of language processing

The central aspect of the diagram is anxiety. Here it is shown as both the consequence of developmental dyslexia (trait anxiety), as well and as the source and consequence of problems experienced at different stages of cognitive processing (language anxiety). Language anxiety (continuous lines) may be present at the stages of cognitive processing in *any* student during foreign language acquisition. It is likely to occur at input, processing and output stages due to the linguistic challenges that a student faces. Apart from this, there is also another type of anxiety viewed as the consequence of language disorders, as originally proposed by Sparks and Ganschow (1993a). It may be considered trait anxiety, which becomes part of the anxious personality of the dyslexic student (Carroll & Illes, 2006), and is a behavioural manifestation of developmental dyslexia. These two types of anxiety cumulate to lead to significant levels of anxiety, observed at stages of cognitive processing in a dyslexic student. The dotted lines show the influence of developmental dyslexia on cognitive processes at the stages of language processing, as well as on the activation of anxiety.

For those who suffer from cognitive disabilities, anxiety reactions are also caused by the experience of learning a language, as supported by the results of the study. Foreign language anxiety, its development and magnitude, cannot be analysed ignoring the role of language deficits. As the findings show, affective differences in students with symptoms of developmental dyslexia, language anxiety among them, are indeed, 'the *result* rather than the *cause* of FL learning problems' (Ganschow *et al.*, 1998, 248).

The basic results of the research can be summed up in the following points:

(1) Students with developmental dyslexia symptoms have a tendency to suffer from higher levels of anxiety at all stages of language processing in comparison to their unimpaired peers.
(2) Their anxiety at the input and processing stages follows the same general path as the anxiety development observed in students without symptoms of developmental dyslexia: it decreases significantly after the first year, remaining stable until the end of a three-year secondary school.
(3) Anxiety at the output stage of students with dyslexia symptoms remains permanently high throughout secondary school education due to processing problems at the preceding stages, and performance deficiencies connected with the affective consequences of developmental dyslexia.

Conclusion and Implications

In spite of the rather discouraging observations of anxiety levels of dyslexic students venturing to study a foreign language presented in this chapter, it is vital to point out that there are good chances for such a student to master a new language irrespective of language deficits and traditional language instruction (see Nijakowska, this volume; Sarkadi, this volume). It is imperative for young people to learn foreign languages for a large variety of reasons; therefore, applying a teaching methodology which caters to the needs of dyslexic students and facilitates their language acquisition in mainstream education is an obvious requirement. In addition, a friendly atmosphere in the classroom, an approachable teacher and supportive classmates may be considered undeniably valuable assets for a dyslexic student. There is also a need to offer social support to students with affective problems caused by developmental dyslexia. The results of the present research highlight the importance of the output stage when the student needs to show what he has learnt. The anxiety experienced in that stage is a critical factor that may give rise to dyslexics' avoidance of taking further risks connected with learning a foreign language. It seems then that many performance difficulties are rooted in affective problems. Consequently, all parties concerned (parents, dyslexics and their peers) need to be educated about ways of coping with anxiety (e.g. how to ask for help, whom to ask, how to manage problems), as well as about applying suitable affective strategies involving knowledge of oneself as the learner (Macaro, 2006), for example taking emotional temperature and building networks of effective emotional behaviours. In this way, by changing the individual's thinking, emotions can be altered to become more positive and thus facilitate the SLA process.

Foreign language teachers' awareness of affective and linguistic problems caused by developmental dyslexia should be raised. A module on learning disabilities in pre- and in-service teacher training would do much to aid this process. Such training cannot be limited to multisensory language instruction but should also include a component aimed at developing, maintaining and increasing positive emotions. Affective feedback helps to prevent, avoid and control negative emotions, aiding the teacher to keep dyslexic students motivated and the students themselves to retain their self-esteem.

The study is certainly not free from limitations. The instrument used for measuring symptoms of developmental dyslexia was the Revised Adult Dyslexia Checklist (Vinegrad, 1994). It is a preliminary tool whose indications need to be confirmed by a team of specialists, which was impossible in this research due to practical reasons. Hence, the dyslexia measurements are tentative and must be treated with caution. Moreover, the multidimensional structure of the scales used to measure anxiety at the input, processing and output stages (MacIntyre & Gardner, 1994a) has been questioned, but their use in a univariate manner remains reliable (Onwuegbuzie *et al.*, 2000), which means that the scales hold adequate psychometric characteristics when analysed separately.

The study offers many interesting paths for further research. One direction could involve investigating the phenomenon of anxiety in the foreign language classroom from the perspective of language deficits, which – so far – has not been fully explored. First of all, it would be worth shedding more light on the interplay of situation-specific anxiety (foreign language anxiety) and anxiety produced by developmental dyslexia. Such studies may also take into consideration participants with different types of developmental dyslexia.

Moreover, the oblique anxiety model in language processing proposed by MacIntyre and Gardner (1994a) does not take into account the importance of the stage that prepares learners for input. Before learners attend to it, they are influenced by various factors connected with the learning process, including motivation, goals, attitudes and beliefs, as well as styles and strategies. These factors come into play during the so-called *preactional* (Dörnyei, 2002) or *pre-processing stage* (Tobias, 1985). Hence, it seems worthwhile to examine the role of these factors in general language processing of dyslexic and non-dyslexic students.

There is also a need to investigate the influence of the first foreign language on the acquisition of a further foreign language (L3), as proposed by studies on trilingualism (e.g. Cenoz *et al.*, 2001). In the literature on dyslexia, it is still unclear whether studying L3 intensifies the probability of failure or of eventual success (Cline, 2000).

Acknowledgements

The study was financed by the Polish Committee for Scientific Research (2004–2007).

References

Arnold, J. and Brown, H.D. (1999) A map of the terrain. In J. Arnold (ed.) *Affect in Language Learning* (pp. 1–27). Cambridge: Cambridge University Press.
Bailey, P., Onwuegbuzie, A.J. and Daley, C.E. (2000) Correlates of anxiety at three stages of the foreign language learning process. *Journal of Language and Social Psychology* 19 (4), 474–491.
Bogdanowicz, M. (2003) Specyficzne trudności w czytaniu i pisaniu – dysleksja rozwojowa [Specific difficulties in reading and writing – developmental dyslexia]. In T. Gałkowski and G. Jastrzębowska (eds) *Logopedia – Pytania i Odpowiedzi* (pp. 491–535). Opole: Wydawnictwo Uniwersytetu Opolskiego.
Bogdanowicz, M. (2005) Fakty i kontrowersje wokół dysleksji rozwojowej [Facts and controversies over developmental dyslexia]. In E. Jędrzejowska (ed.) *Dysleksja Rozwojowa. Obszary Trudności* (pp. 9–26). Brzeg: Andragog.
Bogdanowicz, M. and Krasowicz, G. (1996) Kwestionariusz objawów dysleksji u dorosłych (KODD) [Questionnaire of dyslexia symptoms in adults]. On WWW at http://dysleksja.univ.gda.pl. Accessed 14.01.03.
Carroll, J.M. and Illes, J.E. (2006) An assessment of anxiety levels in dyslexic students in higher education. *British Journal of Educational Psychology* 76 (3), 651–662.

Cenoz, J., Hufeisen, B. and Jessner, U. (eds) (2001) *Cross-linguistic Influence in Third Language Acquisition: Psycholinguistic Perspectives*. Clevedon: Multilingual Matters.

Cline, T. (2000) Multilingualism and dyslexia: Challenges for research and practice. *Dyslexia* 6 (1), 3–12.

Crombie, M. (2000) Dyslexia and the learning of a foreign language in school: Where are we going? *Dyslexia* 6 (2), 112–123.

Dörnyei, Z. (2002) The motivational basis of language learning tasks. In P. Robinson (ed.) *Individual Differences and Instructed Language Learning* (pp. 137–158). Amsterdam: John Benjamins.

Eysenck, M.W. (1979) Anxiety, learning, and memory: A reconceptualization. *Journal of Research in Personality* 13 (4), 363–385.

Eysenck, M.W. and Calvo, M.G. (1992) Anxiety and performance: The processing efficiency theory. *Cognition and Emotion* 6 (6), 409–434.

Fisher, S.E. and DeFries, J.C. (2002) Developmental dyslexia: Genetic dissection of a complex cognitive trait. *Nature Reviews. Neuroscience* 3 (10), 767–780.

Friedman, I.A. and Bendas-Jacob, O. (1997) Measuring perceived test anxiety in adolescents: A self-report scale. *Educational and Psychological Measurement* 57 (6), 1035–1047.

Ganschow, L. and Sparks, R.L. (1995) Effects of direct instruction in Spanish phonology on the native-language skills and foreign language aptitude of at-risk foreign language learners. *Journal of Learning Disabilities* 28 (2), 107–120.

Ganschow, L. and Sparks, R.L. (2000) Reflections on foreign language study for students with language learning problems: Research, issues and challenges. *Dyslexia* 6 (2), 87–100.

Ganschow, L., Sparks, R.L. and Javorsky, J. (1998) Foreign language learning difficulties: An historical perspective. *Journal of Learning Disabilities* 31 (3), 248–258.

Ganschow, L., Sparks, R.L., Javorsky, J., Pohlman, J. and Bishop-Marbury, A. (1991) Identifying native language difficulties among foreign language learners in college: A "foreign" language learning disability? *Journal of Learning Disabilities* 24 (9), 530–541.

Gindrich, P.A. (2002) *Funkcjonowanie Psychospołeczne Uczniów Dyslektycznych [Psychosocial Functioning of Dyslexic Learners]*. Lublin: Wydawnictwo UMCS.

Graziano, A. M. and Raulin, M.L. (1993) *Research Methods. A Process of Inquiry*. New York: Harper & Collins.

Hellendoorn, J. and Ruijssenaars, W. (2000) Personal experiences and adjustment of Dutch adults with dyslexia. *Remedial and Special Education* 21 (4), 227–239.

Hopdapp, V. and Benson, J. (1997) The multidimensionality of test anxiety: A test of different models. *Anxiety, Stress, and Coping* 10 (3), 219–344.

Horwitz, E.K. (2000) It ain't over 'til it's over: On foreign language anxiety, first language deficits, and the confounding of variables. *Modern Language Journal* 84 (2), 256–259.

Horwitz, E.K., Horwitz, M. and Cope, J.A. (1986) Foreign language classroom anxiety. *Modern Language Journal* 70 (2), 125–132.

Horwitz, E.K., Horwitz, M. and Cope, J.A. (1991) Foreign language classroom anxiety. In E.K. Horwitz and D.J. Young (eds) *Language Anxiety: From Theory and Research to Classroom Implications* (pp. 27–36). Englewood Cliffs, NJ: Prentice Hall.

Horwitz, E.K. and Young, D. (1991) Afterword. In E.K. Horwitz and D.J. Young (eds) *Language Anxiety: From Theory and Research to Classroom Implications* (pp. 177–178). Upper Saddle River, NJ: Prentice Hall.

Hwang, W., Chang, C. and Chen, G. (2004) The relationship of learning traits, motivation and performance-learning response dynamics. *Computers and Education* 42 (3), 276–287.

Jeffries, S. and Everatt, J. (2004) Working memory: Its role in dyslexia and other specific learning difficulties. *Dyslexia* 10 (3), 196–214.

Keogh, E. and French, C.C. (2001) Test anxiety, evaluative stress, and susceptibility to distraction from threat. *European Journal of Personality* 15 (2), 123–141.

Liebert, L.W. and Morris, R.M. (1967) Cognitive and emotional components of test anxiety. *Psychological Reports* 20 (3), 975–978.

Macaro. E. (2006) Strategies for language learning and for language use: Revising the theoretical framework. *Modern Language Journal* 90 (3), 320–337.

MacIntyre, P.D. (1995) How does anxiety affect second language learning? A reply to Sparks and Ganschow. MLJ Response Article. *Modern Language Journal* 79 (1), 90–99.

MacIntyre, P. (1999) Language anxiety: A review of the research for language teachers. In D.J. Young (ed.) *Affect in Foreign Language and Second Language Learning. A Practical Guide to Creating a Low-anxiety Classroom Atmosphere* (pp. 24–45). Boston: McGraw-Hill.

MacIntyre, P. and Charos, C. (1995) How does anxiety affect second language learning? A reply to Sparks and Ganschow. *Modern Language Journal* 79 (1), 1–32.

MacIntyre, P. and Gardner, R.C. (1989) Anxiety and second language learning: Toward a theoretical clarification. *Language Learning* 39 (2), 251–275.

MacIntyre, P. and Gardner, R.C. (1991a) Methods and results in the study of anxiety in language learning: A review of the literature. *Language Learning* 41 (1), 85–117.

MacIntyre, P. and Gardner, R.C. (1991b) Anxiety and second language learning: Toward a theoretical clarification. In E.K. Horwitz and D.J. Young (eds) *Language Anxiety: From Theory and Research to Classroom Implications* (pp. 41–55). Englewood Cliffs, NJ: Prentice Hall.

MacIntyre, P. and Gardner, R.C. (1991c) Language anxiety: Its relation to other anxieties and to processing in native and foreign language. *Language Learning* 41 (4), 513–534.

MacIntyre, P. D. and Gardner, R.C. (1994a) The subtle effects of language anxiety on cognitive processing in the second language. *Language Learning* 44 (2), 283–305.

MacIntyre, P. D. and Gardner, R.C. (1994b) The effects of induced anxiety on three stages of cognitive processing in computerized vocabulary learning. *Studies in Second Language Acquisition* 16 (1), 1–17.

Manolopoulou-Sergi, E. (2004) Motivation within the information processing model of foreign language learning. *System* 32 (3), 427–441.

Martínez, R.S. and Semrud-Clikeman, M. (2004) Emotional adjustment and school functioning of young adolescents with multiple versus single learning disabilities. *Journal of Learning Disabilities* 37 (5), 411–420.

McNulty, M. (2003) Dyslexia and the life course. *Journal of Learning Disabilities* 36 (4), 363–381.

Minor, S.W. and Gold, S.R. (1985) Worry and emotionality components of test anxiety. *Journal of Personality Assessment* 49 (1), 82–85.

Onwuegbuzie, J., Bailey, P. and Daley, C. (2000) The validation of three scales measuring anxiety at different stages of foreign language learning process: The input anxiety scale, the processing anxiety scale, and the output anxiety scale. *Language Learning* 50 (1), 87–117.

Orenstein, M. (2000) *Smart, but Stuck: What Every Therapist Needs to Know about Learning Disabilities and Imprisoned Intelligence*. New York: Haworth.

Oxford, R. (1999) Anxiety and the language learner. In J. Arnold (ed.) *Affect in Language Learning* (pp. 58–67). Cambridge: Cambridge University Press.

Pappamihiel, N.E. (2001) Moving from the ESL classroom into the mainstream: An investigation of English language anxiety in Mexican girls. *Bilingual Research Journal* 25 (1&2), 1–8.

Price, M.L. (1991) The subjective experience of foreign language anxiety: Interviews with highly anxious students. In E.K. Horwitz and D.J. Young (eds) *Language Anxiety: From Theory and Research to Classroom Implications* (pp. 101–108). Upper Saddle River, NJ: Prentice Hall.

Reynolds, A.M., Elksnin, N. and Brown, F.R. (1996) Specific reading disabilities: Early identification and long-term outcome. *Mental Retardation and Developmental Disabilities. Research Reviews* 2 (1), 21–27.

Rice, P.L. (1999) *Stress and Health* (3rd edn). Pacific Grove: Brooks/Cole Publishing.

Richards, J.C. and Rodgers, T. (1986) *Approaches and Methods in Language Teaching*. Cambridge: Cambridge University Press.

Riddick, B., Sterling, C., Farmer, M. and Morgan, S. (1999) Self-esteem and anxiety in the educational histories of adult dyslexic students. *Dyslexia* 5 (4), 227–248.

Schneider, E. (1999) *Multisensory Structured Metacognitive Instruction*. Frankfurt am Main: Peter Lang.

Schneider, E. and Crombie, M. (2003) *Dyslexia and Foreign Language Learning*. London: David Fulton.

Scovel, T. (1991) The effect of affect on foreign language learning: A review of the anxiety research. In E.K. Horwitz and D.J. Young (eds) *Language Anxiety: From Theory and Research to Classroom Implications* (pp. 15–23). Englewood Cliffs, NJ: Prentice Hall.

Sparks, R.L., Artzer, M., Ganschow, L., Siebenhar, D., Plageman, M. and Patton, J. (1998) Differences in native-language skills, foreign-language aptitude, and foreign language grades among high-, average-, and low-proficiency foreign language learners: Two studies. *Language Testing* 15 (2), 181–216.

Sparks, R.L. and Ganschow, L. (1991) Foreign language learning differences: Affective or native language aptitude differences? *Modern Language Journal* 75 (1), 3–16.

Sparks, R.L. and Ganschow, L. (1993a) The impact of native language learning problems on foreign language learning: Case study illustrations of the Linguistic Coding Deficit Hypothesis. *Modern Language Journal* 77 (1), 58–74.

Sparks, R.L. and Ganschow, L. (1993b) Searching for the cognitive locus of foreign language difficulties: Linking first and second language learning. *Modern Language Journal* 77 (2), 289–302.

Sparks, R.L. and Ganschow, L. (1996) Teachers' perceptions of students' foreign language academic skills and affective characteristics. *Journal of Educational Research* 89 (3), 172–185.

Spielberger, C.D. (1966) Theory and research of anxiety. In C.D. Spielberger (ed.) *Anxiety and Behaviour* (pp. 3–25). New York: Academic Press.

Spolsky, B. (1989) *Conditions for Second Language Learning*. Oxford: Oxford University Press.

Steinberg, F.S. and Horwitz, E.K. (1986) The effect of induced anxiety on the denotative and interpretive content of second language speech. *TESOL Quarterly* 20 (1), 131–136.

Terry, W.S. and Burns, J.S. (2001) Anxiety and repression in attention and retention. *Journal of General Psychology* 128 (4), 422–432.

Tobias, S. (1985) Test anxiety: Interference, defective skills, and cognitive capacity. *Educational Psychologist* 20 (3), 135–142.

Tobias, S. and Everson, H.T. (1997) Studying the relationship between affective and metacognitive variables. *Anxiety, Stress, and Coping* 10 (1), 59–81.

Vinegrad, M. (1994) A revised adult dyslexia check list. *Educare* 48, 21–23.

Williams, K. and McGillicuddy-De Lisi, A. (2000) Coping strategies in adolescents. *Journal of Applied Developmental Psychology*, 20 (4), 537–549.

Young, D. (1986) The relationship between anxiety and foreign language oral proficiency ratings. *Foreign Language Annals*, 19 (3), 439–445.

Young, D. (1991) Creating a low-anxiety classroom environment: What does the anxiety research suggest? *Modern Language Journal* 75 (4), 426–439.

Chapter 5
Vocabulary Learning in Dyslexia: The Case of a Hungarian Learner

ÁGNES SARKADI

Introduction

Vocabulary acquisition is one of the most problematic areas for dyslexic language learners (Kormos & Kontra, this volume; Schneider & Crombie, 2003), and a number of recommendations have been made about how to help dyslexic learners to acquire words in a foreign language. Nevertheless, few studies have empirically investigated vocabulary learning difficulties of dyslexic learners of English as a foreign language. Most previous studies have concentrated on English speaking dyslexic learners of other modern foreign languages (e.g. Hodge, 1998; Sparks & Miller, 2000) and on adult learners with specific learning disabilities in the target language environment (e.g. Almanza et al., 1996; Gersten et al., 1999). Even research articles describing special teaching programmes for dyslexic learners of English have focused primarily on facilitating spelling and reading in English; therefore they only discuss vocabulary acquisition indirectly (e.g. Nijakowska, 2001, 2004, this volume; Secemski et al., 2000). The present case study tries to provide information about the vocabulary learning problems of a Hungarian dyslexic learner of English, and it examines her reactions to the use of compensatory techniques recommended for teaching English to dyslexics. It is hoped that the presentation of this case will aid teachers of dyslexic language learners to understand the difficulties their students experience in learning words, and that it will provide them with information on techniques that are useful in facilitating their vocabulary learning processes.

An Overview of Dyslexia and Vocabulary Acquisition

Learning a new word is a complex process: it involves the recognition of the auditive and the visual forms of the word, the knowledge of its morphosyntactic and semantic properties and the integration of the word into the mental lexicon (Jiang, 2004; Oxford & Scarcella, 1994). This process is often challenging for language learners even without learning disabilities, which explains why a large body of literature is dedicated to methods facilitating vocabulary learning processes (e.g. Fowle, 2002; Hulstijn, 1997; Schmitt & Schmitt, 1995). Hulstijn (1997) distinguished two types of vocabulary learning: incidental and intentional learning. In the case of intentional learning, the retention of the link between the word's form and its meaning happens through the learner's explicit intention to learn, whereas incidental learning is unintentional. Incidental learning of vocabulary is very difficult for dyslexic learners due to their phonological processing problems, whereas learners with no disabilities are able to acquire words from the input without conscious effort (Schneider & Crombie, 2003). Learning words in English is even more challenging for dyslexic language learners than learning words in some other languages because English is a language with a deep orthography. The English alphabet has 26 letters representing 44 phonemes; however, according to Selikowitz (1993), there are 577 grapheme-to-phoneme correspondences in English, which need to be recognised during the reading process. Nijakowska (2001) describes a dyslexic learner of English who experienced severe difficulties with vocabulary acquisition because of the non-transparent nature of the English language. Similarly, according to the findings of Ormos (2003), learning words was one of the most problematic areas in learning English for Hungarian subjects in a secondary school for dyslexic students. In a case study, Ormos (2004) pointed out that vocabulary learning is challenging even for an otherwise successful dyslexic learner of English.

A number of techniques can facilitate the acquisition of vocabulary for dyslexic language learners (Barr, 1993; Hodge, 1998; Nijakowska, 2001; Schneider & Crombie, 2003; Sparks & Miller, 2000). One of the most frequently used methods is multisensory teaching, which involves the parallel use of perceptual modalities (Barr, 1993), which helps students to take advantage of their stronger learning channels and also to develop their weaker modalities (Hodge, 1998; Schneider & Crombie, 2003). The most commonly recommended multisensory techniques involving kinesthetic/tactile modalities are miming (Robinson-Tait, 2003; Schneider & Crombie, 2003), tracing words on paper, on a desk, and/or in the air (Nijakowska, 2001), and/or using a word processor (Hodge, 1998). As for techniques stimulating the visual channels, the use of flashcards (Robinson-Tait, 2003; Schneider & Crombie, 2003), the preparation of drawings next to words in the vocabulary list (Robinson-Tait, 2003), and the colour-coding of vowels and consonants in words (Hodge, 1998) were also found useful. Special visual organisers called mindmaps, which combine visual and verbal elements and represent information in a holistic way, also facilitate vocabulary acquisition for dyslexics (Gyarmathy, 2001; Kenyon, 2001).

Learning strategies which play an important role in facilitating vocabulary acquisition for dyslexics are mnemonic devices such as those recommended by Schneider and Crombie (2003): visual illustrations (picture mnemonics), sound and letter clues facilitating the recall of pronunciation and spelling, acronyms, crazy stories containing words with difficult spelling and keywords (keywords belong to the learner's active vocabulary in any language; if a new word is mentally linked to them, they can assist the recall of pronunciation, spelling and/or morphology).

Another approach which seems useful for dyslexics is the elimination of homogenous inhibition, which is also called the Ranschburg effect (Ranschburg, 1939). According to this principle, homogenous elements interfere with each other in the learning process and inhibit learning. For example, the Meixner Dyslexia Approach, which is a successful and widespread method for teaching first language (L1) reading and spelling to Hungarian dyslexics, inserts long intervals between the teaching of similar letters to eliminate homogenous inhibition (Meixner, 1993). It seems plausible that the use of long intervals between teaching similar L2 words would also be beneficial.

Empirical studies evaluating the effectiveness of compensatory teaching of English words to dyslexic learners have also been conducted. In her case study of a Polish dyslexic learner of English, Nijakowska (2001) discusses the subject's specific language learning difficulties and the methods applied in her tutoring. The learner had a phonological core deficit and experienced problems in reading and writing in English. Her tutoring was based on an explicit and structured programme which developed phonemic awareness and visual recognition of words through the use of multisensory techniques and cognitive learning strategies.

In the following case study, a dyslexic learner's difficulties in vocabulary acquisition are examined. Apart from the frequently discussed problems with learning the spelling and pronunciation of new words, her difficulties in memorising phonetically and/or semantically similar words and using vocabulary in context are also explored. The chapter also examines the student's experience of and reactions to the use of compensatory techniques recommended by previous studies.

Research Method

My research focused on two main questions: (1) What vocabulary learning difficulties does a successful dyslexic student of English experience? and (2), how does she make use of the compensatory methods taught to her overtly? I chose to conduct a qualitative case study to explore the participant's learning processes, her thoughts, feelings and reactions. The student I had been tutoring for more than three years seemed to be a suitable subject for this research; the length of our teacher–student relationship and the high degree of confidence and trust which characterised it helped me to obtain a good understanding of her case.

The participant

The participant of my research, whom I will refer to under the pseudonym Anna, is a 16-year-old student in a mainstream secondary school in Budapest. She has been studying English for six years, and during this time she has never asked for special treatment in the English lessons, such as extra time during tests or exemption from the evaluation of her written work. Instead, she has been taking private lessons in English to help her cope with the school requirements. I have been tutoring her for more than three years, before which she was taught by a speech therapist for two years. Although after studying English for six years Anna has only reached pre-intermediate-level, she can be considered a successful dyslexic learner of the language. In Hungary dyslexic students are commonly exempted from the evaluation of their foreign language studies (Gyarmathy & Vassné Kovács, 2004), so for one of them to able to meet the requirements of a mainstream school is an indisputable success. Anna is highly motivated to learn the language: she intends to take an intermediate level language exam in two years' time, and she considers herself capable of preparing successfully for this exam.

Procedures

The research presented in this chapter was part of an extensive investigation into Anna's dyslexia-related problems in learning English. The following sources of data were used in the extensive research (Sarkadi, 2005): a learning style questionnaire and an unstructured interview concerning her learning style preferences, my log as a tutor about our sessions, a collection of documents and in-depth interviews with Anna and her mother. The learning style questionnaire, the interview about learning style preferences and the interview with the participant's mother were intended to collect rich and detailed background information about the student. The in-depth interview with Anna was triangulated with the tutor's log and the document review. In the following section these instruments are described from the perspective of vocabulary acquisition since this study describes Anna's case from the point of view of vocabulary learning processes only.

At the beginning of the research, Anna was asked to fill in a learning style questionnaire which was based on the learning style assessment tool described by Hatt and Nichols (1995). The questions were in Hungarian, and the completion of the questionnaire was followed by a short discussion in which Anna commented on some of her answers. The primary aim of this phase of the study was to identify Anna's learning style preferences, which are frequently mentioned in the literature as the basis of effective remedial work (Almanza *et al.*, 1996; Hatt & Nichols, 1995).

During the four months of the research, the author kept a log of the tutorial lessons. The following data were recorded in the log: the activities involved in the lesson; the occurrence of problems in the four skills and in learning spelling; vocabulary or grammar; the use of overt teaching of special compensatory techniques, and Anna's reactions to them.

Three interviews were conducted: two with Anna and one with her mother. The aim of the interview with Anna's mother was to obtain more information about the nature of Anna's dyslexia and her earlier educational experience. The two interviews with Anna were concerned with different aspects of her language learning. In the first interview the focus was on general background information related to the process of language learning. The questions were intended to find out about previous language learning experience, attitude towards studying English and the characteristics of Anna's English lessons in school. I also hoped that Anna's answers would help me to get an insight into the experience of being a dyslexic student in a mainstream class. Part of the second interview was aimed at eliciting detailed information about Anna's acquisition of new lexical items. I asked her about vocabulary learning strategies and techniques, specific problems she had and her use of compensatory methods.

Apart from the data sources listed above, a number of documents were analysed. I used Anna's notebooks to observe the use of certain compensatory techniques and methods recommended for dyslexics and collected some of her written stories, letters and dialogues to study her written self expression and use of vocabulary in writing. Three tasks which involved oral self expression were recorded to provide data about her use of vocabulary in speaking. The three tasks were the following: story-telling based on visuals, summarising the gist of a text, and a spontaneous conversation with the researcher. The total length of the three recordings was 272 words.

The data collection and analysis followed a cyclical approach. In the first stage of my research, I studied my logs, the results of the learning style questionnaire, and the transcribed interview with Anna's mother. This analysis helped me to find the relevant issues in the data, which then guided me in further data collection. At the second stage, I analysed the transcribed interviews with Anna, and I continued the analysis of my log. This was followed by the examination of the collected documents, and the transcription and analysis of the oral tasks. Once all data had been collected and transcribed, they were subjected to content analysis using the constant comparative method (Maykut & Morehouse, 1994). The process of data analysis was aided and the reliability of coding was ensured by expert advice and review by a university lecturer experienced in the field of dyslexia. Three major categories were identified: (1) problems with grapheme-phoneme correspondences; (2) problems with using vocabulary in context; and (3) the student's views regarding the use and usefulness of explicitly taught vocabulary learning techniques. In the following section, I will first introduce Anna as a dyslexic learner, then analyse her approach to learning vocabulary.

Results and Discussion

Anna's language learning history

Anna's mother claimed that the early identification of Anna's learning disability was a major cause of her success at school. The parents noticed their daughter's problems at a very early age, and they consulted a psychologist in time. The first warning sign was a delay in Anna's speech development. At the age of three Anna was examined by a psychologist, who recognised some of the warning symptoms of dyslexia such as speech delay, problems with visual-motor coordination and laterality (preference for one side of the body, e.g. hand, eye, leg, ear preference). After the diagnosis, Anna received therapy for four years. She attended a special kindergarten which was maintained for children with delayed speech development, and in primary school she started her studies in a special education programme where she learned to read through a special dyslexic approach (Meixner, 1993). After finishing the second grade in the special education class, Anna was integrated into a mainstream class since experts suggested that despite her specific learning difficulties she would be able to meet the requirements of a mainstream class. According to Anna's mother, the transition from the dyslexic class to the mainstream class took place without any particular problems.

Anna's first problems at school arose when she started to study English in Grade 4. She did not get good marks in English, and it was sometimes impossible for her to follow what was going on during the English lessons. As Anna failed at the end of the term, her parents had to decide whether to apply for some kind of exemption from English. However, considering Anna's high IQ (128), the psychologist who diagnosed Anna's dyslexia advised that she should take some private lessons in English before the decision about exemption was made. The psychologist recommended a speech therapist, who had an advanced language certificate in English, as a tutor for Anna. The parents decided to give Anna and her tutor a chance.

Anna had two 60-minute lessons with her tutor every week. She really liked these lessons, and her attitude towards learning English also started to change: 'I used to hate learning English. But when she was tutoring me, it was not that bad. Actually, sometimes it was fun.'[1] The private lessons were successful: Anna was able to meet the requirements of her primary school. She got an average grade at the end of the year, and next year she was one of the best students in English. She was even selected to participate in an English competition.

Now Anna studies at a mainstream secondary school (Grades 7–12) where she has four English and four Latin lessons a week. Their English textbook is a pre-intermediate level, monolingual, British publication written for a generic international audience. A rather conservative teaching style characterises the lessons. Most of the teaching is frontal, and pair work or group work are seldom employed. According to Anna, speaking is not practiced too much; most of the lessons are dedicated to studying grammar and doing reading and listening tasks. Grammar is taught in a deductive way, which means that students usually do not discover the rules of grammar on their own but have them presented directly by the teacher. The students are evaluated on the basis of grammar and vocabulary tests. The grammar tests consist of sentence transformations and gap-filling exercises, and the vocabulary tests are based on translating words out of context from one language into the other. The students' speaking skills and written self-expression are seldom evaluated. Unfortunately, Anna does not receive any extra help or special treatment during these English lessons, since she and her mother decided to conceal Anna's dyslexia in secondary school because of some experiences of stigmatisation and humiliation in primary school (Grades 1–6).

She is aware that she has certain problems with learning English and needs tutoring to be able to achieve success in the English lessons:

> I am not too good at learning English words. I find it very hard to study by myself for vocabulary tests. I tend to confuse words ... Sometimes it is also hard for me to understand the explanations of my English teacher when she is talking about grammar. Yes, grammar explanations are very confusing in school, but I usually understand grammar in the private lessons.

Anna usually has two 60-minute lessons of private tutoring a week. It is important for her to make progress in English because she has plans with the language:

> I think you should be able to speak English well to have a good job. I want to take the intermediate level language exam before I leave secondary school. I know it will be more difficult for me than for someone who is not dyslexic, but I think I will be able to pass it, if I work hard.

Summarising the main points of Anna's language learning history, it should be emphasised that Anna is a dyslexic student of English, who can study in mainstream education because of early identification and appropriate therapy. Learning English is more challenging for her than for non-dyslexics, though with the help of her tutor and intensive practice at home, she is successful in it, and she can meet the requirements of a mainstream English class.

Problems with grapheme–phoneme correspondences

When learning new words, Anna relies on her visual processing skills. This is in line with the finding from the extensive study (Sarkadi, 2005) that Anna has a predominantly visual learning style preference and that her auditory processing skills are weaker. Besides, her English teacher's preference for testing vocabulary by administering written quizzes also fosters visual learning.

Anna declared in the interview that she did not like learning new English words and considered it a very difficult and tiring task. Owing to the difference between the pronunciation and the spelling of English words, she said that when she studied a word, she put the main emphasis on memorising its spelling. Learning the correct pronunciation she found more challenging:

> I think learning the correct pronunciation is more difficult than learning the spelling. I can see the spelling in my vocabulary notebook, but I cannot see the pronunciation. If I write the pronunciation next to the word, it helps a bit. The only problem is that I know my school teacher will test the spelling, so I often concentrate only on spelling. I know it is not good. I think pronunciation is more important.

To obtain more information about Anna's problems which originate from the non-transparent orthography of the English language, I asked her to list some problematic and some non-problematic words. First of all, she was asked to mention some words which she could write down and pronounce as well. She listed some basic words (*yes, have, and, the*) and some 'difficult words' which had been discussed in our preceding tutorial lesson (*education, illness, think*). Then she was asked about words which she could spell but could not pronounce: she found it very hard to give examples. She mentioned that for a very long time she had not known how to pronounce words ending in *-tion*, but she had already learnt it. As for words she could pronounce but not spell well, Anna mentioned *between, foot* and *water* (their misspelled versions had been discussed in our preceding lesson) and said that the majority of English words belonged to this category. Finally, Anna was asked to list words which caused her problems in pronunciation and spelling as well. She said that most of the long new words she had not practiced enough belonged to this category, and she mentioned some new words from her vocabulary notebook (*resources, health care, earthquakes*).

Answering the question about what helps her to spell words correctly, Anna said that she tried to recall the word visually:

> When I write down a word, I usually see it. When I have problems with a word, I only see fragments of it. Sometimes I write down a

word, and I see it is not correct because it looks strange. Then I try to correct it.

As for concentrating on pronunciation, Anna told me that considering how words are pronounced sometimes helped her, but she often found pronunciation misleading. Furthermore, she added that it was challenging for her to concentrate on pronunciation, 'Pronunciation may help me in connection with the order of letters, but it requires a lot of concentration. But usually I think pronunciation is misleading. I often misspell a word because I am influenced by its pronunciation.' My notes in the log also provide support for Anna's claim, as my entries reveal that Anna seldom relied on pronunciation as an aid in spelling though I often pointed out to her that some of her mistakes (e.g. omission of *r*, sequential errors, problems with *th*) could be avoided if she concentrated on pronunciation. My log book indicated that if her attention was drawn to a misspelled word, she could usually correct her mistake, but when she was writing on her own, she did not use phonological information to avoid certain errors (e.g. if she had relied on how the following words are pronounced she could have avoided the spelling mistakes *Oxford-Oxfort, presc(r)iption, foot-footh*). She said that listening to certain sounds and writing at the same time was a very difficult task. I also recorded in the log that Anna found it hard to tell whether a word which she can pronounce well contains a specific sound or not (e.g. she could not say whether *thirsty* contains a *t* in the last syllable). These difficulties seem to reflect problems with auditory analysis, and it is very likely that Anna found it hard to concentrate on pronunciation because of her weak auditory processing skills. Similar deficiencies in auditory processing were described by Nijakowska (2001) in her case study of a Polish dyslexic learner of English.

Anna also mentioned some specific features which make spelling especially problematic. The presence of *th* in a word was one of these features:

> I think words which contain *th* are very problematic, for everyone ... I still do not really hear the difference between words that contain *th* and words that contain *t* ... Well, I can hear the difference if I concentrate on it a lot, and someone pronounces the sounds, but I cannot produce the difference in speech myself, and I cannot hear the difference when I am writing.

The other problematic feature which Anna named was the presence of vowel and consonant clusters in words. According to Anna, words containing vowel or consonant clusters are very easy to misspell because she often leaves out or reverses letters in these words. It is interesting to observe that the examples she mentioned as difficult because of their length (*resources, health care, earthquakes*) also contain vowel and consonant clusters.

Problems not directly linked to the non-transparent nature of the English language

Studying my notes about our tutorial lessons, I identified some elements which made vocabulary acquisition difficult for Anna and which could not be directly explained by the non-transparent nature of English orthography. One of these elements was that Anna tended to confuse similar looking and sounding words with each other, which may be explained by the principle of homogenous inhibition. Examples of such confusions were quite frequent. If a new text contained two similar words, Anna was very likely to mix them up. The similarity was usually both phonetic and visual (e.g. *waist-wrist, caught-cough, split-spoil*), but sometimes semantically similar words were also confused (e.g. *bruise-sprain*). These types of confusion deserve special attention since they can lead to serious misunderstanding both in oral and written communication.

The notes in the log reveal that a fairly low degree of similarity was enough for Anna to mix up two words. For example, Anna had problems because she substituted the word *protect* with *practice* in speaking and in writing as well (e.g. she said *Practice the environment* instead of saying *Protect the environment*). At first glance these words were only similar in their first two sounds; however they share some other features which may influence Anna: *c* and *t* follow each other in both words, and they both have a *t* in the middle. To distinguish these two words from each other may not be problematic for most learners of English, but it is a difficult task for Anna.

In the interview, Anna was asked to list some words she had studied many times, but still occasionally confused, 'I often forget what distinguishes *water* and *weather* and *waiter* and *weather*... Now I can pronounce them, and I know what they mean because I practiced them a lot. But I am not sure about their spelling.'

There was another problem which aggravated vocabulary acquisition. Both the interview data and the notes in the log indicate that Anna sometimes misread the words she was studying and then memorised the misread versions (*electricat* for *electrician, preoparti* for *prepare*). These problems often occurred in connection with polysyllabic words, especially when she encountered the item in the context of a reading passage, or when the pronunciation of new words was not discussed in class. It should be mentioned that the vocabulary notebook Anna used at school contained numerous spelling mistakes (about 15% of the words were misspelled), which also made learning words difficult for her. She said that her school English teacher often did not write new words on the blackboard; this made it very hard for her write down words correctly. In order to avoid the memorisation of misspelled word forms, we regularly checked her notebook in the tutoring sessions. Occasionally she was given a typed glossary at school, which she considered useful because this way she did not have to worry about the spelling mistakes. However, these glossaries were lengthy (they contained 80–100 words), and they were supposed to be learnt within a week, which was extremely challenging for Anna.

Problems with using vocabulary in context

It is interesting to observe the mistakes Anna made in oral self expression. In order to study her use of vocabulary when speaking, I audio-recorded three tasks which involved oral speech production. The three tasks were the following: construction of a narrative based on visuals, summarising a text, and a spontaneous conversation with the researcher. Most of her mistakes were due to vocabulary confusion, which may be explained with reference to the principle of homogenous inhibition. She confused words with similar pronunciation and/or orthography in speech. For example, she said *they said George* instead of *they saved George*. Anna also confused derived word forms. For example, she used *injured* instead of *injury* (George has a very dangerous *injured*), optimist instead of optimistic (Kaku is *optimist* about the future).

It seems that some of the confusions were triggered by proximity. If two similar words were relatively near to each other (usually within a unit of two or three sentences), Anna occasionally confused these words in speech, 'We have *one world language* called English. We will have a *one government* (instead of world government).' *One* and *world* are next to each other in the first sentence, in the second sentence *world* was confused with *one*. In another example, Anna was speaking about a *hot knife* and a *candle*. At the beginning of the task, she used these words correctly, however, after a short time she started to use the word (*knef*) to refer to *candle*.

Finally, some of her oral mistakes consisted of adding extra sounds to the word forms (*dressert* instead of *desert*, and *organis* instead of *organs*), which may be explained by that fact that she could not recall the visual image of these words correctly, or she may have memorised misread versions of these word forms.

As for self expression in writing, I did not observe vocabulary confusion and distorted word forms similar to her oral mistakes in the collected documents. However, Anna confirmed that she sometimes had problems with mixing up words in writing as well.

The use of compensatory techniques facilitating vocabulary acquisition

During the tutorial sessions, a variety of vocabulary teaching methods recommended for dyslexics were introduced. These methods were chosen after the analysis of the interview with Anna on her vocabulary learning difficulties. It is important to mention that I did not measure the improvement in Anna's vocabulary acquisition, I only recorded her comments about the compensatory methods and my observations about her reactions. At the end of the four-month teaching period, I asked Anna to reflect on the new methods.

The result of the learning style questionnaire, according to which Anna had a predominantly visual learning style with some kinaesthetic elements, guided me in choosing appropriate multisensory techniques. Therefore, when tutoring Anna, I mainly applied activities stimulating the visual and the kinaesthetic channels. During the tutorial lessons, I had the impression that the use of methods involving visual modalities was well received by Anna, and their application could significantly enhance the efficiency of her vocabulary learning. As I noted in my log, if the introduction of new words was accompanied by pictures and other visuals, it made memorisation and recall easier. When she was given thematic lists of vocabulary to learn at school, I used pictures to illustrate the words. Similarly, I used illustrations when I taught new words before reading a text. Anna also remarked in the interview that the use of visuals made vocabulary learning less difficult for her, 'It is easier to learn words, if I can link pictures or illustrations to them.'

Some other specific methods stimulating the visual channels also proved to be useful. One of them was colour-coding vowels and consonants (recommended by Hodge, 1998). All words entered in the vocabulary notebook used in our tutorial lessons were colour-coded. The consonants were written in black or blue, and the vowels in red. Anna found this technique very helpful, and she started to apply it in her school notebook as well. She summarised the advantages of this method in the following way, 'The use of different colours helps me. This way the words do not look that long, and it is easier to remember them.'

Another helpful method was putting drawings next to problematic words (proposed by Robinson-Tait, 2003). For example, Anna illustrated words with drawings when they studied long lists of thematic vocabulary such as words in connection with the topic of health. An important advantage of engaging the learner in drawing is that it helps to ease the tension which is experienced when learning words. Anna considered this method useful, and she also remarked that these drawings made orientation in her vocabulary notebook easier and helped her to recall words. Upon inspecting Anna's vocabulary notebook, I found that she put drawings next to about 20% of the words.

Techniques involving kinesthetic and tactile modalities also facilitated vocabulary acquisition. One of the methods which Anna found especially useful was tracing words in the air (*cf.* Nijakowska, 2001). As I noted in my log, at first Anna was quite unwilling to apply this strategy because she considered it childish. However, her attitude changed quickly when she found that it was effective, and she applied it during memorisation and recall as well: 'I was really surprised that this technique could help me. It is indeed useful if I learn difficult words.' When she used this technique, she only traced the problematic parts of the words (e.g. recalling the correct spelling of *message* she traced *eae*), and her movements were small, so it was not easy to notice when she was tracing words. As noted in my log, during the four-month observational period Anna used this tracing technique in connection with 10 different words such as *prescription, leather* and *courage* during the lessons. She also mentioned that she occasionally used this technique when memorising words at home, and tracing helped her to spell, for example, the word *advance* accurately in a word test at school.

Another method involving the tactile-kinaesthetic modalities was the so-called 'memory game.' Problematic words and their Hungarian equivalents were written on cards in capital letters. The letters of the words were colour-coded (consonants: black, vowels: red). Anna played the well-known memory game with these cards. The only extra feature of this memory game was that Anna was asked to say the English or the Hungarian equivalent of the word after picking up a card. First I prepared the cards for her, but later she applied this technique twice on her own when she had to memorise difficult words for school tests. She found this technique useful:

> These cards can be made very quickly. And what I like about them is that if you play memory with eight very difficult words, you will be able to remember five or six of them very well.

Finally, I also tried miming to make memorisation and recall more efficient and varied (*cf.* Robinson-Tait, 2003; Schneider & Crombie, 2003). However, as I noted in my log, Anna was quite shy about miming; therefore this method was applied only twice. When she was asked to reflect on the 'new learning methods', she said she did not find this method useful. A technique similar to miming was, however, useful when she studied the parts of the body and the different organs. During memorisation Anna pointed at the location of different words on herself, and she considered this efficient:

> It was good when I practiced the parts of the body this way. I remember I had problems confusing *eyebrows, eyelid, eyelashes,* and I sometimes confused *lips* and *eyelid*. It helped me a lot when I showed these words on myself.

Without the use of mnemonic devices, learning vocabulary would be a heavy burden for Anna. Three years ago when I started to teach her, and it became obvious that she found learning vocabulary very difficult, I occasionally used keywords to help her to memorise words. Keywords are very useful mnemonic devices to facilitate the memorisation of new words (Schneider & Crombie, 2003), so when I saw that learning a word was problematic for Anna, I tried to look for an appropriate keyword in her active vocabulary. For example, *rain* was an appropriate keyword to teach the spelling and the pronunciation of the word *complain*, which Anna kept spelling as *complen*. To help her, I pointed out that *complain* and *rain* contain the same vowels, and they are spelt in the same way. She could link the two words semantically as well (*I complained about the rain*). During the period of the research, keywords were used in every second lesson to facilitate vocabulary acquisition. Most of the time, I was the one who provided the keywords, but in the last two weeks of the research, my student came up with five keywords of her own. For example, *rain* as a keyword for *sprain* and the Hungarian *vél* (presume) as a keyword for *whale*. When Anna reflected on the different compensatory techniques, she said that keywords provided by her tutor often helped her to recall problematic words; however, she considered it very difficult to find keywords on her own.

I also used some other mnemonic devices recommended by Schneider and Crombie (2003). One of these methods which seemed to be useful was writing stories and dialogues incorporating problematic vocabulary. For example, this method helped Anna to distinguish between *weather, waiter* and *water*. She was asked to write and memorise a short and interesting story containing these words. She also drew a picture about the story and named the problematic words on her drawing. This relatively short activity helped Anna to overcome a problem which she had been struggling with for more than two years. Funny stories also proved useful for learning collocations with the same verb. For example, Anna learnt that the verb *make* is used in the idiom *make up one's mind*, and that *make* is also used in collocations with *sure, a reservation,* and *a complaint* by incorporating these expressions in a story. During the four-month research period, Anna was asked to write stories with problematic words five times. I gave her the words to be incorporated in the stories, and Anna found the method useful; however she did not use it on her own. She spoke about the advantages of the method in the following way: 'If I write and memorise a story containing difficult words, it usually helps a lot ... I could remember the differences between *weather, waiter* and *water* when I recalled the story.'

Schneider and Crombie (2003) also suggest the use of visual cues to facilitate the memorisation of new vocabulary. I modelled this technique to Anna, and during the teaching period she applied it on her own on one occasion, when she invented the following subtle visual clue for learning the meaning and the spelling of the word *commute*:

> *Commute* is in connection with movement. The two *m-s* in the middle of the word can represent the two legs of a person – who moves (commutes) with his two legs ... Of course, people who commute usually travel by car or train ... But it helps me to remember the word and its spelling.

The explicit teaching of grapheme-phoneme correspondences is also an essential part of successful vocabulary acquisition for dyslexic learners (Schneider, 1996). About 80% of the tutoring lessons involved the discussion of problematic words, and the analysis of grapheme–phoneme correspondences always had an important role in these discussions. Anna considered this technique useful, 'It is good if I see that there is some relation between spelling and pronunciation. This way spelling is less chaotic.'

The syllabification of difficult words (*cf.* Nijakowska, 2001) also helped Anna to notice grapheme-phoneme correspondences, and it aided the acquisition of the spelling and the pronunciation of polysyllabic words. Anna said that she sometimes used syllabification when she was preparing for vocabulary quizzes at home. She also mentioned that her former tutor used this method quite frequently, and it helped her:

> She had coloured cards with syllables on them, and I had to put them in the right order. I think it helped me to learn the words. Now, I only divide words into syllables if they are very long. It is easier to remember them that way.

I also started to apply some activities which focused on grapheme–phoneme correspondences. These were gap-filling exercises with missing letters and exercises in which Anna had to find examples of given spelling patterns. Anna noted that these activities were difficult at the beginning and required a lot of attention. Another type of activity which I used was 'rhyming games' (recommended by Nijakowska, 2001). Although these types of activities are useful, they were challenging for Anna, and she did not enjoy them. In my opinion, Anna's problems with these activities may be explained with reference to her difficulties with auditory processing and phonemic awareness. She spoke about her problems with these activities in the following way:

> It is very difficult for me when I have to find a word which rhymes with another word. Sometimes it is also difficult for me to decide whether I hear a specific sound in a word or not. I mean I can decide on it, but I have to concentrate a lot.

Apart form the above mentioned methods, I also applied some techniques to reduce the occurrence of vocabulary confusion. These techniques were the isolated presentation of new vocabulary items before reading or listening to a text, the use of relatively long intervals between the teaching of similar words, and the pre-selection and discussion of problematic words.

I noted in my log several times that Anna confused words frequently if new lexical items in a text had not been discussed prior to a reading activity. However, if the new words of a reading task were pre-taught with the help of visuals, brainstorming or some other pre-reading activities (*cf.* Gábor, 2003; Root, 1994), I observed that it prevented the memorisation of misread versions and reduced the number of problematic words. Unfortunately, the new vocabulary of textbook reading texts was usually not pre-taught in Anna's English lessons at school, which, as I noted, often led to vocabulary confusions and the memorisation of misread word forms. In these cases I had to reteach the vocabulary in the tutoring sessions.

Leaving relatively long intervals between the teaching of similar words also seemed to be useful. In her recommendations on teaching Hungarian reading and writing to dyslexic learners, Meixner (1993) proposed that the teaching of similar letters should be separated by long intervals in order to eliminate homogenous inhibition. Long intervals also seem to be beneficial in the case of words in a foreign language. In the pre-teaching period for reading tasks, I never taught similar looking or similar sounding words one after the other, and I tried to increase the interval between teaching similar words as much as possible when the aim of the lesson was vocabulary development. As recommended by Meixner for learning to identify letters in the process of acquiring L1 literacy, it also seemed important that similar words should not be written after each other in the vocabulary notebook, and as the entries of my log revealed, the teaching of more than four similar words in one session was unsuccessful. Anna herself noted in the interview that leaving long intervals between similar words helped her to acquire new vocabulary:

> If I hear or read two similar words one after each the other, I am very likely to confuse them. So, it helps me a lot if I do not learn similar words together, and if they are not near to each other in the vocabulary notebook.

Unfortunately, the words in Anna's school vocabulary notebook were sometimes in alphabetical order; therefore a large number of similar words followed each other. In these cases the vocabulary section was rewritten in a different order in our tutorial lessons.

Another technique that I used with Anna was the pre-selection and discussion of problematic words. I usually asked Anna to reflect on new words before she started learning them. She was asked to choose the ones which were likely to cause problems and we discussed the reasons for the problems (e.g. 'This word is likely to be hard to learn because I do not know how to pronounce it/it is similar to another word/it contains a silent *e*/a *th*/a lot of syllables.'). Using this technique, I also came to understand Anna's problems with learning vocabulary better. For example, I found it surprising that certain words which did not seem to be similar to me were considered to be similar (and therefore problematic) by Anna. For example, according to her, the words *recover* and *cancer* are easy to confuse because they are visually similar. As learning words was problematic for Anna, and in her English lessons at school vocabulary tests were frequently used to measure achievement, these discussions were quite frequent in our tutorial sessions.

It is very important to note about all the above-mentioned compensatory techniques that the four-month teaching period of the research was only enough for the modelling and training of these compensatory techniques. Anna reacted positively to most of them, but except for a few cases she did not start to apply the techniques on her own. A possible reason for this is that she was not asked explicitly to apply these techniques by herself while preparing for school English lessons as I did not want to impose them on her. On the basis of this research, it cannot be predicted which compensatory techniques Anna will regularly use in the future.

Conclusion

The results of the study reported in this chapter indicate that Anna experienced several problems in vocabulary acquisition, which she was able to overcome only with considerable effort. Her difficulties with vocabulary acquisition seemed to be related to a number of different factors. It is indisputable that the deep orthography of the English language played a very important part in the problem. Another factor which can be related to Anna's problems in spelling is that due to her difficulties with auditory processing, she found it very hard to rely on the pronunciation of words in deciding how to spell a word correctly. These findings revealed that the confusion of similar words and the memorisation of misread word forms also resulted in severe difficulties and lead to misunderstandings in oral self expression.

The findings concerning the application of compensatory methods suggest that there are a number of techniques which can facilitate vocabulary acquisition for dyslexic students. As Anna had a dominantly visual learning style with some kinesthetic elements, the multisensory approach involving visual, kinesthetic and tactile modalities was especially useful. The use of mnemonic devices and the explicit teaching of grapheme–phoneme correspondences also enhanced the efficiency of vocabulary acquisition. A number of techniques were found to be useful in reducing the occurrence of vocabulary confusions. The pre-teaching of new reading vocabulary in isolation, the elimination of homogenous inhibition, and the pre-selection and discussion of 'difficult words', helped to prevent the memorisation of misread word forms and reduced the number of problematic words.

As for the applicability of the findings in other contexts, it is important to remember that Anna's case is unusual from many points of view. Anna is an early-identified dyslexic, and she had been given special therapy to manage her problems in her native language. One may suspect that dyslexics who are diagnosed at a later stage experience more severe difficulties in learning foreign vocabulary than those diagnosed in early childhood. Furthermore, Anna's supportive family background also facilitated her language learning. It also has to be noted that Anna seemed to have problems mainly with auditory processing, and her visual learning channels were only slightly impaired. It is quite likely that another student whose dyslexia manifests itself in problems with visual processing would have different problems in learning English words and would benefit from different compensatory techniques than Anna. The investigation of the vocabulary learning processes of dyslexic language learners who have difficulties with visual processing and those who were not given special therapy in their mother tongue would be possible directions to pursue in further research.

Despite the above-mentioned limitations of this study, the description of Anna's special vocabulary learning difficulties may be useful for English teachers teaching dyslexic students in mainstream classrooms, as most of the methods which facilitated language learning for Anna can easily be incorporated in the teaching repertoire of these teachers. For example, the teaching of certain mnemonic devices and the use of multisensory techniques has been found to be applicable in classroom settings (see Nijakowska, this volume). By finding out more about the problems of dyslexic language learners and the compensatory techniques which facilitate vocabulary acquisition, English teachers may be able to offer a real alternative to exemption from the foreign language requirement and provide effective help to dyslexics. This would be an important step in enhancing the future possibilities of dyslexic people in tertiary education and in the labour market as well.

Note
1. Anna's words are cited in the author's translation.

Acknowledgements
The writing of this chapter has been sponsored by the Equal Rights in Foreign Language Education project of the Hungarian National Bureau of Research and Technology (NKTH B2 2006-0010).

References
Almanza, D., Singleton, K. and Terril, L. (1996) Learning disabilities in adult ESL: Case studies and directions. On WWW at http://www.cal.org/caela/esl_resources/LDcase.html. Accessed 15.04.08.

Barr, V. (1993) *Foreign Language Requirements and Students with Learning Disabilities*. Washington, DC: ERIC Clearinghouse on Language and Linguistics. (ERIC Document Reproduction Service No. EDO-FL-93-04.)

Fowle, C. (2002) Vocabulary notebooks: Implementation and outcomes. *ELT Journal* 5 (4), 380–388.
Gábor, Gy. (2003) Teaching English to dyslexics. On WWW at http://www.diszlexia.hu/Teaching.html. Accessed 15.04.08.
Gersten, R., Baker, S., Marks, S.U. and Smith, S. B. (1999) Effective instruction for learning disabled or at-risk English-language learners: An integrative synthesis of the empirical and professional knowledge bases. On WWW at http://www.ld.org/research/osep_at_risk.cfm. Accessed 15.04.08.
Gyarmathy, É. (2001) Gondolatok térképe [Mindmaps]. *TaníTani* 18–19, 108–115.
Gyarmathy, É. and Vassné Kovács, E. (2004) Dyslexia in Hungary: A guide to practice and resources. In I. Smythe, J. Everatt and R. Slater (eds) *International Book of Dyslexia. A Cross-language Comparison and Practice Guide* (pp. 116–121). Reading: British Dyslexia Association.
Hatt, P. and Nichols, E. (1995) *Links in Learning. A Manual Linking Second Language Learning, Literacy and Learning Disabilities*. Ontario: MESE Consulting.
Hodge, M.E. (1998) Teaching foreign language to at-risk learners: A challenge for the new millennium. On WWW at http://www.vccaedu.org/inquiry/inquiry-spring98/i21hodge.html. Accessed 15.04.08.
Hulstijn, J.H. (1997) Mnemonic methods in foreign language vocabulary learning. In J. Coady and T. Huckin (eds) *Second Language Vocabulary Acquisition* (pp. 203–224). Cambridge: Cambridge University Press.
Jiang, N. (2004) Semantic transfer and development in L2 vocabulary acquisition. In P. Bogaards and B. Laufer (eds) *Vocabulary in a Second Language: Selection, Acquisition and Testing* (pp. 101–127). Amsterdam: John Benjamins.
Kenyon, G. (2001) Mind mapping can help dyslexics. On WWW at http://news.bbc.co.uk/1/hi/education/1926739.stm. Accessed 15.04.08.
Maykut, P. and Morehouse, R. (1994) *Beginning Qualitative Research: A Philosophic and Practical Guide*. London: The Falmer Press.
Meixner, I. (1993) *A dyslexia prevenció, reedukáció módszere [The Method of Dyslexia Prevention and Re-education]*. Budapest: Bárczi Gusztáv Gyógypedagógiai Tanárképző Főiskola.
Nijakowska, J. (2001) Teaching English as a foreign language to a Polish dyslexic child – a case study. Paper presented at the 5th BDA International Conference, 18–21 April, 2001, University of York, UK.
Nijakowska, J. (2004) Teaching English as a foreign language to Polish dyslexic students. Paper presented at the 6th BDA International Conference, 27–30 March, 2004, University of Warwick, UK.
Ormos, E. (2003) Teaching English as a foreign language to dyslexic children. Unpublished MA thesis, Eötvös Loránd University.
Ormos, E. (2004) Egy sikeres diszlexiás nyelvtanuló [A successful dyslexic language learner]. In E.H. Kontra and J. Kormos (eds) *A nyelvtanuló: sikerek, módszerek, stratégiák [The Language Learner: Successes, Methods, Strategies]* (pp. 145–160). Budapest: Okker.
Oxford, R. and Scarcella, R. (1994) Second language vocabulary learning among adults: State of the art in vocabulary instruction. *System* 22 (2), 231–243.
Ranschburg, P. (1939) *Az emberi tévedések törvényszerűségei [Regularities in Human Errors]*. Budapest: Novák Rudolf és Társa.
Robinson-Tait, C. (2003) Dyslexia and modern language teaching. On WWW at www.dyslexia-parent.com/mag46.html. Accessed 15.04.08.
Root, C. (1994) A guide to learning disabilities for the ESL classroom practitioner. On WWW at www.writing.berkeley.edu/TESL-EJ/ej01/a.4.html. Accessed 15.04.08.

Sarkadi, Á. (2005) Dyslexia and achieving success in studying English as a second language. Unpublished MA thesis, Eötvös Loránd University.
Schmitt, N. and Schmitt, D. (1995) Vocabulary notebooks: Theoretical underpinnings and practical suggestions. *ELT Journal* 49 (2), 133–143.
Schneider, E. (1996) *Teaching Foreign Languages to At-Risk Learners*. Washington, DC: ERIC Clearinghouse on Languages and Linguistics. (ERIC Document Reproduction Service No. ED402788.)
Schneider, E. and Crombie, E. (2003) *Dyslexia and Foreign Language Learning*. London: David Fulton.
Secemski, S., Deutsch, R. and Adoram, C. (2000) Structured multisensory teaching for second language learning in Israel. In R. Peer and G. Reid (eds) *Multilingualism, Literacy and Dyslexia: A Challenge for Educators* (pp. 235–242). London: David Fulton.
Selikowitz, M. (1993) *Dyslexia and Other Learning Difficulties: The Facts*. Oxford: Oxford University Press.
Sparks, R. and Miller, K. (2000) Teaching a foreign language using multi-sensory structured language techniques to at-risk learners: A review. *Dyslexia* 6 (2), 124–132.

Chapter 6
An Experiment with Direct Multisensory Instruction in Teaching Word Reading and Spelling to Polish Dyslexic Learners of English

JOANNA NIJAKOWSKA

Introduction

Dyslexia in Poland affects about 10–15% of the student population according to recent statistics (Bogdanowicz, 2003; Bogdanowicz & Adryjanek, 2004). Dyslexic learners constitute a part of special educational needs (SEN) students, whose special rights at school are guaranteed by the regulations of the Ministry of Education and Sport. Provision of special pedagogical and psychological help in the form of correction-compensation work in therapeutic groups and on an individual basis is available free of charge, but only to students with official assessment (Bogdanowicz & Krasowicz-Kupis, 2005).

The following definition of developmental dyslexia is widely used in Poland and constitutes the basis for the diagnosis of the disorder:

> Dyslexia is one of several distinct learning disabilities. It is a specific language-based disorder of constitutional origin characterised by difficulties in single word decoding, usually reflecting insufficient phonological processing. These difficulties in single word decoding are often unexpected in relation to age and other cognitive and academic abilities; they are not the result of generalised developmental disability or sensory impairment. Dyslexia is manifested by variable difficulty with different forms of language, often including, in addition to problems with reading, a conspicuous problem with acquiring proficiency in writing and spelling. (Bogdanowicz, 2003: 497; Ott, 1997: 4; Reid, 1998: 3)

This is an example of a research-based definition which describes a construct that can be measured directly and can clearly indicate when an individual may be diagnosed as dyslexic (Reid, 1998). This definition is also clinical since it pertains to the characteristic symptoms of specific difficulties in reading and writing (Bogdanowicz, 2003). Difficulties in processing linguistic stimuli are stressed, indicating language malfunctions in the pathomechanism of dyslexia. Problems in single word decoding that result from insufficient phonological processing are claimed to constitute a cause of incomplete development and great difficulty in accurate and/or fluent word reading, writing and spelling. Still, it is believed that despite the core deficit connected with poor phonological processing, developmental dyslexia can result from the visual-spatial processing deficit (Bogdanowicz, 2003; Bogdanowicz & Adryjanek, 2004; Stein, 2001; Stein et al., 2001) and perceptual-motor integration deficit (Bogdanowicz, 1997, 2004).

Specific difficulties in reading and writing can manifest themselves in normal, healthy children, despite conventional instruction, adequate intelligence and the absence of environmental and educational negligence. In Poland the assessment of the disorder is conducted in pedagogical-psychological dispensaries. Estimating the intellectual ability (IQ) of the child is a precondition for the process of dyslexia diagnosis. If the IQ is within or above the average range, one can proceed to the subsequent stages of diagnosis, which involve thorough assessment of the functions that underlie the ability to read and write, namely visual-spatial and auditory-linguistic functions (as they relate to attention, perception and memory), motor functions, lateralisation, perceptual-motor integration, and finally, motivation and emotional development. Reading and spelling skills are also examined.

At school, teachers are obliged by law to adjust their requirements towards the needs and abilities of dyslexic students. Some accommodations are also introduced into the external examination procedures providing special conditions for dyslexics, for example more time for completing exam tasks and reduced requirements as regards the orthographic correctness of work. Finally, students with deep dyslexia can be exempted from learning a second foreign language (Bogdanowicz & Krasowicz-Kupis, 2005). Since knowing foreign languages is of great importance in present day Europe, and the number of children recognised as dyslexic is steadily growing, researchers can offer significant help to teachers by suggesting ways of overcoming the difficulties dyslexic students experience in foreign language learning.

Dyslexia and Foreign Language Learning

It is widely accepted (Jurek, 2004; Ott, 1997; Sparks et al., 1992a) that dyslexic students tend to face difficulties in foreign language instruction and that, in fact, the problem is associated with native language learning. Ganschow and Sparks (Ganschow et al., 1998; Sparks, 1995; Sparks et al., 1989, 1998a) convincingly argued that for dyslexic students native language learning poses variable difficulties which then translate into similar problems in foreign language learning (FLL). It follows that an individual's skills in the native language components of linguistic coding – phonological, syntactic and semantic – are the cornerstone of a successful FLL process. Crucial to this process, as well as being its most problematic aspect, is phonemic awareness, which involves the ability to isolate and consciously manipulate the sounds of a language and to relate them to the appropriate written symbols.

As has been mentioned, the most pronounced dyslexic difficulty in L1 relates to the lack of phonological/orthographic awareness and the poor phonological/orthographic processing skills that negatively affect reading and spelling performance (Schneider, 1999). Nicolson and Fawcett (2001) consider the most crucial factor behind fluent word reading to be the ability to recognise letters, spelling patterns and entire words effortlessly and automatically. Furthermore, the influence of phonemic training on reading acquisition is deemed especially strong when phonemes are taught together with the letters by which they are represented (Reid, 1998). The fact that poor grapheme–phoneme conversion is a key problem among poor readers has also been highlighted by Kappers (1997). Training in sound–letter correspondences has been found to have more impact on reading progress than phonemic awareness training or the teaching of the phonological strategy, which involves only oral activities but does not teach how too assign sounds to their graphic representations (Bogdanowicz, 2002). Therefore, in order to minimise the literacy problems of dyslexic children, it is necessary to automatise their skills through carefully designed and monitored long-term training (Nicolson & Fawcett, 2001).

In the modern FL classroom, where emphasis is put on authentic situational contexts (Schneider, 1999), the almost exclusive use of the target language and the inductive acquisition of grammar, pronunciation and spelling, the needs of dyslexic students are hardly catered for. Dyslexic learners require explicit and structured instruction. A direct multisensory structured learning approach (henceforth: MSL), which integrates perceptual-motor functions, has proved to be successful in teaching dyslexics not only their native, but also a foreign language (Bogdanowicz, 1997; Ganschow et al., 1998; Miller & Bussman Gillis, 2000; Schneider, 1999; Sparks & Ganschow, 1993; Sparks et al., 1989, 1992b, 1998a, b).

Włodarski (1998) conducted comparative studies on the effectiveness of mono-modal and multi-modal perception, and his results indicate that multi-modal perception is usually more beneficial than mono-modal as regards both the amount of the remembered material and the pace of learning. The simultaneous presentation of linguistic material via as many sensory channels as possible is believed to be beneficial for dyslexic individuals. In the multisensory approach it is assumed that the more modalities are involved in the learning process, the more effective it is.

Multisensory methods utilise the simultaneous engagement of several sensory channels and the synthesis of stimuli coming from these channels. Teaching reading and writing with the help of multisensory methods is realised through the integration of visual, auditory, kinaesthetic and tactile stimuli and involves simultaneous presentation of information coming from various senses. Thus, multisensory teaching is based on the constant use of the following: what a letter or a word looks like, what it sounds like and how the speech organs and hand feel when producing it (Bogdanowicz, 1997; Ott, 1997). A dyslexic person learns how to read and spell words by hearing, seeing and pronouncing them, by making models out of plasticine, forming them from wooden, sponge or plastic letters; finally, by tracing them on various surfaces such as paper, carpet, floor, sand, and by writing them. The more perceptual channels are open, the greater the possibility of forming associations between the graphic (visual) and phonetic (auditory) aspects of a word as well as its meaning. If a stimulus is complex, it activates several receptors, and the perception of information is realised simultaneously through several sensory channels. The following methods involving perceptual-motor integration are used in the pedagogical therapy of dyslexic children: visual–auditory (VA), visual–auditory–kinaesthetic (VAK) and visual–auditory–kinaesthetic–tactile (VAKT). The greater the difficulties in learning to read and write and the more severe the disorders of psycho-motor functions are, the more intensive and diversified the therapy that should be provided. In the most severe cases the VAKT method is necessary (Bogdanowicz, 1997).

In languages with a deep orthography like English, the grapheme–phoneme relations are especially difficult to learn. For a Polish learner, it seems difficult to understand, first, the capacity of a single sound to be graphically represented by more than one letter; second, the fact that a single sound may be represented by different letters or letter combinations in different words (inconsistent spelling); and third, that a given letter or a combination of letters may represent more than one sound and that there are numerous exceptions and irregular words which need to be learned. Studies have shown that the awareness of grapheme–phoneme correspondences acquired during instruction with MSL produces an automatic response to familiar letters and letter sequences. This allows students to shift attention from perceptual aspects such as recognition of letters and their order in words to the semantic aspects (Robertson, 2000).

In order to test the applicability of the above assertions in a Polish context, the aim of the research described in this chapter was to investigate the application of MSL to teaching reading and spelling to Polish dyslexic learners of English. The study sought answers to the following research questions:

(1) Do Polish dyslexic learners experience greater difficulties in learning the English phonological-orthographic system than their non-dyslexic peers?

(2) Does direct, multisensory and structured instruction in selected grapheme-phoneme correspondences and spelling rules improve dyslexic learners' ability to decode and encode the language?

The proposed hypotheses for the present study were as follows:

Hypothesis 1. Polish dyslexic learners experience greater difficulties in learning the English phonological–orthographic system with the use of traditional instruction than their non-dyslexic peers.

Hypothesis 2. Direct, multisensory and structured instruction in selected English grapheme–phoneme correspondences and spelling rules improves dyslexic learners' ability to decode and encode the language (read and spell).

Hypothesis 3. Pre-post test comparisons in the experimental group show significant differences indicating a considerable gain.

Hypothesis 4. Pre-post test comparisons in the control group with dyslexia do not reveal significant differences, indicating no gain.

Hypothesis 5. Pre-post test comparisons in the control group without dyslexia reveal significant differences, indicating a considerable gain.

Hypothesis 6. There are no significant differences between the results of the spelling and reading pre-tests in the experimental group and the control group with dyslexia. Significant differences between the results of the spelling and reading post-tests in the experimental group and the control group with dyslexia would be found. The experimental group would show greater pre-post test gains than the control group with dyslexia.

Hypothesis 7. Significant differences between the results of the spelling and reading pre- and post-tests in the experimental group and the control group without dyslexia will be found. Despite considerable progress and gain in the knowledge of English grapheme–phoneme correspondences, the experimental group would still lag slightly behind the control group without dyslexia or, in other words, will not show greater pre-post test gains.

Hypothesis 8. Significant differences between the results of the spelling and reading pre- and post-tests in the control group with dyslexia and the control group without dyslexia will be found. The control group without dyslexia shows greater pre-post test gains than the control group with dyslexia.

Method

Participants

To elucidate the operation of MSL, and, specifically, to show the rationale for the explicit teaching of the grapheme-phoneme conversion rules, three discreet groups of English language learners were selected. One group, defined as experimental, consisted of five individuals diagnosed as dyslexic. The remaining two groups were labelled as control groups: the first one was made up of 10 individuals diagnosed as dyslexic, and the second of 10 students without developmental dyslexia.

The study took place in a secondary school in one of the major cities in Poland, where 15 students were randomly chosen from a dyslexic group of 100 – the number amounting to about 12% of the school population – and assigned to two groups. Five students (two males, three females, mean age 17.6) formed the experimental group and 10 students (eight males, two females, mean age 17) formed one of the control groups. In further selection, 10 students (five males, five females, mean age 17) from the non-dyslexic part of the school population were assigned to the second control group. All the students from the experimental group and the control group with dyslexia had an up-to-date assessment indicating specific difficulties in learning to read and write, that is, they were diagnosed as dyslexic. They had clearly non-general learning difficulties but limited and specific difficulties in learning to read and spell. Their mental development was normal, and so was their intelligence, which ranked average or above average. There were no emotional or personality disorders, nor any hearing or sight deficits. Finally, no environmental or educational negligence was observed. All the dyslexic students were receiving compensatory teaching services in their native language, in the form of self-contained classes run by the school's teacher–therapist. However, no compensatory teaching to minimise foreign language difficulties was officially provided. All three groups were enrolled in their regular English classes at school, conducted with the use of traditional foreign language methodology by the same teacher, who refrained from devoting time to explicit presentation of orthographic and phoneme–grapheme conversion rules, claiming that students inferred these relations naturally and spontaneously from the input they received in the language classroom. The author provided tutorial sessions for the experimental group, whereas the control groups with and without dyslexia attended no such sessions.

As far as their ability to read and spell in the native language is concerned, no additional tests were given to the dyslexic participants in the study apart from the formal assessment they had undergone in the pedagogical-psychological dispensary. Interviews with the teacher of Polish and the teacher-therapist who ran the correction–compensation classes were conducted in order to collect qualitative data on the estimated level of the participants' skills in Polish. The dyslexics' native language skills were described as considerably poorer than the skills of the non-dyslexic participants of the study, in most cases lower than satisfactory.

Prior to the introduction of training in the experimental group, skills in English as a foreign language of all the students participating in the study

Table 6.1 Results of the assessment of skills in English in the experimental group, the control group with dyslexia and the control group without dyslexia

Group	Assessment by	Mean	Max	Min	SD	Reading aloud mean	Spelling mean
Experimental	Teacher	2.7	3.2	2.0	0.5	2.2	2.8
	Students	2.9	3.5	1.2	0.9	2.2	2.0
Control with dyslexia	Teacher	2.5	3.8	1.4	0.9	2.8	2.1
	Students	3.0	3.7	1.5	0.7	2.8	2.4
Control without dyslexia	Teacher	3.5	5.1	1.5	1	3.9	3.3
	Students	3.4	4.3	2.0	0.6	3.6	3.3

were evaluated by their teacher of English on a 6-point scale where 1 denoted unsatisfactory, while 6 stood for excellent. Additionally, all the students were asked for self-assessment applying the same criteria. The following aspects were assessed: reading aloud, reading silently with comprehension, listening comprehension, speaking, written assignments, pronunciation, vocabulary, spelling and grammar (see Table 6.1 for descriptive statistics). Additionally, apart from the overall mean score, the mean scores relating to the two aspects most relevant for the study, namely the ability to read aloud and spell, are included in Table 6.1 as well. Students with dyslexia were assessed by their teacher of English as very poor learners of English, usually representing the level lower than satisfactory. Dyslexic students perceived themselves as poor foreign language learners as well. Generally, dyslexic students were assessed by the teacher of English as much poorer learners of English than their non-dyslexic peers participating in the study.

Procedures

In order to verify the proposed hypotheses, the research was conducted using an experimental procedure intended to produce an observable gain in the experimental group stemming from the introduction of an innovative factor responsible for improvement of learning and teaching (Komorowska, 1982). The independent variable in the present study was the direct multisensory language instruction in the English phonological/orthographic system. The dependent variable was made up of the results attributable to teaching the English grapheme/phoneme correspondence with the use of the MSL approach. Thus, the dependent variable was operationalised as the test scores after the training in the experimental group.

Table 6.2 The design of the study

Experimental group	→	PRE-S, PRE-R	→	Treatment	→	POST-S1, POST-R1	→	POST-S2, POST-R2
Control group with dyslexia	→	PRE-S, PRE-R	→	–	→	POST-S1, POST-R1	→	POST-S2, POST-R2
Control group without dyslexia	→	PRE-S, PRE-R	→	–	→	POST-S1, POST-R1	→	POST-S2, POST-R2

The design of the study departed slightly from the experimental scheme of the classic type which normally involves a pre-test, a post-test and a control group (Komorowska, 1982). The present research employed two different control groups and two post-tests, as displayed in Table 6.2.

In Table 6.2 PRE-S denotes a spelling pre-test, PRE-R a reading pre-test, POST-S1 the first spelling post-test and POST-R1 the first reading post-test (administered immediately after the treatment) and finally, POST-S2 stands for the second spelling post-test and POST-R2 for the second reading post-test, administered two weeks after the treatment.

The pre-test (PRE-S and PRE-R) and the post-test 1 (POST-S1 and POST-R1), as well as the post-test 2 (POST-S2 and POST-R2), consisted of a word-level reading and a spelling task. The pre-test and post-test 1 involved exactly the same words, whereas post-test 2 featured a different list (see Appendix 1). The words included in the pre- and post-tests were carefully selected to contain all the phoneme–grapheme regularities and spelling choices covered in the programme. Furthermore, the number of words with the same spelling patterns was equal across the tests.

Before the introduction of the experimental factor in the experimental group, the spelling and reading pre-tests were administered in all three groups. Each group was tested separately: the spelling test was in written form and was conducted with the whole group. The reading test was administered individually and students were recorded. A list of 63 words was first dictated to the students; then, after a break, they were recorded reading the same list of words. Each word was dictated in isolation twice, interspersing the dictation with a single reading of the word in sentence context to increase meaningfulness. The students had to write down individual words on the form provided. There was no difference between the groups regarding the time allotted for testing, nor were any time limits set. A special education teacher who works at the school where the study took place assisted in the administration of the pre-test. In the assessment of the students' performance, only the words which were spelled and read correctly were accepted. One point was given for each correctly spelled or read word. The handwriting of all the students participating in the study was intelligible enough, so there were no dubious cases. The students scored a point for every read word as long as they could make themselves understood. Even though 63 words make up a long list, testing did not seem to wear out the students, on the contrary, they were eager to co-operate throughout.

In the next stage of the research, the experimental group was exposed to the operation of the experimental variable, which was not applied to the control groups. The classes for the experimental group were conducted by the author herself. They were all 90-minute contact sessions, which took place once a week over a period of six months. During the treatment in the experimental group, direct multisensory teaching of the phoneme–grapheme relations and spelling rules of English was conducted in a structured, step-by-step fashion. The specific problem areas covered during the training were the same as in the pre- and post-tests (for a list see Appendix 1). Small amounts of material were presented at a time, and their thorough mastery was accomplished by the use of multisensory techniques: simultaneous saying, seeing, hearing and writing, the use of movable devices and repetition. Auditory, visual and tactile-kinaesthetic pathways were simultaneously engaged in the perception of linguistic items. The information processed via unaffected channels and integrated through intensive practice, drill and repetition could then lead to the development of written language skills. Attention was paid to the complexity of the activities as well as to the perceptual abilities of a given child. The teacher moved from simple elementary exercises to more complex tasks involving the mastery of more and more teaching content. Moving towards more difficult tasks was conditioned by the ability to complete the simple ones. Attractive techniques and tasks as well as regular, systematic work proved to be successful and motivating for the students in the experimental group. A sample lesson plan with a detailed description of the task types, procedure, teaching aids and worksheets used during the lesson can be found in Appendix 2.

Immediately after the treatment had ended, the spelling post-test 1 and the reading post-test 1 were administered in all three groups. Two weeks later the spelling post-test 2 and the reading post-test 2 were administered to all participants.

The current data analysis consists of the pre- and post-test comparisons both within and between the groups. The pre- and post-test comparisons for each group were generated by determining the means and standard deviations. The differences between the pre- and post-test means were analysed with the use of the Wilcoxon Test. The pre- and post-test comparisons between groups were generated by determining the means and standard deviations. The Mann–Whitney U-test was used to determine the possible existence of any significant differences between the experimental group, the control group with dyslexia and the control group without dyslexia (Jóźwiak & Podgórski, 1994; Luszniewicz & Słaby, 2001; Stanisz, 1998). It has to be noted, however, that the results described in the following section are accurate as far as the actual participants are concerned but cannot be generalised owing to the small sample.

Results

Table 6.3 gives the results of all the tests in all three groups. The pre-test results were low in all three groups, but it can also be seen that the non-dyslexic group performed better in both spelling and reading than their dyslexic peers. It is also observable that spelling posed more severe difficulties for these dyslexic learners than reading: the experimental and the dyslexic control groups achieved 27.62% and 24.60% respectively on spelling but almost 60% each on reading.

Pre-post comparisons within groups

Experimental group

In the experimental group, the POST-R1 resulted in the highest mean score (87.62%). The low mean score of the PRE-S (27.62%) and the relatively high mean scores of the POST-S1 (71.74%) and the POST-S2 (82.86%) indicated an improvement in spelling skills in the experimental group. Analogously, the low mean score of the PRE-R (57.46%) and the relatively high mean scores of the POST-R1 (87.62%) and POST-R2 (83.81%) marked an improvement in reading skills.

Table 6.3 Results of the spelling and reading pre- and post-tests in the experimental group, the control group with dyslexia and the control group without dyslexia

Test	Experimental group			Control group with dyslexia			Control group without dyslexia		
	Mean points (max 63)	Mean %	SD	Mean points (max 63)	Mean %	SD	Mean points (max 63)	Mean %	SD
PRE-S	17.4	27.62	6.47	15.5	24.60	8.06	24.2	38.41	8.13
PRE-R	36.2	57.46	7.16	37.3	59.21	7.83	48.2	76.51	6.73
POST-S1	45.2	71.74	13.54	16.5	26.19	8.10	29.2	46.35	9.54
POST-R1	55.2	87.62	6.76	39.3	62.38	5.85	50.0	79.37	6.31
POST-S2	52.2	82.86	7.85	17.5	27.78	8.58	30.7	48.73	11.62
POST-R2	52.8	83.81	3.56	36.2	57.46	8.97	47.1	74.76	5.76

Statistically significant differences emerged between the results of the following pairs of variables: PRE-S and POST-S1, PRE-S and POST-S2, PRE-R and POST-R1 as well as PRE-R and POST-R2 (in all cases $T = 0.0$, $p = 0.04$). Conversely, no significant differences were found between the results of the following pairs of tests: POST-S1 and POST-S2 ($T = 0.0$, $p = 0.07$), POST-R1 and POST-R2 ($T = 2.0, p = 0.14$).

Control group with dyslexia

Students in the control group with dyslexia achieved the highest mean score on the POST-R1 (62.38%) and the lowest on the PRE-S (24.60%). The mean scores of all the spelling tests PRE-S (24.60%), POST-S1 (26.19%) and POST-S2 (27.78%) had similar values, which indicated no improvement in spelling skills in the control group with dyslexia. The mean scores of all the reading tests PRE-R (59.21%), POST-R1 (62.38%) and POST-R2 (57.46%) had similar values, which shows, again, no improvement in reading skills in the control group with dyslexia either.

In contrast to what was observed in the experimental group, there were no statistically significant differences between the results of the following pairs of tests in the control group with dyslexia: PRE-S and POST-S1 ($T = 11.5$, $p = 0.36$), PRE-S and POST-S2 ($T = 9.0$, $p = 0.21$), PRE-R and POST-R1 ($T = 12.0$, $p = 0.21$) as well as PRE-R and POST-R2 ($T = 13.0$, $p = 0.26$).

Control group without dyslexia

The highest mean score was yielded by the POST-R1 (79.37%), the lowest by the PRE-S (38.41%). The mean score of the PRE-S (38.41%) was lower than the mean scores of the POST-S1 (46.35%) and the POST-S2 (48.73%), which might indicate some enhancement of spelling skills in the control group without dyslexia. Even though the differences were not as substantial as in the experimental group, they were still significant in statistical terms. The mean scores of all the reading tests: PRE-R (76.51%), POST-R1 (79.37%) and POST-R2 (74.76%) had similar values, which showed that the reading skills in the control group without dyslexia underwent no improvement.

There were statistically significant differences between the results of the PRE-S and POST-S1 ($T = 0.0$, $p = 0.007$), as well as the PRE-S and POST-S2 ($T = 1.0, p = 0.01$). No statistically significant differences emerged between the PRE-R and POST-R1 ($T = 5.0$, $p = 0.07$), or between the PRE-R and POST-R2 ($T = 11.0$, $p = 0.33$) in the control group without dyslexia.

Pre-post comparisons between groups

The results of the PRE-S ($U = 23.5$, $p = 0.85$) and PRE-R ($U = 20.0$, $p = 0.54$) indicated no differences between the experimental group and the control group with dyslexia. In contrast, statistically significant differences were observed between the results of all post-tests, with the experimental group outperforming the control group with dyslexia (POST-S1 ($U = 2.0$, $p = 0.005$), POST-S2 ($U = 0.0$, $p = 0.002$), POST-R1 ($U = 2.5, p = 0.006$) and POST-R2 ($U = 1.0, p = 0.003$)).

As regards the comparison between the experimental group and the control group without dyslexia, significant differences were yielded on three measures: PRE-R ($U = 4.0$, $p = 0.01$) in favour of the control group without dyslexia, POST-S1 ($U = 8.0$, $p = 0.04$) and POST-S2 ($U = 3.5$, $p = 0.008$) both in favour of the experimental group. The observable differences between the means of the other tests were small and of no statistical significance: PRE-S ($U = 18.0$, $p = 0.39$), POST-R1 ($U = 11.0$, $p = 0.09$), POST-R2 ($U = 9.5, p = 0.06$).

As anticipated, the control group without dyslexia performed better on all measures than the control group with dyslexia. The differences were statistically significant between the results of the PRE-R ($U = 12.5$, $p = 0.005$), POST-S1 ($U = 15.0$, $p = 0.008$), POST-S2 ($U = 18.0$, $p = 0.015$), POST-R1 ($U = 10.5, p = 0.003$) and POST-R2 ($U = 18.5, p = 0.02$). However, there were no statistically significant differences between these two groups as far as the result of PRE-S ($U = 27.5$, $p = 0.09$) is concerned.

Discussion

Polish dyslexic learners experience greater problems in learning the English phonological-orthographic system than their non-dyslexic peers, as was revealed by the poorer results of the word spelling and reading pre-tests in the experimental group and the control group with dyslexia in comparison to the control group without dyslexia. This has been further confirmed by the poor achievement in the spelling and reading post-tests of the dyslexic control group (Hypothesis 1).

Hypothesis 3 was also supported as the pre-post test comparisons within the experimental group revealed significant differences between the results of the pre- and post-tests, which indicated a considerable gain. A very low mean score on the PRE-S (27.62%) and relatively high mean scores on the POST-S1 (71.74%) and POST-S2 (82.86%) indicated the improvement of spelling skills in the experimental group. A similar situation was found for the reading task – a low mean score on the PRE-R (57.46%) and relatively high mean scores on the POST-R1 (87.62%) and POST-R2 (83.81%) meant enhanced reading skills in the experimental group. Moreover, the above differences were all statistically significant. Thus the experimental group performed significantly better after the completion of the training than at the onset of the instructional programme. Hence, the increased efficiency of the students in the experimental group on the spelling and reading tasks after training, as compared to their scores before, can be attributed predominantly to the adopted teaching method rather than to other factors (Hypothesis 2).

The above assertion is supported by the fact that no significant differences between the mean scores on the spelling and reading pre- and post-tests were found in the control group with dyslexia. Such a finding had been anticipated in view of the absence of MSL instruction. The mean scores on all the spelling tests had similar values, which indicated no improvement in the spelling skills of this group. Likewise, the values of the mean scores of all the reading tests were similar, which, again, indicated no improvement. Finally, no statistically significant differences emerged between the following pairs of variables: PRE-S and POST-S1, PRE-S and POST-S2, PRE-R and POST-R1, as well as PRE-R and POST-R2. Thus it can be concluded that despite the traditional instruction the group received at school, they did not make any progress in terms of their word spelling and reading skills (Hypothesis 4).

In the control group without dyslexia statistically significant differences were found between the results of the PRE-S and the POST-S1, as well as the PRE-S and the POST-S2, which indicates some improvement in the spelling skills in this group. However, one should not lose sight of the fact that they were, from the start, in a much more beneficial position than the other groups since they demonstrated no specific developmental reading or spelling disorders. It could then be assumed that as regards spelling the traditional instruction was successful in their case. Interestingly enough, the mean scores on all their reading tests had similar values with no statistically significant differences, which indicated no improvement in the reading skills of this group after six-months of regular instruction. In other words, the control group without dyslexia did not achieve any progress in their word reading skills. Hence Hypothesis 5, that the pre-post test comparisons in the control group without dyslexia would reveal significant differences between the results of the pre- and post-tests, was only partially supported.

The results of the spelling and reading pre-tests were poor in the case of the experimental group and the control group with dyslexia, and the scores did not differ significantly between these two groups. In contrast, Hypothesis 6, that there would be significant differences between the results of the spelling and reading post-tests, received clear confirmation, as did the comparative postulate that the experimental group would show greater pre-post test gains than the control group with dyslexia. Both groups received traditional instruction in English as a foreign language during the experiment, but the control group with dyslexia, unlike the experimental group, did not undergo the MSL training, which could be the reason why they did not make any progress on the spelling and reading post-test. Apparently, the experimental group demonstrated enormous progress in acquiring the relationships between the graphemes and phonemes and, consequently, in word reading and spelling (Hypothesis 2).

The role of the direct multisensory instruction in the success of the experimental group cannot thus be overestimated.

Surprisingly, Hypothesis 7, that significant differences would occur between the results of the spelling and reading pre- and post-tests in the experimental group and control group without dyslexia – the scores favouring the control group, was only partially validated. To our even greater surprise, the ensuing hypothesis that, despite making considerable progress, the experimental group would still be lagging, however slightly, behind the control group without dyslexia, was not verified either. The latter hypothesis was based on recent empirical findings suggesting that, in spite of explicit instruction in phonological/orthographic skills, at-risk learners are still likely to continue to lag behind good foreign language learners in terms of their phonological/orthographic skills (Sparks *et al.*, 1991, 1997). As can be seen from the present study, however, dyslexic students (experimental group) may perform no worse than their non-dyslexic peers; in fact, they may well be capable of achieving better scores in spelling and reading tests. It needs emphasising that the experimental group's scores on the post-tests after the implementation of direct multisensory training, a performance markedly better than that of the control group without dyslexia, was the most surprising outcome of the study. Even allowing for a considerable gain, the experimental group was still rather expected to situate itself on the achievement scale slightly behind the non-dyslexic students.

Hypothesis 8, that there would be significant differences between the control group with dyslexia and the control group without dyslexia, was confirmed by the results of all the spelling and reading pre- and post-tests. The control group without dyslexia achieved much higher scores. There were statistically significant differences between the results of all of the tests, apart from the spelling pre-test. These findings prove that students with developmental dyslexia experienced greater difficulties in learning English as a foreign language with the use of traditional instruction than their non-dyslexic peers, as supposed in Hypothesis 1.

Although originally weaker, the students from the experimental group showed considerable improvement in their performance on all the spelling and reading tests. Both the magnitude of their academic growth and its rapidity indicate the effectiveness of direct, multisensory instruction in the area of the grapheme/phoneme correspondences and spelling rules in English (Hypothesis 2).

Implications

The results of the study yield several implications for teaching foreign languages to dyslexic students. They support the effectiveness of direct multisensory instruction in the phonology/orthography of the English language. A growing body of evidence indicates that the difficulties, whether subtle or overt, experienced by a great majority of foreign language learners labelled as 'poor', are of phonological nature (Sparks & Ganschow, 1993). Thus, dyslexic learners, who hardly benefit from methodologies that expect them to intuitively discover the phonological structure of a new language, will most probably profit from direct instruction in the phonology of the target language. Nevertheless, although the outcome of the study is decidedly encouraging, it must be treated cautiously due to the small sample size. This definitely limits any generalisability of the results, which should be considered tentative and subject to further investigation. Another issue that would certainly require more thorough investigation is the degree of difficulty that the individual students had in Polish reading and spelling, as this might have been a relevant factor affecting the outcome of the study. Moreover, it would have been interesting to find out whether the multisensory direct instruction in English phonology had any influence on the native language skills of the dyslexic students in the experimental group. Furthermore, it seems necessary to carry out longitudinal research upon dyslexic versus non-dyslexic students, to study the effects – regarding both native and foreign language skills – of direct multisensory instruction as opposed to the more traditional approaches.

The reluctance of foreign language educators to accept the importance of explicit multisensory instruction in phonology and grammar is, presumably, a natural consequence of their being good language learners themselves (Sparks *et al.*, 1991). Arguably, more attention should be paid to acquainting pre-service and in-service teachers of English with the constitutional nature of dyslexic difficulties in the first place, as well as with effective teaching methods and techniques that could be employed while working with dyslexic students. By far the most important and basic issue seems to be raising awareness of developmental dyslexia, especially in the light of the latest regulations of the Polish Ministry of Education concerning the conditions and ways of assessing, classifying and promoting students, as well as conducting exams. Teachers are now obliged to adjust their educational requirements to the individual needs and abilities of students with specific learning difficulties. They are required to make the conditions and forms of external exams suit dyslexic students. However, since under the law dyslexic students belong to the group of children with special educational needs (SEN), which hinders their reception of a standard educational programme, their abilities and needs ought to be catered for in the individualised pace of work, teaching programmes and requirements, all of them controlled by specially qualified teachers (Bogdanowicz, 1995; Tomaszewska, 2001).

Another regulation concerning the principles of provision and organisation of psychological-pedagogical help in public kindergartens, schools and institutions, suggests that any special help for students with specific learning difficulties should be organised in the form of correction–compensation classes. However, the law does not make any mention of foreign language instruction, so currently dyslexic students do not receive any specialised help in language learning. To offset the negative consequences of this, another regulation has been implemented to the effect that students with deep dyslexia can be exempted from learning a second foreign language (an L3), temporarily or even permanently. As a result, facing the uninviting alternative of their children's failure in learning another foreign language, parents of dyslexic students will naturally take advantage of this option. Arguably, the application of MSL instruction could help stop such a trend.

To further benefit dyslexic students, there should be more collaboration between special educators and foreign language teachers. Since native and foreign language skills are interrelated, weak native language skills, especially phonological ones, have a natural impact on foreign language learning. Direct multisensory instruction in a foreign language not only substantially improves foreign language learning but also has a potential to increase native language phonology (Ganschow & Sparks, 1995; Sparks *et al.*, 1992b). Moreover, improvements in the students' performance on the sound identification and manipulation tasks, and in their awareness of the spelling choices in their native language, may have a positive effect on their foreign language skills: it has been shown that students with stronger native language reading and spelling skills achieve higher grades in foreign language courses and are more verbally proficient in a foreign language (Sparks *et al.*, 1995).

It also has to be noted that the results of the study indicate that direct multisensory instruction in English as a foreign language might also be beneficial for non-dyslexic students, as it would allow them to achieve even greater success in their spelling and reading skills. While it was beyond the scope of this study to investigate such a possibility, the specific effects of MSL instruction on non-dyslexic students should still be determined in future research. This study has been an attempt to inspire further experimentation with the use of the direct multisensory approach, an activity which promises, in the long run, more successful foreign language instruction for dyslexic learners and potentially non-learning disabled students as well.

It goes without saying that, if an individual constantly faces an impossible challenge, gets discouraged and confused by inadequate teaching materials and by requirements that cannot be fulfilled, learning will not become a source of joy and satisfaction. Raising awareness, sensitivity and understanding of students' difficulties and exploring ways of overcoming them seems to be a good way to steer clear of such a danger.

References

Bogdanowicz, M. (1995) Uczeń o specjalnych potrzebach edukacyjnych [A student with special educational needs]. *Psychologia Wychowawcza* 3, 216–223.

Bogdanowicz, M. (1997) *Integracja percepcyjno-motoryczna: teoria – diagnoza – terapia [Perceptual-Motor Integration: Theory – Diagnosis – Therapy]*. Warszawa: Centrum Metodyczne Pomocy Psychologiczno-Pedagogicznej Ministerstwa Edukacji Narodowej.

Bogdanowicz, M. (2002) *Ryzyko dysleksji. Problem i diagnozowanie [The Risk of Dyslexia. The Problem and Its Diagnosis]*. Gdańsk: Wydawnictwo Harmonia.

Bogdanowicz, M. (2003) Specyficzne trudności w czytaniu i pisaniu [Specific difficulties in learning to read and write]. In T. Gałkowski and G. Jastrzębowska (eds) *Logopedia. Pytania i odpowiedzi. Wydanie drugie poprawione i rozszerzone [Logopaedics. Questions and Answers. Second Edition]* (pp. 491–535). Opole: Wydawnictwo Uniwersytetu Opolskiego.

Bogdanowicz, M. (2004) Integracja percepcyjno-motoryczna w dysleksji [Perceptual-motor integration in dyslexia]. In A. Grabowska and K. Rymarczyk (eds) *Dysleksja: od badań mózgu do praktyki [Dyslexia: From Brain Research to Practice]* (pp. 272–290). Warszawa: Instytut Biologii Doświadczalnej im. M. Nenckiego PAN.

Bogdanowicz, M. and Adryjanek, A. (2004) *Uczeń z dysleksją w szkole. Poradnik nie tylko dla polonistów [Dyslexic Student at School. A Guide Not Only for Polish Language Teachers]*. Gdynia: Wydawnictwo Pedagogiczne Operon.

Bogdanowicz, M. and Krasowicz-Kupis, G. (2005) Diagnoza dysleksji rozwojowej [Diagnosis of developmental dyslexia]. In T. Gałkowski, E. Szeląg and G. Jastrzębowska (eds) *Podstawy neurologopedii [Introduction to Neurologopaedics]* (pp. 967–985). Opole: Wydawnictwo Uniwersytetu Opolskiego.

Ganschow, L. and Sparks, R. (1995) Effects of direct instruction in Spanish phonology on the native-language skills and foreign-language aptitude of at-risk foreign-language learners. *Journal of Learning Disabilities* 28 (2), 107–120.

Ganschow, L., Sparks, R. and Javorsky, J. (1998) Foreign language learning difficulties: An historical perspective. *Journal of Learning Disabilities* 31 (3), 248–258.

Jóźwiak, J. and Podgórski, J. (1994) *Statystyka od podstaw [Introduction to Statistics]*. Warszawa: Państwowe Wydawnictwo Ekonomiczne.

Jurek, A. (2004) Trudności w nauce języków obcych uczniów z dysleksją rozwojową [Difficulties in foreign language learning in dyslexics]. In M. Bogdanowicz and M. Smoleń (eds) *Dysleksja w kontekście nauczania języków obcych [Dyslexia in the Context of Foreign Language Learning]* (pp. 98–120). Gdańsk: Wydawnictwo Harmonia.

Kappers, E.J. (1997) Outpatient treatment of dyslexia through stimulation of the cerebral hemispheres. *Journal of Learning Disabilities* 30 (1), 100–125.

Komorowska, H. (1982) *Metody badań empirycznych w glottodydaktyce [Methods of Empirical Research in Glottodidactics]*. Warszawa: Państwowe Wydawnictwo Naukowe.

Luszniewicz, A. and Słaby, T. (2001) *Statystyka z pakietem komputerowym STATISTICA PL [Statistics with a Computer Program STATISTICA PL]*. Warszawa: Wydawnictwo C.H. Beck.

Miller, S. and Bussman Gillis, M. (2000) The language puzzle: Connecting the study of linguistics with a multisensory language instructional programme in foreign language learning. In L. Peer and G. Reid (eds) *Multilingualism, Literacy and Dyslexia. A Challenge for Educators* (pp. 218–228). London: David Fulton.

Nicolson, R.I. and Fawcett, A.J. (2001) Dyslexia as a learning disability. In A.J. Fawcett (ed.) *Dyslexia. Theory and Good Practice* (pp. 141–159). London: Whurr.

Ott, P. (1997) *How to Detect and Manage Dyslexia. A Reference and Resource Manual*. Oxford: Heinemann.

Reid, G. (1998) *Dyslexia. A Practitioner's Handbook*. Chichester: Wiley.
Robertson, J. (2000) Neuropsychological intervention in dyslexia: Two studies on British pupils. *Journal of Learning Disabilities* 33 (2), 137–149.
Schneider, E. (1999) *Multisensory Structured Metacognitive Instruction. An Approach to Teaching a Foreign Language to At-Risk Students*. Frankfurt am Main: Peter Lang.
Shemesh, R. and Waller, S. (2000) *Teaching English Spelling. A Practical Guide*. Cambridge: Cambridge University Press.
Sparks, R. (1995) Examining the linguistic coding differences hypothesis to explain individual differences in foreign language learning. *Annals of Dyslexia* 45, 187–214.
Sparks, R. and Ganschow, L. (1993) The effects of multisensory structured language instruction on native language and foreign language aptitude skills of at-risk high school foreign language learners: A replication and follow-up study. *Annals of Dyslexia* 43, 194–216.
Sparks, R., Ganschow, L. and Pohlman, J. (1989) Linguistic coding deficits in foreign language learners. *Annals of Dyslexia* 39, 179–195.
Sparks, R., Ganschow, L., Kenneweg, S. and Miller, K. (1991) Use of an Orton-Gillingham approach to teach a foreign language to dyslexic/learning-disabled students: Explicit teaching of phonology in a second language. *Annals of Dyslexia* 41, 96–118.
Sparks, R., Ganschow, L., Javorsky, J., Pohlman, J. and Patton, J. (1992a) Test comparisons among students identified as high-risk, low-risk, and learning disabled in high school foreign language courses. *Modern Language Journal* 72, 142–159.
Sparks, R., Ganschow, G., Pohlman, J., Skinner, S. and Artzer, M. (1992b) The effects of multisensory structured language instruction on native language and foreign language aptitude skills of at-risk high school foreign language learners. *Annals of Dyslexia* 42, 25–53.
Sparks, R., Ganschow, L. and Patton, J. (1995) Prediction of performance in first-year foreign language courses: connections between native and foreign language learning. *Journal of Educational Psychology* 87 (4), 638–655.
Sparks, R., Ganschow L., Artzer, M. and Patton, J. (1997) Foreign language proficiency of at-risk and not-at-risk learners over 2 years of foreign language instruction: A follow-up study. *Journal of Learning Disabilities* 30 (1), 92–98.
Sparks, R., Artzer, M., Ganschow, L., Siebenhar, D., Plageman, M. and Patton, J. (1998a) Differences in native-language skills, foreign-language aptitude, and foreign-language grades among high-, average-, and low-proficiency foreign-language learners: Two studies. *Language Testing* 15 (2), 181–216.
Sparks, R., Artzer, M., Patton, J., Ganschow, L., Miller, K., Hordubay, D. and Walsh, G. (1998b) Benefits of multisensory structured instruction for at-risk foreign language learners: A comparison study of high school Spanish students. *Annals of Dyslexia* 48, 239–270.
Stanisz, A. (1998) *Przystępny kurs statystyki [An Easy Course in Statistics]*. Kraków: StatSoft.
Stein, J.F. (2001) The magnocellular theory of developmental dyslexia. *Dyslexia: An International Journal of Research and Practice* 7 (1), 12–36.
Stein, J.F., Talcott, J.B. and Witton, C. (2001) The sensorimotor basis of developmental dyslexia. In A.J. Fawcett (ed.) *Dyslexia. Theory and Good Practice* (pp. 65–88). London: Whurr.
Tomaszewska, A. (2001) *Prawo do nauki dziecka z dysleksją rozwojową w świadomości nauczycieli [Teachers' Awareness of Dyslexic Students' Right to Learn]*. Kraków: Oficyna Wydawnicza 'Impuls'.
Włodarski, Z. (1998) *Psychologia uczenia się [Psychology of Learning]*. Warszawa: Wydawnictwo Naukowe PWN.

Appendix 1

Words used in the pre-test, post-test 1 and post-test 2

No.	Pre-test and Post-test A	Problem area	Post-test B
1	tag	Short vowel sounds, CVC words	fan
2	fix		bin
3	mug		rug
4	shift	Initial and final consonant blends and digraphs	shed
5	crush		blush
6	such		much
7	whip		when
8	chick		chin
9	flint		cloth
10	froth		twist
11	slick		crisp
12	thin		theft
13	clamp	Nasal sounds, assimilation	plump
14	trench		clench
15	shunt		print
16	frond		brand
17	clink		blink
18	prong		cling
19	thrust	Initial triple consonant blends	strung
20	strand		shrimp
21	sprung		spring
22	shrink		splash
23	miss	Doubling rule – single vowel followers	spill
24	fuzz		buzz
25	stiff		sniff
26	swan	'W' rules	swamp
27	wharf		ward
28	word		worm
29	lark	Vowel/consonant digraphs	smart
30	cord		north
31	fern		verb

(Continued)

No.	Pre-test and Post-test A	Problem area	Post-test B
32	have	'V' rules	live
33	cover		glove
34	cane	'Magic e' rule	flame
35	cube		duke
36	pine		kite
37	dole		rope
38	pick	Spelling of the /k/ sound	track
39	clinic		bark
40	kilt		kettle
41	cactus		clip
42	milk		basic
43	quit		quest
44	mix		fax
45	gypsy	Spelling of the /dʒ/ and /tʃ/ sounds	gender
46	jug		junk
47	edge		lodge
48	large		wage
49	fetch		stretch
50	fry	Spelling of the long vowel sounds /ai/, /ei/, /əʊ/, /ju:/, /u:/, /i:/	spy
51	sight		flight
52	tray		bay
53	brain		fail
54	grow		blow
55	moan		soak
56	glue		clue
57	grew		flew
58	boot		broom
59	keep		wheel
60	east		meal
61	copy		windy
62	niece		piece
63	receive		ceiling

Appendix 2

Sample lesson plan.
Lesson 11 (90 min).
Topic: 'Magic e' rule.
Aims: After the lesson: Students will be able to compare short and long vowels and perceive the differences between them. Students will understand the 'magic e' rule. Students' visual and auditory perception and memory of words with the 'magic e' pattern will improve. The processes of visual and auditory synthesis and analysis of words with the 'magic e' pattern will improve. Visual–auditory–kinaesthetic integration of words with the 'magic e' pattern will be consolidated. Technique and speed of reading and writing words with the 'magic e' pattern as well as their meaning will be consolidated.

No. I	Type of task II	Realisation of task III	Teaching aids IV	Comments V
(1)	• Introduction	• The teacher greets the students, asks what their day has been like, how they feel. • The teacher checks the additional exercises the students were supposed to work on at home after the previous lesson.		
(2)	• Progress test – 'doubling rule'.	• In the first part of the test words and sentences are dictated. Then students are asked to read words and sentences.	• Test form.	• e.g. *buzz, sniff, jazz, grill, ball* *I often miss my bus. He pushed her off the cliff. The alarm will buzz at two. It is hard to spell well.*
(3)	• Short and long vowels – comparison.	• The students are reminded that short vowels say their sounds and the long vowels say their names. • The teacher elicits the names of the five vowels and writes the vowel letters on the board. • Then she asks the students to give the key words to unlock the sounds of		• The rules and the explanations are provided in Polish.

	short vowel sounds. The words: apple, egg, Indian, octopus, umbrella are written on the board. The students are asked to read the words and say what the beginning sound in each of them is. The teacher stresses that they are short vowel sounds and writes the corresponding symbols of phonetic transcription – /æ/, /e/, /ɪ/, /ɒ/ and /ʌ/. The students are asked to provide some examples of words containing short vowel sounds, e.g. hat, hen, zip, hot, nut. • The teacher elicits from the students the names of vowels (they revise the alphabet if necessary). The teacher writes the following on the board: 'a'–/ei/, 'e'–/iː/, 'i'–/ai/, 'o'–/ðʊ/, 'u'–/juː/ or /uː/.		Short vowel sounds	Vowel letters	Long vowel sounds
			/æ/	a	/ei/
			/e/	e	/iː/
			/ɪ/	i	/ai/
			/ɒ/	o	/ðʊ/
			/ʌ/	u	/juː/ /uː/
(4) Auditory differentiation between short and long vowel sounds – minimal pairs.	• It is explained to the students that a minimal pair is a pair of words that differ only in one sound. Here they differ in a vowel sound. • The students listen to the teacher reading minimal pairs of words (the consonants remain the same but the vowel sound differs) and decide in which word they hear a short vowel sound and in which one a long vowel sound.	• A list of minimal pairs.	• e.g. (a) ship-sheep, (b) note-not, (c) bed-bead, (d) fit-fight, (e) read-red, (f) cut-cute, (g) bat-bait
			Minimal pair	Short vowel sound	Long vowel sound
			a	1	2
			b	2	1
			c	1	2
			d	1	2

(Continued)

No. I	Type of task II	Realisation of task III	Teaching aids IV	Comments V
(5)	• Auditory differentiation between short and long vowels – odd one out.	• The students listen to the teacher reading sets of one-syllable words containing either short or long vowels and choose the odd one out. Each set consists of four words. The students mark their answers in the chart.		• e.g. cut sun nut **cute** wine five **win** nice hop hot **hope** cot 	No.	I	II	III	IV
1				v
2			v	
3			v		
(6)	• Auditory differentiation between short and long vowel sounds.	• The students listen to the teacher reading a list of one-syllable words and decide which vowel sound they hear in which word. They put a tick in the chart under the appropriate heading.	• A list of words.	• e.g. (1) ship, (2) shape, (3) shop, (4) sheep, (5) cup, (6) mine, (7) hen, (8) hope, (9) rat, (10) cute | No.	a		e		i		o		u	
	S	L	S	L	S	L	S	L	S	L
---	---	---	---	---	---	---	---	---	---	---
1										
2	v									
3								v		
4				v							

(7)	'Magic e' – rule – introduction	• It is made explicit to the students that there are several ways of spelling long vowel sounds but we will concentrate on one of them – 'magic, silent or lengthening e'. • The teacher draws the chart* on the board with the headings and the first column filled up. Then she says the words *mad, met, win, hop, cut* and asks the students whether they contain short or long vowel sounds and to indicate in which row of the second column they should be written. Next the teacher asks the students to write these words again adding the 'e' at the end of each of them in the corresponding rows of the third column. The teacher reads the words from the third column and then the minimal pairs and asks the students what spelling pattern they can see in the words from the third column. We add the 'e' after the final consonant and this makes the vowel long (or say its name).	• Rule card: *Adding the 'e' after the single final consonant of a one-syllable word makes the vowel in the middle of that word long (or say its name).*	• The rules and the explanations are provided in Polish. *<table><tr><th>1</th><th>2</th><th>3</th></tr><tr><th>Vowel</th><th>Short sound</th><th>Long sound</th></tr><tr><td>a</td><td>mad</td><td>made</td></tr><tr><td>e</td><td>met</td><td>mete</td></tr><tr><td>i</td><td>win</td><td>wine</td></tr><tr><td>o</td><td>hop</td><td>hope</td></tr><tr><td>u</td><td>cut</td><td>cute</td></tr></table>
(8)	The /aɪ/ sound spelled 'i-e'	• The teacher writes the following words on the board: *white, time, write, five, nice, pine, like* and reads them. The students are asked what spelling pattern they can see in these words. The teacher highlights the 'i-e' pattern in all the words and writes the 'i-e' rule on the board.	• Rule card **'i-e'**: *When we hear the sound /aɪ/ ('i' saying its name) in the middle of a one-syllable word followed by a single consonant sound ('e' is silent), we most frequently spell it with the letters 'i-e'.*	• The rules and the explanations are provided in Polish.

(*Continued*)

No. I	Type of task II	Realisation of task III	Teaching aids IV	Comments V
(9)	• Reading drill – 'i-e'.	• The students are given flash cards with 'i-e' words for reading practice. They look at the underlined letter, say the sound it makes and read a word.	• Flash cards with 'i-e' words.	• The sound /ai/ is printed at the left top corner and a word in the middle of a flash card (lower case letters are used). The letters used to spell a given sound are printed in bold type. There is a Polish translation of the word on the other side of the flash card. e.g. /ai/ /ai/ /ai/ t**i**me n**i**ce sm**i**le
(10)	• Hands on activity – 'i-e'.	• (a) The students are given movable devices – slides. The task is to form and read the words with the /ai/ sound. Later they write the words into the chart. The consonants are already filled in, the missing element in all words is the 'i-e' pattern. '*i-e*'–/ai/ 		i	e	 |---|---|---|---| 	1	t	s		 	2	s	z		 	3	n	c			• Slides. Colour coding is used to enhance visual perception.	• e.g. (a) (slide device showing t_s, m_z, n_c with i and e)

		(b) The students are provided with a movable device comprising four piles of flash cards joined at the top with a spring. The first pile consists of white cards with consonants or initial consonant blends or digraphs, the second pile consists of a green card with the letter 'i', the third pile includes white cards with consonants and the forth pile consists of a green card with the letter 'e'. The students are asked to form words by moving the cards, to read and write them. There are numbers and Polish translations of words on the reverse side of the white cards so that the students can check whether they have formed a correct word.	• Movable teaching device comprising four piles of cards in different colours joined at the top with a spring.	• e.g. (b) t /ai/ m E i
(11)	• Auditory/ visual perception.	• The students are given charts with the 'i-e' pattern written, they listen to the teacher reading the words and fill in the missing consonants.	• Worksheet.	• e.g. | 1 | _ i _ e | time | | 2 | _ i _ e | wine | | 3 | _ i _ e | like |
(12)	• Picture crossword.	• The students are asked to do the crossword. Pictures are the clues.	• Worksheet adapted from Shemesh and Waller (2000).	• To make the exercise easier the list of words can be provided for students.

(Continued)

No. I	Type of task II	Realisation of task III	Teaching aids IV	Comments V

(13)	• Grid.	• The students are asked to solve the clues on the left and write the words in the boxes on the right.	• Worksheet adapted from Shemesh and Waller (2000).	• e.g.
				
				  | A number, half of ten | | i | e |
				  | A colour | | i | e |
				  | Belongs to me | | i | e |
				  | A reward | | i | e |
				
				• To make the exercise easier the list of words can be provided for students.

(14)	• Letter leads.	• The students solve the clues and write the letters in the boxes, one letter in each box. The letter in the marked box will be the first letter of the next word.	• Worksheet adapted from Shemesh and Waller (2000).	• e.g.
				The river of Egypt.
				  | N | I | L | E |
				A citrus fruit.
				  | L | I | M | E |
				A measure of distance.
				  | M | | | |
				• To make the exercise easier the list of words can be provided for students.

(15)	• Visual perception, orientation in space.	• The task is to find the answers to the clues in the grid. The students have to start at the letter given (in the grid it will have a dot in the top left corner of the square) and then move one square in any direction – up, down, left or right – changing direction when necessary, in order to discover the words.	• Worksheet adapted from Shemesh and Waller (2000).	• e.g. It starts with P – a reward: _ _ _ _ _ - PRIZE | E | L | I | | Z | I | M | | •P | R | •S |
(16)	• Dictation – 'i-e'.	• Minimal pairs are dictated (the words differ in the vowel sound, they include either short or long 'i'), the students write the words into the chart. It is important that they write the words in the order they hear them.	• Worksheet.	• e.g. (1) pill-pile, (2) shine-shin, (3) bite-bit, (4) pin-pine, (5) Tim-time | No. | a | b | | 1 | pill | pile | | 2 | shine | shin |

Chapter 7
Deaf EFL Learners Outside the School System

ÁGNES BAJKÓ and EDIT H. KONTRA

Introduction

The need to speak a foreign language, especially English, is of central importance in present day Hungarian society as well as in many other new EU countries. However, there are very few forums dealing with the issue of foreign language education for people with special needs, and one group, that of the Deaf,[1] seems to be particularly far from the focus of attention, probably due to their special status regarding spoken language itself.

In Hungary, no special methodology has been developed for teaching foreign languages to the Deaf, and the officially sustained oralist method in Deaf education leaves the foreign language teacher very little room for experimentation with fundamentally different approaches. English teacher training at universities and colleges hardly ever deals with the issue. Thus, very little is known about principles of teaching English as a foreign language to the Deaf, and very little – if any – effort is made towards investigating how to improve or adjust to the special needs of Deaf learners the semi-communicative, eclectic method that is currently being applied at mainstream schools. Moreover, in state education there are doubts about whether foreign languages should be taught to Deaf people at all, and students with a hearing impairment are often exempted from foreign language classes (Bartha & Hattyár, 2002).

This study describes a group of Deaf adults learning English as a foreign language in a private language school. By introducing the applied methodology, it attempts to show a different perspective for English language teachers of the Deaf and to provide some basis for further research and development in the field. It is hoped that it will also demonstrate that although teaching foreign languages to the hearing impaired is a considerable challenge, it is a challenge well worth meeting.

Deafness and Deaf Communication

In order to provide the reader with some background information on the Deaf, this section gives a brief overview about deafness itself, including its definitions according to the degree, the types, and the onset of hearing loss. It also explains how the Deaf relate to language and introduces the means of communication they use, their mother tongue, and its status in Hungary. Finally, it describes the present state of education of the Deaf, including the major methods that are available and the ones that are currently employed in Hungary.

Deafness

In the hearing world two opposing views regarding deafness prevail: the *pathological* and the *sociocultural* view. The former defines deafness as an auditory deficiency, a medical problem that should be remedied in order that the deaf individual should become as similar to a hearing person as possible. For this reason it advocates the use of hearing aids and cochlear implants and promotes the teaching of lip-reading and speech production. The sociocultural view, on the other hand, recognises the Deaf as a sociocultural minority, which shares characteristics with other minorities, and its representatives regard the problems of the Deaf as human rights issues (Reagan, 1995 cited in Skutnabb-Kangas, 2000a).

Two main types of hearing loss can be distinguished medically: partial loss of hearing and deafness. People with a partial loss of hearing are referred to as hard-of-hearing, and their hearing loss is between 30–90 dB. In face-to-face communication they rely on speech and lip-reading, and they utilise their residual hearing, enhanced by a hearing aid, when talking on the phone. They rarely use or even know visual languages. Many hard-of-hearing people, however, will identify themselves as Deaf and will use sign language for communication (Lane *et al.*, 1996).

A deaf person has a hearing loss of 90 dB or more and relies on the visual aspects of language in communication: lip-reading, facial expressions, gestures, signs or written language. Deaf people might also have some residual hearing, but it is so little that they cannot make use of a hearing-aid and can only perceive the very loudest sounds. Deafness can be hereditary but can also be a consequence of a disease or an accident, or a side-effect of certain medicines. Most Deaf couples have hearing children and the majority of Deaf children are born to hearing parents (Lane *et al.*, 1996). In some cases hearing can be restored by surgery using cochlear implants (National Institute on Deafness and other Communication Disorders, 2006) – though many Deaf people would not agree to such an intervention, since they do not see their deafness as an impairment or a disease to be cured but rather as a state on the basis of which they belong to a separate cultural group: the Deaf (Lancz, 1999; Lane *et al.*, 1996; PBS, 2007).

From the perspective of acquiring spoken language, an important factor is the age at which the deaf person 'lost' his or her hearing. *Congenital deafness* occurs if a person becomes deaf at or before birth. If a person who was born to hearing parents loses his or her hearing before the end of the normal language acquisition period – that is, before approximately three years of age – we talk about *pre-lingual* deafness. Children with pre-lingual deafness learn spoken language as a foreign language, with the help of a speech therapist in preschool and in school. If, on the other hand, hearing loss occurs after the completion of the language acquisition process – that is, after approximately three years of age – it is called *post-lingual* deafness. The effect of post-lingual deafness on speech, reading, writing and lip-reading depends on the individual and the age at which the hearing loss occurred (Bartha & Hattyár, 2002; Kósa, 2002; O'Neill, 1998).

Deaf communication

Contrary to the common belief that all Deaf people communicate in one and the same way, there are many ways in which they can express themselves. The communication channel a Deaf person chooses depends on many factors such as age, the onset of deafness, the type of deafness, language skills of both the listener and the speaker, the degree of residual hearing, lip-reading skills, fluency in speech, personality, family background, schooling, intelligence personal preference and who they are communicating with (Kósa, 2002; Woll, 2005).

First of all, the Deaf can use *sign language*, which is a visual-gesticular language, using hand shape, position and movement, body movements, gestures, facial expressions and other visual cues to form words and expressions. Linguists assert that sign language fulfils all the criteria for a natural language (Bartha & Hattyár, 2002; Branson & Miller, 2007; Sutton-Spence & Woll, 1999). Sign language has its own structure, grammar and vocabulary, different from but equivalent to spoken languages (Liddell, 2003). It also has its own word order, and expresses grammatical features differently than spoken languages (National Institute on Deafness and Other Communication Disorders, 2006). It is primarily the language of the Deaf, who use it for the same communicative purposes as hearing people use oral/aural languages. It is very important to note here that sign language is not international, but that each Deaf community has its own sign language. The sign languages of some nations resemble each other in structure, yet there are such significant differences in lexis that we talk about different languages (Litavecz, 1996; Woll, 2005). What is more, sign language is usually not uniform even within one country; it has different varieties, similarly to the dialects of spoken language in most countries. Like any other language, sign languages also develop and change.

Signed speech, also referred to as a manual signed code system, is somewhat different from sign language: it is a manual supplement to lip-reading which supports lip movement with hand-positions. Unlike sign language, it attempts to follow the syntax of spoken language and uses its grammatical forms, articles and linking words. Manual sign codes have been used to teach the dominant oral/aural language to Deaf children. The ideology underlying manual sign codes is the pathological approach, which ranks languages in a hierarchy with oral languages at the top, sign languages at the bottom, and manual sign codes in between them. Thus most Deaf communities reject the use of manual sign codes (Lane *et al.*, 1996; Reagan, 1995 cited in Skutnabb-Kangas, 2000a).

Fingerspelling is different from signs in that a handshape represents a printed alphabetic letter. It is one way to represent sequences of letters that form words. Most Deaf people are familiar with the print of the majority language in their country. Fingerspelling is used mainly between the Deaf and hard-of-hearing or in communication with hearing people. It is also used within the Deaf community when there is no sign for a word – usually names of places or people, or acronyms – or when the sign is not known by everybody present. In finger-spelling, letters are represented by the fingers, every hand-position denoting a different letter. It is rather slow, so Deaf people prefer not to use it as a main form of communication.

The mother tongue of the Deaf

There are different views concerning the mother tongue of the Deaf and its relation to spoken language. These originate from the two views already described: the pathological and the sociocultural. According to the pathological view, the mother tongue of the Deaf is the oral/aural language of the country they live in. Representatives of this view do not accept sign language as a language in its own right (Skutnabb-Kangas, 2000a).

The sociocultural view, on the other hand, sees sign language as a legitimate language which is the mother tongue of the Deaf, and considers the spoken language of the majority as a foreign or second language. Sign language is the primary means of communication between Deaf people, so for them it fulfils the role of the mother tongue. Linguists agree that the Deaf form a linguistic minority group (Bartha *et al.*, 2006; Branson & Miller, 2007), and based on this, they should be given the opportunity to express their opinion and communicate in this language in official forums. Unfortunately this right is granted in only very few societies (Szabó, 1998).

In our view, Deaf children learn the spoken language of the majority as a foreign language. Knowledge of the first language (mother tongue) greatly supports the learning of a foreign language (Cummins, 1989). Thus, if Deaf children acquire sign language as their mother tongue before the age of three, it supports the development of their overall language competence, which can ease the process of learning a foreign language for them (Grosjean, 1999; Muzsnai, 1997). The earlier a child is exposed to and begins to acquire language – any language – the better that child's communication skills will become (Lane et al., 1996). Research suggests that the first six months are the most crucial to a child's development of language skills. If hearing loss is identified in this very early period, and appropriate intervention begins, language development can be normal no matter how severe the hearing loss is (Arehart & Yoshinaga-Itano, 1999; Sacks, 1989). On the other hand, as Fisher (1994, cited in Muzsnai, 1999) points out, delayed exposure to sign language also delays primary socialisation and may affect the development of the child's personality.

Sign language is clearly a minority language in a majority culture that tends not to understand or respect sign languages. Many Deaf people grow up with ambivalent attitudes toward their own language, often conditioned to feeling 'inferior to hearing persons' (Kannapell, 1976: 11, cited in Holcomb & Peyton, 1992), even in the United States, where American Sign Language has a much greater legitimacy than sign languages anywhere else. The Deaf also have ambivalent feelings toward the spoken language of the majority (Holcomb & Peyton, 1992). Most Deaf people, however, do not think of their deafness as a handicap or a problem to be eliminated. For many of them it is rather a 'state'. They consider themselves people who, apart from not hearing, are in no way different from the hearing majority. A Deaf community typically uses sign language, and this makes it a linguistic-cultural minority: a community held together by the language, and not by the pathological qualification of hearing loss.

The Deaf in Hungary

In Hungary approximately 10% of the population have some kind of hearing loss, with 60,000 of them being Deaf, and 300,000 severely hard-of-hearing. According to national statistics, the Deaf constitute the third largest minority group in Hungary (Bartha et al., 2006), however, their cultural identity and the question of their mother tongue remains a debated and unresolved problem even today. Three per cent of the hard-of-hearing and 28% of the Deaf have no school qualifications. Only 4.6% of the hard-of-hearing and 0.6% of the Deaf have a high school diploma, 83.5% of the hard-of-hearing do manual work, and 16.5% of them are white-collar workers. Among the Deaf, 98.1% are blue-collar and 1.9% are white-collar workers. While 23.3% of hard-of-hearing people hold a leading post, there are no Deaf in managerial positions (Kósa & Lovászy, 2002).

The special educational needs of the Deaf are seldom recognised and catered for at schools. Hungarian Sign Language (HSL) is not taught in Hungarian institutions for Deaf children, nor is it a required subject at the

Special Teacher's College for future teachers of the Deaf and hard-of-hearing. In pre-school programmes and at school, children learn spoken Hungarian, and since most of them come from hearing parents, they acquire HSL informally from their signing peers outside the classroom (Lancz, 1999). Muzsnai (1999: 284) cites his own experience at the Budapest School for the Deaf, where he teaches, saying that in 1997 'none of the pupils in a class of six-year-olds had aquired an L1 language base by the beginning of their school career'. Without a fully established language – spoken or signed – prior to learning to read, Deaf children have more difficulties during their studies than those whose parents use sign language at home (Wilbur, 2002, cited in Kárpáti, 2002). This results in the fact that most Deaf high school graduates at the age of 20 read the majority language roughly at third or fourth grade level – an observation which corresponds to international findings of research using standardised reading assessment (Allen, 1986; King & Quigley, 1985, cited in Holcomb & Peyton, 1992). They frequently make vocabulary and structural errors in their writing and have difficulties with complex sentence structures (Kárpáti, 2002). As a direct consequence of these limited literacy skills, Deaf adults are often confined to low-level jobs and experience a variety of disadvantages irrespective of the fact that the measure of their literacy skills is not per se a measure of what a Deaf person knows and is able to do.

At present, there are eight primary schools for the Deaf in Hungary. There are three vocational secondary schools but no secondary grammar schools for the Deaf or hard-of-hearing students, and there is only one school where there are separate, self-contained classes for the hearing-impaired. Besides this, Deaf and hard-of-hearing students only have the opportunity to study in integrated classrooms in regular secondary schools. Deaf or hard-of-hearing students can take part in higher education only in integrated groups. Very few Deaf students go to college or university. Those who do continue their studies experience disadvantages in several situations, apart from having to spend about twice as much time in preparation for lessons compared to their hearing peers. This is mainly due to insufficient attention being paid to their special needs.

Regarding the education of the Deaf, two conflicting views prevail: manualism and oralism. Manualists are those who view the use of manual signs (either sign languages or, most often, manual codes) as 'normal or most appropriate for deaf people' (Senghas, 1998: 542, cited in Skutnabb-Kangas, 2000b). Oralists, on the other hand, try to teach Deaf people to communicate verbally, often completely forbidding the use of sign language (Baker & Jones, 1998). The oralist approach, developed in Germany, was embraced by (hearing) educators and dominated the education of the Deaf for most of the 20th century both in Europe and the United States, until attitudes toward signing started to change in the 1970s and 1980s (Woll, 2005).

Deafness in Hungarian education is still considered a pathological condition. Due to their inability to hear, Deaf people are considered mentally and educationally deficient and in need of special education (Muzsnai, 1999). In accordance with this view, the education of the Deaf is based primarily on the oralist approach, and there are very few teachers who are able and willing to use sign language in teaching. The prevailing educational policy does not accept sign language as the first language of severely hard-of-hearing and Deaf students, but treats spoken Hungarian as their mother tongue. Using Hungarian as the medium for teaching foreign languages practically means teaching one foreign language through another. Kárpáti (2002) was granted access to one of the three Hungarian vocational schools which have Deaf classes and offer a choice of English or German as a foreign language in their curriculum. Of the two English teachers who were observed, only one could communicate with the students using HSL in the classroom. The other teacher, who used the oralist approach, was unable to understand her Deaf students, who could only understand her with the help of sign interpretation by hard-of-hearing classmates, which resulted in frustration on both sides.

Bartha and Hattyár (2002) provide a detailed discussion of the legal documents that govern the education of Deaf students in state schools. They quote the National Core Curriculum, which declares that students with a hearing impairment can be exempted from the compulsory study of a foreign language. If they do learn a foreign language, they can ask to be exempted from the oral part of accredited proficiency exams. Various accomodations and provisions are available for Deaf students at school exams as well, such as the possibility of taking a written exam instead of an oral one, extended preparation time for working on test tasks, and the obligation on schools to provide a sign language interpreter if so requested by the student (Kárpáti, 2002).

Since the foreign language requirement is usually waived for Deaf students in primary and secondary education, those who are motivated to learn a foreign language often do so as adults with the help of private tutors. The authors are aware of only two private language schools in the capital city of Budapest which have recently experimented with organising English as a foreign language courses specifically for Deaf learners with signing tutors. There are successful language learners among the Deaf in Hungary, for example the three adult cases in Kárpáti's (2002) study, who mastered English at an intermediate or upper-intermediate level. They each have a certificate in English; one of them achieved a high enough score on the TOEFL to be admitted to an American university.

This study introduces five Deaf adults taking a course at a private language school who are also determined to learn English and even to take an examination in it. Their case is another small piece of evidence that it is worth teaching foreign languages to the Deaf.

Method

In order to gain a deeper understanding of the issues involved in teaching English to the Deaf, data were gathered over a period of one semester using multiple methods of data collection. Since the use or non-use of sign language constitutes a key issue in Deaf education, a series of observations were carried out to establish what the participants used sign language for and how often they did so. Data were also collected regarding the methods and materials their teacher employed, and both student and teacher interviews were conducted to investigate the views of participants concerning the teaching of English as a foreign language to the Deaf. The two researchers participated in the investigation to different degrees: the first author did all the fieldwork since she is the one with sufficient knowledge of sign language. The second author was involved in the design of the instruments, and in the analysis and interpretation of the data.

The research focus was initially defined as follows: 'How does the teaching and learning of English take place in a group of Deaf adult language learners, with special attention to the use of sign language and teaching materials?'

In order to operationalise this broad research question, it was broken down into the following sub-questions:

(1) What motivates these Deaf students in learning English?
(2) How do the teacher and students make use of sign language in the teaching and learning process?
(3) What methods and materials does the teacher use in order to meet the special needs of Deaf students?
(4) Do small group-size and non-integrated teaching play a role in the effective teaching of a foreign language to Deaf students?

In order to obtain answers to the above questions and to gain a deep insight into the relevant issues, a qualitative approach was taken. The case under investigation was defined as a small group of five learners, which was observed closely with the purpose of understanding the various aspects of the teaching-learning process from the perspective of the participants themselves, that is, the Deaf students and their teacher. The selection of the participants was purposeful: one group of five Deaf adult learners studying English at a private language school and their teacher.

Research was conducted using multiple data sources. In order to gain an insider's perspective and to gather enough information in the field, the first researcher regularly visited the group's language classes over a period of five months, during which she took field notes and filled out observation sheets. Besides this, she often had informal conversations with the students and the teacher. She extensively examined and discussed with the teacher the materials she used for teaching this group. The students were asked to fill out a detailed questionnaire about their language learning, and formal interviews were conducted with them, as well as with their teacher.

The use of multiple data sources, the researcher's extended stay in the field and the thick description of the findings in the Analysis section were each intended to contribute to the trustworthiness (Guba, 1981; Lazaraton, 2003) of the research and to the transferability of the results.

Participants

The students

In 2003 the Hungarian Ministry of Education launched a project to support the language learning of individuals with special needs in both the state and the private sectors. It was within the framework of this project that the language school where our research took place won a grant to design and implement an English course for the Blind and one for the Deaf and hard-of hearing. Participation in the course was made possible for the students by the grant covering 70% of the tuition fee. One of the course-participants was an acquaintance of the first researcher, who thus managed to establish contact and gain access to the group and their teacher. The actual data collection was carried out in 2005.

Originally there were seven members in the group, but two of them rarely participated and attended inconsistently, and therefore were not included in the study. The remaining five members, three male and two female students, attended classes on a regular basis. In order to preserve their anonymity, they are introduced below under given pseudonyms.

Nikolett

She is a young woman of 28, who is severely hard-of-hearing and uses hearing aids, but culturally identifies with the Deaf. Her hearing loss is attributed to medication she received as a baby. She has a college degree in packaging technology but works in the small ads section of a newspaper. Before joining this group, she studied English for about six months at a course organised by the Hungarian Association for the Deaf and Hard of Hearing, and also studied German at primary school for three years. Her command of Hungarian is very good, though her pronunciation is a little distorted. However, she asserts that her mother tongue is HSL, and she feels more comfortable interacting with Deaf people.

Melinda

Melinda is a 21-year-old female. She became deaf due to an illness when she was approximately eight months old. Although she is qualified as a software operator, she enrolled in a teacher training college in September

2005. Melinda never studied English before joining this programme, but she studied German at secondary school for a year. Though very helpful, she is reserved by nature, and the fact that she is not very talkative came to light in the interview. She gave relatively short answers to the questions and often had to be prompted two or even three times to provide as much information as the same question elicited from the other participants. She speaks Hungarian well, with a wide range of vocabulary and good grammar, but her pronunciation is very distorted: it is almost impossible to understand her speech. She maintains that her mother tongue is HSL.

Aron

Aron is a 27-year-old male. His hearing loss was probably inherited from his parents, since they are Deaf as well. He grew up signing with them from the very beginning. He has a university degree in information technology and is an office worker. Aron never studied English or any other foreign language before. He has a wide range of vocabulary both in Hungarian and in Sign Language. His knowledge of Hungarian grammar is very good, and his speech is quite easy to understand.

Imre

Imre was born deaf and is 25 years old. He holds a degree from a technical university and is currently employed as an information technologist. When he was a child, his father taught him some German, but he says he has forgotten most of it. Imre attempted to study English a number of times, but could not complete any of his courses either because they were broken off, or because the school exempted him from attending foreign language classes. Finally, he decided to make a fresh start in English in the present language course. Like Aron, Imre is very intelligent and friendly. In spite of his many disappointing experiences, he is still very ambitious and enthusiastic about English. His pronunciation of Hungarian, like Melinda's, is almost impossible to understand. However, his vocabulary in both English and Hungarian is extensive, and his knowledge of Hungarian grammar is at an intermediate level.

Robi

Robi is a 32-year-old man who was born deaf. His deafness is said to be caused by faulty genes, suggesting his hearing loss is hereditary. He is a high-school graduate, and he works as a software developer for hospitals. He studied some German in primary school. Robi is much less well-educated than the others. During the interview, instead of trying to answer the questions, he often just said whatever came to his mind. Thus questions often had to be repeated in different forms, but sometimes with little success. His knowledge of Hungarian vocabulary is quite poor, as is his knowledge of Hungarian grammar, but he is able to express himself well in his mother tongue, HSL, although also with a limited vocabulary.

The teacher

Tímea is a young teacher in her 20s. She has a teaching degree in English but does not have any training or qualifications in teaching people with special needs. Tímea has been teaching English since her graduation, most of the time in language schools. She has never taught in a state school and had never taught Deaf or other people with special needs before meeting this group in October 2003. At the time of data collection, it seemed she had not lost any of her initial enthusiasm for the programme. She knows sign language at an approximately intermediate level because she completed a course in HSL on her own initiative in preparation for teaching these and other Deaf students.

The language school

The private language school where the fieldwork was carried out is situated close to the centre of the capital. Permission to conduct the research was received from both the educational management of the school and the individual course participants.

The school is situated on the ground floor of a big apartment building. It has a very friendly atmosphere, created by both the school's interior and the people working there. The classrooms are designed for teaching small groups. They are decorated with English posters which display useful vocabulary, pronunciation charts and cultural information. The desks are arranged in a U-shape, so everyone can see each other. Overall, the classrooms provide a favourable learning environment.

Instruments

Altogether four different instruments were used for collecting data: an observation sheet, a long and detailed student questionnaire, and two interview guides – one for the students, and one for the teacher. Finally, the materials, worksheets, handouts and visual aids prepared by the teacher were also examined. Each of the instruments is introduced below in detail.

Observation

The first author had the opportunity to observe nine 90-minute lessons with the group. The first observed lesson served as an opportunity to collect basic information for planning future observations, which were to be more systematically organised. One important observation confirmed the researchers' initial expectation, namely that contrary to preferred practice in state schools, the use of sign language is a natural part of language learning for Deaf students. Based on the field notes taken during the first visit, an observation sheet was designed for taking notes on the details of sign language use. It was essentially a large-sized chart designed to register the learning activities as well as the frequency and the purpose of the students' and the teacher's use of sign language. The following seven categories were anticipated for the use of sign language: *Instruction, Explanation, Feedback, Question, Answer, Translation between two students* and *Translation between student and teacher*. Besides these, there was a column to mark whether the use of sign language took place parallel to (P) or consecutive of (C) the use of spoken language. The chart had 90 rows for the 90 minutes, and the intended procedure was to put a mark into the corresponding boxes for each minute: one mark to indicate which participant (S1, S2, S3, S4, S5, T) used sign language, and another to indicate the purpose of its use.

The second visit was used for trying out the chart and for gaining some practice in using it. Following the piloting of the instrument a number of changes were made to simplify its structure and use: the indication of the participants was reduced to *Teacher* (T), and *Student* (S), and the categories for the purpose of using sign language were reduced from seven to four: *Question-Answer, Instruction-Explanation, Translation* and *Speech without sign language*. The parallel vs. consecutive aspect was eliminated as irrelevant since sign language turned out to be used simultaneously with spoken language most of the time. Finally, in the revised version some space on the right hand side of the sheet was left for the observer's notes and comments. This version proved to be adequate, and no more changes were needed. Observation notes to be used in the analysis were taken during the remaining seven visits, which comprised 630 minutes of class-time.

Questionnaire

The use of a questionnaire for data collection was motivated by a number of factors. Owing to the communication difficulties between the researcher and the participants, it was considered important to reduce the interview time to a reasonable length and to gather as much information as possible by other means. Questionnaires are easy to administer, and filling them out takes up relatively little of the participants' free time. The impersonality of the questionnaire format is another advantage: some factors, like language learning anxiety and group dynamics, seemed to be easier to investigate via written means because participants were less likely to give answers that they thought would be pleasing to the interviewer. Last but not least, gathering as much initial information as possible about the participants' thoughts and feelings regarding their language learning experiences would make it possible to draft a more meaningful and more focused interview guide. The language of the questionnaire was Hungarian.

In terms of content, the questionnaire focussed on three areas of individual differences: learner beliefs (30 items), motivation (55 items), and learning styles and strategies (24 items). The first area, learner beliefs, was considered very important since we have very little direct information about what Deaf learners think about learning foreign languages or their own ability to achieve success. When drafting the items, the authors made use of Horwitz's (1987) 'Student Beliefs About Language Learning Inventory', a well known and widely used instrument which deals with five areas of student beliefs: Foreign Language Aptitude, The Difficulty of Language Learning, The Nature of Language Learning, Learning and Communication Strategies and Motivation. Probing into the same areas as those included in Horwitz's inventory allowed us to examine the beliefs of these students about language learning against the backdrop of the beliefs of their hearing peers.

For investigating motivation, the questionnaire extensively used in Hungarian motivation research was taken as a model (*cf.* Clément et al., 1994; Dörnyei, 2001). It was thought appropriate since it had been developed for a Hungarian sample, was originally written in Hungarian, and covered a variety of dimensions of motivation such as external and internal motives, instrumental and integrative orientations, the learners' attitudes toward American or English people, foreign language anxiety, and the role of the group in motivating or demotivating learners. This part of the questionnaire yielded information on why our Deaf participants devote their free time to studying a foreign language, and whether their motivational characteristics are similar to those of hearing language learners. Some examples for our items on motivation (translated into English) are:

- Studying English is important to me because I might need it in the future for a new job or for a degree.
- Studying English is important to me because I need a foreign language certificate.
- Knowing English will help me when travelling.
- I always feel that my group-mates know English better than I do.
- I always feel uneasy when I have to speak in an English class.
- My English group is composed of people who fit together well.

Both in the learner beliefs part of the questionnaire and in the section on motivation, the students were asked to give their answers on a six-point Likert-type scale using the following dimensions: *1 – definitely disagree, 2 – do not really agree, 3 – have some reservations about it, 4 – agree to a certain extent, 5 – roughly agree, 6 – definitely agree.*

The third part of the instrument contained a checklist of statements, each describing a particular learning strategy shown to be effective in enhancing foreign language learning by previous research (O'Malley & Chamot, 1990; Oxford, 1990; Rubin, 1975) such as guessing, inferencing the meaning from context, translating into Hungarian, using the dictionary, rehearsing, practicing, etc., and the participants were asked to mark which strategies they applied when studying English. For example:

- I revise my notes from the lesson.
- I look for opportunities to use the language.
- I translate everything into (spoken) Hungarian.
- I infer the meaning of the unknown words from the context.
- I rehearse the new material by speaking/signing to myself.

This checklist was included in the questionnaire to find out if there is any peculiarity in the way these Deaf students study English and to see what areas the interview questions should probe further.

Student interviews

All five of the student interviews were conducted on the premises of the Hungarian Association of the Deaf and Hard of Hearing. Each interview lasted from 20 to 30 minutes, the total time being approximately 130 minutes. Even though the first researcher, who conducted the interviews, knows HSL at an intermediate level, an interpreter was used for two reasons. First, this allowed the interviews to be audio-recorded, which ensured that no information would be lost. Secondly, by not having to use her hands for signing or taking notes, the interviewer was able to pay full attention to the interviewees. The interpreter translated the questions into HSL and the students' answers into spoken Hungarian. The fact that the participants already knew both the interpreter and the researcher ensured an open and friendly atmosphere for the interviews.

The semi-structured interview guide contained 20 open-ended questions, which covered four main areas: (1) background information; (2) use of sign language in class; (3) students' opinion about ideal group structure and course material; and (4) views on the English language and learning English. Since it was a semi-structured interview, the researcher sometimes changed the order of the questions or asked additional ones that were not originally included in the guide if it seemed necessary.

Teacher interview

One semi-structured and one free interview were conducted with the teacher, in one of the rooms of the language school where she works. Each interview lasted approximately 60 minutes, and was audio-recorded from beginning to end. The first interview included 19 questions to cover four main areas: (1) biographical information; (2) personal experience in teaching English to Deaf people; (3) teaching methods; and (4) future plans for the group and its teacher. The whole of the second interview was taken up by the teacher presenting and explaining the materials she used for teaching the group of Deaf people.

Analysis

The data analysis followed the principles of qualitative research (Patton, 2002). It was part of the cyclical nature of the research design that the data collected in one phase of the investigation should be at least partially analysed right away so that the results could inform the design of the next phase. Thus the observations aided the structuring of the questionnaire, and both the observation and the questionnaire results influenced the content of the interviews.

The observation data were analysed by calculating frequencies. The number of marks in each observation category was added up for all of the lessons. This yielded total figures indicating the amount of time during which sign language was used by teacher and students. For the purpose of a meaningful comparison between categories, these sums were divided by the total number of observed minutes and averages were calculated for each of the observed purposes: *Question-Answer, Instruction-Explanation, Translation* and *Speech without sign language.*

The questionnaire data were analysed by calculating means for the Likert-scale items, and frequencies for the checklist items. As regards the interviews, first the audio-recordings were transcribed – that is, the Hungarian translation provided by the sign language interpreter. Following this, the data were subjected to content analysis using the constant-comparative method as described by Maykut and Morehouse (1994). The trustworthiness of the research was ensured by data triangulation, peer-review, and by leaving an audit trail (Guba, 1981).

Results and Discussion

In the presentation of the results first an overall picture of the participants' beliefs and attitudes towards learning English will be discussed. This will include their views about their abilities and their goals and also a description of how they see their own learning techniques and strategies. This will lead to the central issue of this study, namely the use of sign language in the teaching and learning of English, which will be further linked to the students' and the teacher's views on group size and on learning English in integrated vs. non-integrated groups. Finally some teaching methods and materials suitable for teaching the Deaf will be presented.

Learner beliefs

The participants' beliefs about learning English were primarily investigated with the help of the written questionnaire described in the Method section above. The responses were recorded on a scale of 1–6, and the results were averaged. Although the group was small, the mean values are informative and are therefore provided in parentheses. In the interviews the students elaborated further on these issues and gave examples. The quotes from the interviews are presented in the authors' translation.

The participants found that some languages were easier to learn than others ($M = 5.2$), and that learning English was important for Hungarians ($M = 5.2$). When asked if she liked the English language, Melinda gave the following response:

> To my mind the question is not whether you like it or not. Everybody has to learn a foreign language at a certain level so that for instance when they go abroad they can rely on that knowledge.

In comparison to other languages, only one of the students thought English was difficult, all the others considered it a language of medium difficulty. They agreed that some people have a special ability to learn foreign languages ($M = 5.2$), and most of them were confident that they too can learn English well ($M = 4.6$). Another sign of their confidence was that most of them said they were not intimidated by speaking English to other people ($M = 2.6$) and did not think that speaking English with errors was a problem ($M = 1.8$). Their low level of anxiety was observed during the class visits of the first researcher and was also supported by their teacher's opinion. They were not at all anxious in the company of English speaking people, and they did not feel ashamed to speak in front of their group mates or in front of an outside observer in the English lessons either.

It comes as no surprise that the members of this group found reading and writing easier than speaking or understanding spoken English ($M = 5.8$). This is self-explanatory, in view of the fact that speaking and understanding any language other than sign language is strongly connected to oral and lip-reading skills, which cause considerable difficulty for Deaf people. Consequently, the participants also agreed that learning English is best done in an English speaking country ($M = 5.4$). Robi expressed this in the interview as follows:

> I learn for the course what I have to, but it would be good to practise speaking with a Deaf person who knows English. And then sign language could be linked to it, and so I could practise better. It would be good to practise abroad; that already would help me practise English better. If I could spend a year abroad and study there, learning English would be easier.

In the interviews each of the students elaborated on the issue of oral skills and pronunciation. These were the skills that they found the most difficult to acquire although it is known from case studies (Kárpáti, 2002, 2004) that with the help of training and strong determination even the Deaf can learn to produce English speech. When Aron was asked in the interview what the most difficult part of learning English was for him, he named pronunciation without a moment's thought:

> With the Deaf the teacher should not insist on practicing pronunciation. The basics need to be taught, but learning to pronounce need not be pushed. I do not deal with pronunciation, really. In England, when I meet Deaf people, then it is sign language and lip-reading ... so we do not 'talk' anyway.

Melinda echoed the same belief when she said: 'I do not deal with pronunciation because I am Deaf. Even if I learn English well, I will not have a good pronunciation.' Robi shared these views, but he also expressed his dissatisfaction with the situation and his helplessness saying:

> English is easier to learn via reading than learning pronunciation. [...] Pronunciation is difficult. I cannot listen to it, so I cannot practise pronunciation through hearing. Even on television, if the program is closed captioned, I can understand what is written, but the pronunciation I cannot learn even then. [...] So I lag behind very badly because of that, I am very concerned about pronunciation.

The extent of Robi's concern could indeed be seen from the fact that in the interview he kept returning to the subject. He thought that if he could study abroad and practice English with Deaf English people, his pronunciation would improve. At least this was what he had heard from colleagues, and he was eager to find out for himself:

> I wonder how it would work out in real life if I met a foreign Deaf, and let's say my pronunciation is not good, and then how would the conversation work out. My colleagues told me that they had already met English Deaf and that pronunciation was easier to learn by talking to Deaf than to hearing people. That they have a better feel for how to talk to each other than the hearing do. Pronunciation is easier to learn from the Deaf.

Aron also found lip-reading in English a very difficult task, and Melinda said she would resort to writing even when she thought she could be understood otherwise:

Interviewer: And when you were abroad and used English, did you always use it in writing?
Melinda: Yes, always. The Deaf always have paper and a pen on them. When they are abroad, twice as much paper, twice as many pens. When I ask something, like where I need to go, or ask for a map, I would be understood in English everywhere, but I write it down.

The above results show that the beliefs of these Deaf students about language learning are in line with those of their hearing peers (*cf.* Kontráné Hegybíró & Kormos, 2004). This is important because it shows that there is no particularly negative belief which would act as an obstacle to these students acquiring English. These Deaf participants hold two beliefs which are not characteristic of hearing learners, both of which derive logically from their hearing impairment: they consider writing and reading English easier than speaking and understanding it, and they consider pronunciation an extremely difficult skill to acquire.

Motivation

The instrumental motivation of these Deaf students was much higher than their integrative motivation. All of them mentioned the usefulness of English for travelling, and nearly all were aware of the need for English in their jobs or in advancing their career. This was especially true for those students who work with computers like Aron. He read work-related materials in English and said he would like to get in touch with foreign Deaf people. Robi also used English in his work, and he could memorise the words related to the use of the computer better than everyday language, which he did not really use outside of class. He was happy that he knew a little English already and enjoyed the fact that as a result of the course, he knew the meaning of a lot of English signs in the street which he had not understood before.

Most students in the group wanted to learn English well ($M = 4.2$). They associated the ability to speak English with better job opportunities, and their answers reflected an awareness of the importance of speaking English as a strong expectation in Hungarian society. Nikolett's goal in fact was to obtain a language certificate because she hoped to be able to make use of it when looking for a job. Imre, who frequently attended the international conferences of the Deaf, the language of which is English, voiced his opinion as follows:

> The government should support the language learning of the Deaf, and not merely issue waivers from language classes at school. In foreign countries, Sweden or Austria, the Deaf know English. The Deaf could be taught English at school. That would be good. Now we are in the EU, and we would need English.

Melinda also thought that the education system should provide better opportunities for the Deaf to learn foreign languages:

> It would be good if foreign language learning was introduced at an early age like it is for hearing students, who are taught languages in the primary school. Not like it is now for the Deaf that at the age of 30, they realize they should learn English. It should be introduced at school gradually as a compulsory subject [...] Then I am sure, a lot of Deaf would know foreign languages.

From their questionnaire answers we could also see that they wanted to learn English in order to get to know American/English people better ($M = 4.2$) and that they were interested in making American friends ($M = 4.2$). Some of them had already taken part in exchange programs with Deaf from abroad, for example in Wales or Portugal, and were motivated to learn English in order to keep in touch with friends or relatives abroad. The students in the group viewed a second language environment as highly facilitative of language learning; however, cultural knowledge seemed to be less important for them. It was interesting though that when asked about course books and supplementary materials, Aron mentioned that he would be interested in materials on Deaf culture and sign languages.

Even though the students admitted both during the interviews and in their questionnaires that they did not have much time to spend on studying English, their need for achievement was quite high. Their goal was to attain a lower-intermediate level in English. They were observed to work hard during the lessons, and they usually did their homework conscientiously. They rarely did extra work on their own initiative; however, they said they would not mind getting more homework and declared that if their teacher gave them some extra tasks, they would do them willingly.

Almost all of these Deaf students were content with the dynamics of the group. Some of them even thought that the atmosphere in this group was better than in others. A few of them admitted that sometimes there was some tension in the group that hindered learning, but during the observations no sign of this could be seen. The group seemed to be able to work very well together, and it appeared that the motivation resulting from the composition of the group played an important role in the learning process of these students.

Learning strategies

The participants reported using a wide variety of strategies which have been identified by research on good language learners (Kontráné Hegybíró & Kormos, 2004; O'Malley & Chamot, 1990; Oxford, 1990; Rubin, 1975). They unanimously supported the view that repetition and formal practice are important in learning a foreign language ($M = 6.0$), and considered grammar ($M = 5.2$), vocabulary ($M = 5.0$) and translation from the native language into English ($M = 4.4$) the most important elements of foreign language learning. The most common learning strategy applied by the group for studying at home was going through and revising their notes. They also tended to organise the new material, use a dictionary for looking up the meaning of new words, and check the grammar section of the course book for explanations on grammar. When asked about how he did his homework, Robi emphasised some of his metacognitive strategies, such as advance preparation, monitoring and checking as well:

> I looked the words up in the dictionary, and that is how I did the written homework. I always revised, always checked the definitions in the monolingual dictionary and only then did I write the tasks that Timi [the teacher] gave me.

Melinda thought that for the Deaf it would be important to have the grammar rules and explanations in the course books in a language they already knew, so that they could study independently:

> [The course book] should give the grammar rules in Hungarian, and not only in English so that one should not always have to ask the teacher. If there is a person who studies at home on her own and would like to learn the rules from the book, those are not included in Hungarian, which makes it more difficult.

The participants looked for opportunities to use the language, and monitored the other students during the lessons, correcting their mistakes to themselves. They often read English texts on the Internet, and they tried to infer the meaning of the unknown words from the context. These are all strategies that characterise successful and autonomous language learners (Kontráné Hegybíró & Kormos, 2004). On the other hand, these learners rarely talked the material over with others: they all preferred to study alone. What none of them did was to copy the new material several times for practice, although copying is usually thought to be a useful strategy in practicing English spelling. They said they did not use what they had learnt by talking to themselves in English, which is a strategy that hearing people often find effective. They also said they never used their hands for signing when they studied English at home, but they signed 'in their head', that is, they mentally pictured the act of signing.

Regarding the strategy use of these learners, we can conclude that they employed a wide variety of learning strategies which they applied consciously and autonomously. An issue of particular interest is the use of sign language in the learning process, which is dealt with in the following section.

The use of HSL

Since the use of HSL is not promoted in mainstream education of the Deaf, one of the goals of this research was to get an insight into this issue through the eyes of those who are directly involved: the learners and their teacher. During the lessons the first researcher visited, she recorded how often the teacher and the students spoke without sign language, and how often they used it for instruction/explanation, question/answer and

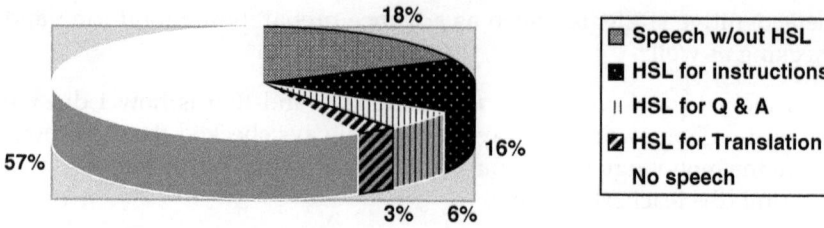

Figure 7.1 The teacher's use of HSL

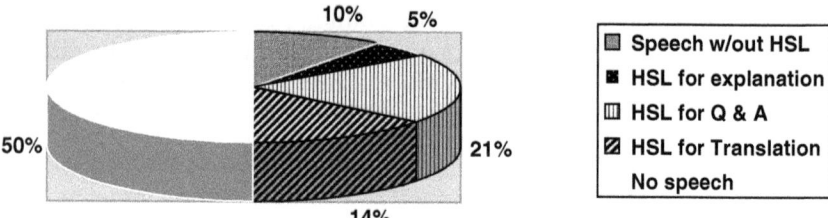

Figure 7.2 The students' use of HSL

translation. Naturally there were also minutes when nobody spoke, and there were minutes when more than one person was talking.

After adding up the minutes for each category, the total values were divided by the total time of observation, that is 7×90 minutes = 630. The results are displayed in Figure 7.1 with percentages to show the comparative ratios.

As can be seen in Figures 7.1 and 7.2, the teacher used more of her time to speak without sign language (in 18% of the lessons) than the students (in 10% of the lessons). This was mainly because during lip-reading practice it was her turn to speak and the students' job was to 'listen', so she needed to speak more without sign language than her students did. Tímea most often used HSL during her lessons for giving instructions or explanations (16%), while the students used it the most often for translation (14%) – either when reading a text and signing at the same time, or when translating English words or phrases to their group mates during all types of exercises. The teacher used HSL the least often for asking questions (6%) and translation (3%), that is, repeating with signs what was said orally in English. The students used sign language the least often for giving explanations to their group mates or the teacher (5%). In approximately half of the observed time, nobody spoke: the students worked in silence. This included working on dialogues as well, since the students practiced dialogues by writing them down in their notebooks in pairs.

As the diagram shows, a great deal of 'talking time' was spent with speech accompanied by sign language, which, the students admitted, contributed greatly to their better understanding of the material, and to their feeling less anxious and frustrated during the lessons. The fact that Tímea was able to teach with the help of HSL made a tremendous difference for these students, which they expressed in the interviews in many different ways. Aron said: 'This way the lessons were easier to understand. It is very difficult to lip-read English because of its pronunciation. The use of sign language helped a lot in this'.

The use of sign language also helped the group to make faster progress with the material during the lessons, as pointed out by Robi:

> Without sign language learning would take longer, because then it is much more difficult to understand the words and expressions. This way I make quicker progress ... And I understand pronunciation better with signs than if it was taught only orally.

Robi also added that if their teacher could not use HSL, he did not think she would be able to teach a foreign language to the Deaf at all. When asked what advice the participants would give to an English teacher who is about to start teaching Deaf students, they unanimously suggested that the teacher should learn sign language in the first place.

Most of the students had very negative experiences of learning foreign languages without the use of sign language, and they each elaborated on what it was like in detail. Imre, for instance, needed English for his degree, but he had to restart learning English over and over again without making much progress. He enrolled in two courses at the Association of the Deaf, but the teachers of those courses were unable to sign, and so the participants lost interest, the groups disintegrated, and the courses were discontinued. Then at the university he attended the language course for hearing students for a year and a half, but finally he had to give it up because he just could not lip-read in English. He was so determined that he also took some private lessons from someone who had a Deaf sibling and could thus teach English 'in the Deaf way', but for this he had to travel to his hometown for the weekends. Finally the university waived the foreign language requirement in his case, admitting that they could not provide the right kind of training for him.

Robi had negative experiences from the high school where he had been taught English in a mixed group of two hard-of-hearing and four Deaf students:

> In the first year the teacher just talked and talked. I asked him to slow down but he always forgot and had to be reminded all the time. And a lot of times. And this went on in every class. The lessons were boring because we could not understand them. [...] Signing matters a lot. Because then we can pay attention, then there is interest.

Tímea, the teacher also had some experiences regarding teaching the Deaf without signing, and in the interview she talked about them at great length. She had visited a few lessons at a school for the Deaf, and had been disappointed by what she had seen:

> The teacher was standing with an amplifier hung around her neck, and the students wore hearing aids ... the teacher was yelling, and she was impatient and unsympathetic ... and the students did not understand her ... and what came through to me from all that was that you cannot teach like this ... because the teacher: she used no sign language at all. The students were signing among themselves, they were trying to sign with the teacher, and the teacher shouted back – but this was not simply a raised voice, but, in my opinion, a kind of reproof.

Of course, not all foreign language lessons at the schools for the Deaf are like this – however, the five different lessons Tímea visited all looked the same. The use of an amplification device seemed to be completely superfluous since it made no difference to the deaf or severely hard-of-hearing students in those lessons. They had so little residual hearing that they could not make use of it or understand anything even when such devices were used.

When amplification devices are not used in the lessons for the Deaf, teachers try to rely on articulation in communication with the students. However, what usually happens – as narrated by our interviewees – is that the Deaf students do not understand what the teacher says, and they get bored. If there are hard-of-hearing students in the classroom, they usually act as mediators between the Deaf students and the teacher: they sign to the students what the teacher said, and they translate to the teacher what the students said. Unfortunately most of the time, Deaf students lose their motivation and do not even ask for help, but try to study the material in their books.

If it is hard for the Deaf to lip-read Hungarian, it is even harder for them to lip-read English. Thus, if the teacher speaks in English, they have even more difficulty understanding him or her, which can be very demotivating. It was when she realised this that Tímea decided to teach her Deaf group English by using their mother tongue, HSL. She talked to many Deaf people before starting to teach the group, and all of them complained about the oralist method used at schools for the Deaf. Her classroom observations supported those opinions as well. In the interviews she expressed her conviction that sign language helped her to understand what the students were trying to say in English. The students appreciated this solution, they felt more at ease using their mother tongue instead of Hungarian, and they found the lessons much easier to follow and more interesting.

Another reason why Tímea applied HSL was her conviction that signing was necessary for building a relationship with her students:

> ... it helped me to fit into the group. Because a huge gap will remain between you and them that you cannot cross if you do not at least try to speak their own language. Why should they talk to me in English if I cannot sign? So, I think there is no doubt that I needed sign language for this. This was not even a question.

Signed Hungarian was used by the teacher to explain the syntactic features of English. For example, normally the Deaf say 'I go home' with only one or at most two signs, where the subject of the sentence 'I' is not obvious, but in the English lesson they signed all three words instead. The students did not object to this solution; rather, it helped them to understand and memorise English grammatical structures.

There were two types of activities in Tímea's lessons for which they consistently did not use either HSL or signed Hungarian. One was when they practiced lip-reading. Then neither the teacher nor the students used signs, but only articulation. The other type of activity was when the students had to act out dialogues. Instead of articulating to each other and relying on lip-reading, they wrote down the dialogues in their 'dialogue notebooks' in pairs, taking turns. This method will be explained in more detail below.

Group size and integrated teaching

The Deaf students who took part in this research all supported small group size because it allows faster progress, and more attention can be paid to the special needs of the students if their number is low. Whereas for hearing learners a group size of eight to ten students is considered ideal in most Hungarian language schools, Tímea explained that she did not think she could work with so many Deaf students effectively, and put the optimal group size for Deaf students at six. 'With four people it would be boring, but six are ideal', she said. It was also important for her that their number should be even, so that pairwork could be employed without difficulty.

One of the arguments for smaller groups comes from the differences in the students' knowledge of Hungarian, since, as Tímea said, 'there is no Deaf group with a homogeneous knowledge of Hungarian'. Given that the grammar of sign language is so different from the grammar of spoken languages, the knowledge of the structure of a spoken language, in our case the first foreign language, Hungarian, provides Deaf students with a foundation for learning a second foreign language. The fewer the students, the easier it is to cope with the mixed quality of their language base.

Concerning the question of integrated teaching, the students gave unanimous answers. All of them insisted that for the Deaf it is best to learn in a homogeneous environment, that is, among other Deaf students, rather than learning with hard-of-hearing and/or hearing students in integrated groups. One of the main reasons the students gave for their preference for studying with other Deaf students was that there is a common basis for learning, namely their mother tongue. Imre said:

> For me it does not depend on the group, but on the teacher, how he/she likes to teach. It depends on the teaching method. If he/she can use sign language, then it is better to learn in that group.

From Aron's answer we concluded that the use of sign language during the lessons not only made learning easier for the students, but also made the teacher's work less complicated:

> Of course, for me it is easier to learn with the Deaf. There isn't as big a gap in communication. There everybody studies in sign language, that is, they are taught in sign language, and everyone understands it. This way it is also easier and quicker. And it is easier for the teacher as well, because she doesn't have to apply two kinds of methods, like if the group was mixed – then she would apply the oralist method and sign language simultaneously.

Even though it would seem to be easy to apply the two methods – oral and visual – at the same time, Aron was right in pointing out that it is not that simple. While for hearing or hard-of-hearing students oral speech in English would provide enough input, the Deaf (who either see the accompanying signs and thus a translation of the speech or have to cope with difficulties in lip-reading) need more reading in order to get the same amount of input. Similarly, the hearing or hard-of-hearing students' utterances need to be translated, especially if they are in English, or else the Deaf do not understand anything and the lessons become boring and useless for them as illustrated by Tímea in the following example:

> ... Viktor [a severely hard-of-hearing student who did not attend the classes regularly], when he talked to me, did not use sign language ... The students nagged him, asked him to translate, because they did not understand what he said. So if such a student is in the group, and the others often do not understand what he or she says, then it is boring for them ... When I had a dialogue with him, it went quickly, but it was boring for the Deaf because they didn't understand it. They could not lip-read my speech that quickly either. Not to mention Viktor's. So, in my opinion, integrated teaching in this sense is not possible.

If the hard-of-hearing students know sign language, the common language base can be sign language. However, if sign language is not the mother tongue of the hard-of-hearing students, then, even though they could accompany their speech with signs, they would in fact have to use two foreign languages – English and sign language – at the same time, which is very difficult, and is thus an unfair requirement. This is what happened to Viktor, the hard-of-hearing student in Tímea's class. Nikolett, the severely hard-of-hearing student, did not have this kind of problem, since her mother tongue is sign language: 'Since I am hard-of-hearing and know sign language as well, for me it is easier with the Deaf ... I wouldn't like to be in the same group with hearing students ... Surely, it is not good'.

Finally, sociological considerations come into the picture. The Deaf often feel uncomfortable and inferior in the same group with hearing people due to the fact that they are not accepted as a linguistic minority but regarded by society as handicapped people (Muzsnai, 1999). This is surely not a suitable environment for language learning: 'It is better to learn with the Deaf, because we are equal', Melinda said.

Teaching methods and materials

A key issue in designing a course for students with special needs is the selection and design of learning materials. For lack of a more appropriate choice, this group used a popular course book which was written for hearing students and claims to be communicative. The students criticised this book on several grounds, but primarily because they did not consider it suitable for self-study. They did not appreciate the tasks which required listening to the tape or working with a partner in class. Imre voiced the opinion of the whole group when he talked about his preferences as follows:

> [title of the course book] I do not like. There are too few explanations in it, everything is in English, and it bothers me when I see that I should listen to the cassette ... it is not for me. A book which has reading, writing and grammar practice, that is better. [...] You cannot use this one on your own, only with the teacher. There are tasks in it that you can only do in groups. So it is not suitable for studying on your own.

To replace listening tasks, Tímea used speech-comprehension in the form of lip-reading practice. Usually at the beginning of the lessons she asked some short questions in English without using sign language, that is, 'What is the weather like today?' and the students had to answer likewise. Due to the shortness of these questions and answers, the students did not become bored even if they were not able to lip-read what was said by their peers: it was soon their turn, so they needed to pay attention all the time. When asked about what activities he particularly liked, Aron mentioned this question-and-answer practice as one 'from which you can learn a lot'.

In appreciation of the students' needs, no lesson passed without the use of supplementary materials taken from picture dictionaries and storybooks, or worksheets designed by the teacher. The stories often came from children's books, which have copious illustrations and little text. Whenever one of the students was reading a part of the text, he or she was also signing it in HSL at the same time. Since the Deaf have a much wider field of vision than their hearing peers, the group did not even need to stop after every sentence to look at the reader and see his or her translation, because they could see the signing out of the corner of their eyes, while following the text as well. With her knowledge of sign language the teacher could immediately see if the students understood what they were reading. Melinda liked these stories very much and talked about them in the interview as follows:

> It is easier to understand and remember tasks which are linked to stories [...] When we read fairy tales, they also have new words, we learn from them as well. And then we write sentences or compositions based on the stories we have read, that is what I like the best. [...] We read lots of fairy tales – at those times I always feel like I am a child again. [...] We read them together. We read them in English, and we sign them in Hungarian [i.e. HSL]. These are for me the best experiences.

All the students emphasised what they thought was a general dislike on the part of the Deaf for dry theory and boring exercises and their preference for colourful, practical, creative and intellectually challenging tasks and games. They liked guessing words from pictures, picture dictation, matching sentence halves, creating sentences from word-cards, working with antonyms and synonyms and practicing dialogues.

For situational dialogues Tímea came up with two techniques that the group found both useful and enjoyable. To practice situations in the group, they could not use HSL, because then it would have been an immediate translation of what was said, and thus there could not have been any practice of English. So the teacher decided to have the students write down the conversations, taking turns in pairs. Going around in the classroom, she checked and monitored each pair's work, just as a teacher of hearing students goes round to listen a little to each student's speech. They had a separate 'dialogue notebook' for this conversation-writing practice.

As another way of practising the typical form of sentences in dialogues, Tímea often wrote dialogues up on the board, and after the students had read them, she erased some words. Then the students had to read out the dialogues, including the missing words. They did this until the whole dialogue had disappeared from the board, and the students had to reproduce the whole text orally from memory.

Instead of dealing with grammar explanations in the book, the teacher gave the students worksheets, and, after a simple explanation of the grammatical structures, she let them understand and learn by doing the exercises. She decided to do so mainly because in her experience Deaf people learn much better by being active than by passively trying to understand something. Her familiarity with HSL helped her a great deal in this area of the language as well. The students needed plenty of practice of such simple grammar features as the pronouns, since in HSL they are much simpler. For example, HSL does not differentiate between 'my' and 'to me', and it does not have different signs to differentiate between possessive forms like 'my' and 'I have' (in HSL, both are expressed by putting the palm on one's chest).

For useful practice of structures, the students mentioned activities on word order, question formation, the use of question words and auxiliaries. Robi enjoyed it when the rules about asking questions in English were written on the blackboard like 'a cheat-sheet to make sure we do not mix up the word order'. Imre also liked completion exercises with question words, conjunctions, adverbs or verbs. Nikolett mentioned the task of sorting out the mixed-up word order in sentences as something she particularly enjoyed. In order to make these structural exercises more attractive, Tímea often used coloured word-cards. Various kinds of guessing games and activities that involved touching or manipulating objects were all popular with this group of Deaf students. Though nobody else mentioned the issue of assessment, for Imre the best and most memorable experience was when there was a test, and he performed well.

Conclusion

Working on this project has convinced us that teaching English to the Deaf is indeed possible. They have as much legal right to access to foreign language education as any other minorities in the EU. The participants in the study testify to the fact that the Deaf have as much motivation to learn foreign languages as anybody else in the country, and they believe in their abilities to cope with the task. Instead of issuing waivers under the false pretence of doing them a favour, educational institutions should find the means to provide adequate and appropriate language courses for Deaf individuals. These adult participants and their teacher allowed us to see their language learning-teaching process through the eyes of an insider. What we could see from this perspective is that for the Deaf, learning languages is an enormous challenge, and that the effort these students invest in the task is an invaluable motivating force for the teacher.

On the basis of our results we can say that teaching Deaf students successfully does require the use of their mother tongue, which is HSL. The students use and rely heavily on HSL when learning English: they use it in class for translations, to help each other to understand the foreign language, to mediate between a non-signing teacher and students, and even as a learning strategy when studying alone and signing 'mentally'.

This implies that Hungarian teachers of the Deaf should be trained in HSL. This is not only necessary in order to ease communication with the students but is also a pre-requisite for building a good student-teacher rapport and for creating a relaxed and anxiety-free atmosphere in the classroom.

It is also clear that in order to be a teacher of the Deaf, it is necessary to understand how the Deaf communicate and what the structural differences between visual and oral languages are. These differences need to be taken into account when designing teaching materials.

Another lesson learnt was that having course books specifically written for Deaf learners would be useful. These course books should take into account such characteristics of Deaf learners as their preference for self-study and analytical thinking, their need for explicit grammar rules and explanations, interesting stories to read and challenging tasks to perform.

Although there is a lot to be said for educating learners with special needs in integrated classrooms, it is important for educational policy makers and course designers to know that Deaf students are likely to prefer non-integrated language classes because they feel that their needs will be better catered for and that they can make better progress in non-integrated teaching.

Although this study has its limitations, we hope that our findings may serve as a stepping stone for further research in the field. Further studies are needed to design new methods and materials that match the special needs of Deaf language learners. We also hope that more attention will be paid to the special needs of Deaf learners in teacher education, and that the new generations of teachers-to-be will be given ample opportunity to learn about Deaf learners and receive appropriate training for teaching them.

Acknowledgements

The authors would like to thank Prof. Robert Hoffmeister for his invaluable suggestions and comments on an earlier version of this paper. We are also grateful to the five participants and their teacher, as well as to the Hungarian Association of the Deaf and Hard of Hearing, for their generous support and encouragement. The second author was supported in writing this paper by the Equal Rights in Foreign Language Education project of the Hungarian National Bureau of Research and Technology (NKTH B2 2006-0010).

Note

1. We share the belief that the Deaf constitute a separate cultural group and their language is a language in its own right, which is not inferior to other, spoken languages (Ladd, 2003). For this reason, we have decided to use a capital 'D' to indicate a person who follows Deaf culture, and a lowercase 'd' to refer to the physical nature of deafness.

References

Allen, T. E. (1986) Patterns of academic achievement among hearing impaired students: 1974 and 1983. In A. Schildroth and M.A. Karchmer (eds) *Deaf Children in America* (pp. 161–206). San Diego, CA: College-Hill Press.

Arehart, K.H. and Yoshinaga-Itano, C. (1999) The role of educators of the Deaf in early identification of hearing loss. *American Annals of the Deaf* 144 (1), 19–23.

Baker, C. and Jones, S. (1998) *Encyclopedia of Bilingualism and Bilingual Education.* Clevedon and Philadelphia: Multilingual Matters.

Bartha, Cs. and Hattyár, H. (2002) Szegregáció, diszkrimináció vagy társadalmi integráció? – A magyarországi siketek nyelvi jogai [Segregation, discrimination or social integration? – The language rights of the Deaf in Hungary]. In H. Hattyár and M. Kontra (eds) *Magyarok és nyelvtörvények [Hungarians and Language Laws]* (pp. 73–123). Budapest: Teleki László Alapítvány.

Bartha, Cs., Hattyár, H. and Szabó, M.H. (2006) A magyarországi siketek közössége és a magyar jelnyelv [The Deaf community in Hungary and Hungarian Sign Language]. In F. Kiefer (ed.) *Magyar nyelv [Hungarian Language]* (pp. 852–906). Budapest: Akadémiai Kiadó.

Branson, J. and Miller, D. (2007) Beyond 'language': Linguistic imperialism, sign languages and linguistic anthropology. In S. Makoni and A. Pennycook (eds) *Disinventing and Reconstituting Languages* (pp. 116–134). Clevedon: Multilingual Matters.

Clément, R., Dörnyei, Z. and Noels, K. A. (1994) Motivation, self-confidence, and group cohesion in the foreign language classroom. *Language Learning* 44 (3), 417–448.

Cummins, J. (1989) *Empowering Minority Students.* Sacramento, CA: California Association for Bilingual Education (CABE).

Dörnyei, Z. (2001) *Teaching and Researching Motivation.* Harlow: Longman.

Fisher, S. (1994) Critical periods: Critical issues. In B. Schick and M.P. Moeller (eds) *Proceedings of the Tenth Annual Conference on Issues in Language and Deafness* (pp. 1–11). Omaha: Boys Town National Research Hospital.

Grosjean, F. (1999) A siket gyermek joga a kétnyelvűvé válásához [The right of the Deaf child to become bilingual]. *Modern Nyelvoktatás* 5 (4), 5–8.

Guba, E. (1981) Criteria for assessing the trustworthiness of naturalistic inquires. *Educational Communication and Technology Journal* 29 (2), 75–91.

Holcomb, T. and Peyton, J.K. (1992) ESL literacy for a linguistic minority: The Deaf experience. *ERIC Digest*: On WWW at http://www.ericdigests.org/1993/deaf.htm. Accessed 19.04.08.

Horwitz, E.K. (1987) Surveying student beliefs about language learning. In A. Wenden and J. Rubin (eds) *Learner Strategies in Language Learning* (pp. 111–129). New York: Prentice Hall.

Kárpáti, D. (2002) Teaching English as a foreign language to Deaf learners. Unpublished MA thesis, Eötvös Loránd University.

Kárpáti, D. (2004) Az angol mint idegen nyelv tanítása siket nyelvtanulóknak [Teaching English as a foreign language to Deaf learners]. In E.H. Kontráné and J. Kormos (eds) *A nyelvtanuló: Sikerek, módszerek, stratégiák [The Language Leaner: Successes, Methods and Strategies]* (pp. 161–174). Budapest: Okker.

Kontráné Hegybíró E. and Kormos, J. (eds) (2004) *A nyelvtanuló: Sikerek, módszerek, stratégiák [The Language Leaner: Successes, Methods and Strategies].* Budapest: Okker.

Kósa, Á. (2002) Hogyan kommunikáljunk a siket emberekkel? [How to communicate with the Deaf]. On WWW at http://www.C3.hu/~sinosz/sikomm.htm. Accessed 19.04.08.

Kósa, Á. and Lovászy, Á. (2002) *Rövid történeti áttekintés a hallássérültekről* [A short historical overview of the hearing impaired]. On WWW at http://www.motivacio.hu/Magyar/Hirlanc/Hirlanc2/kosa2a.htm. Accessed 30.10.05.
Ladd, P. (2003) *Understanding Deaf Culture*. Clevedon: Multilingual Matters.
Lane, H.L., Hoffmeister, R. and Bahan, B. (1996) *A Journey into the Deaf-world*. San Diego, CA: Dawn Sign Press.
Lancz, E. (1999) *A magyar jelnyelv szótára [A Dictionary of Hungarian Sign Language]*. Budapest: SINOSZ.
Lazaraton, A. (2003) Evaluative criteria for qualitative research in applied linguistics: Whose criteria and whose research? *The Modern Language Journal* 87 (1), 1–12.
Liddell, S.K. (2003) *Grammar, Gesture and Meaning in American Sign Language*. Cambridge: Cambridge University Press.
Litavecz, A. (1996) Ismeretek a hallássérültekről [Information about the hearing impaired]. On WWW at http://www.c3.hu/~sinoszib/jelny.htm. Accessed 19.04.08.
Maykut, P. and Morehouse, R. (1994) *Beginning Qualitative Research*. London: The Falmer Press.
Muzsnai, I. (1997) Kinek az érdekét hivatott szolgálni a szurdopedagógia? [Whose interest does surdopedagogy serve?]. *Gyógypedagógiai Szemle* April–June, 139–142.
Muzsnai, I. (1999) The recognition of sign language: A threat or the way to a solution? In M. Kontra, R. Phillipson, T. Skutnabb-Kangas and T. Várady (eds) *Language: A Right and a Resource* (pp. 279–296). Budapest: Central European University Press.
National Institute on Deafness and Other Communication Disorders (2006) *American Sign Language*. On WWW at http://www.nidcd.nih.gov/health/hearing/asl.asp. Accessed 19.04.08.
O'Malley, M. and Chamot, A.U. (1990) *Learning Strategies in Second Language Acquisition*. Cambridge: Cambridge University Press.
O'Neill, R. (1998) Using bilingual methods to train teachers of British Sign Language. *Language Issues* 10 (1), 24–27.
Oxford, R. (1990) *Language Learning Strategies: What Every Teacher Should Know*. Boston, MA: Heinle and Heinle.
Patton, M.Q. (2002) *Qualitative Research and Evaluation Methods* (3rd edn). Thousand Oaks, CA: Sage.
PBS (2007) Sound and fury: Cochlear implants. On WWW at http://www.pbs.org/wnet/soundandfury/cochlear/index.html. Accessed 19.04.08.
Rubin, J. (1975) What the 'good language learner' can teach us. *TESOL Quarterly* 9 (1), 41–51.
Sacks, O. (1989) *Seeing Voices. A Journey into the World of the Deaf*. London: Picador.
Skutnabb-Kangas, T. (2000a) *Linguistic Genocide in Education – or Worldwide Diversity and Human Rights?* Mahwah, NJ & London: Lawrence Erlbaum Associates.
Skutnabb-Kangas, T. (2000b). Sign languages – how the Deaf (and other sign language users) are deprived of their linguistic human rights. On WWW at http://www.terralingua.org/DeafHR.html. Accessed 30.03.08.
Sutton-Spence, R.L. and Woll, B. (1999) *The Linguistics of British Sign Language: An Introduction*. Cambridge: Cambridge University Press.
Szabó, M.H. (1998) A siketség alkalmazott nyelvészeti vonatkozásai [Issues of Applied Linguistics in Deafness]. *Modern Nyelvoktatás* 4 (4), 28–33.
Woll, B. (2005) Issues at the interface between British Sign Language (BSL) and education. *Language Issues* 17 (2), 2–8.

Chapter 8
Hungarian Teachers' Perceptions of Dyslexic Language Learners

JUDIT KORMOS and EDIT H. KONTRA

Introduction

Dyslexia is one of the most frequent learning disabilities among Hungarian school-children affecting approximately 7–10% of the population (Smythe & Everatt, 2000). This rough estimate is based on the incidence of dyslexia in European countries as no exact data are available for our country (Torda, 2004). The definition of dyslexia applied in Hungarian special education follows the guidelines of the European Union and is based on 'The classification of Educational Programs for Students with Special needs' (OECD, 2002, cited in Gordosné Szabó, 2004). In this definition dyslexia is seen as a type of developmental disorder in which students experience difficulties in reading despite adequate intellectual capacities (translated from Gordosné Szabó, 2004).[1] Dyslexia has occupied a special position in the Hungarian system of special education since the beginning of the 20th century as Ranschburg (1916, cited in Torda, 2004) was among the first researchers in Europe who investigated the neural processes of students with reading disabilities and who argued for the biological origin of dyslexia. As a consequence of the studies conducted by Ranschburg, compensatory programmes for dyslexic schoolchildren were started in the 1930s. Institutional and organised help, however, was not provided to children with reading difficulties until the Education Act in 1993 included dyslexia among special educational needs. Since then, in settlements where nursery schools employ speech therapists, children have been screened with the help of a dyslexia quick-test around the age of five. If the child is suspected of exhibiting signs of possible learning disabilities, he or she is entitled to participate in a compensatory programme free of charge. The compensatory classes are held either in the child's nursery school or in the regional special education centres or in educational advisory centres. In order to help dyslexic children once they start school, a number of public elementary schools organise special groups for dyslexic learners. Compensatory programmes continue to be available for children when they reach school age either at their schools or in the previously listed educational centres (for a detailed description of the Hungarian special education system, see Gordosné Szabó, 2004). Compensatory programs are based on therapies such as phonological awareness training, the Sindelar (for a description in English see Sindelar, 2000) and Frostig therapy (Frostig & Horne, 1964), and the pedagogical programme by Meixner (1993) developed especially for Hungarian dyslexic learners.

As can be seen from this short description of the Hungarian educational programmes for students with learning disabilities, the institutional and legal system in Hungary ensures that dyslexic students are provided with a number of opportunities to become successful at school. Torda (2004), however, rightly points out that several problems have remained unsolved. First of all, there is no national diagnostic protocol for learning disabilities, the consequence of which is that still a considerable proportion of students remain under-diagnosed and do not receive dyslexia compensatory education. Second, in a high number of elementary schools the special educational needs of dyslexic learners are not taken into consideration due to financial reasons and the lack of a modified pedagogical programme. The situation is even less favourable in the field of language teaching. Students diagnosed with learning disabilities have the right to be exempted from evaluation in foreign language classes (Educational Act of 1993, cited in Sarkadi, 2006) and often from learning foreign languages in general, instead of being given extra help in overcoming the difficulties they experience in language learning. This puts Hungarian dyslexics at a serious disadvantage on the job market. Hungary is a small country in central Europe that is largely dependent on international investments and foreign trade; therefore, it is almost impossible to find a well-paying job if someone does not speak at least one foreign language. In addition, a certificate of intermediate level of proficiency in a foreign language is also a prerequisite for obtaining a university degree. Although students diagnosed with dyslexia are given some minor allowances in taking language exams, these allowances are far from sufficient for ensuring equal opportunities for most dyslexic language learners in successfully passing a proficiency test (Sarkadi, 2006).

Research Aims and Rationale

The 'Equal Opportunities in Foreign Language Learning' research group was set up at Eötvös Loránd University, Budapest in 2006 in order to investigate the situation of foreign language learners with special needs in the present Hungarian educational context. The ultimate aim of the project is to initiate changes in foreign language teaching, teacher education and educational policy which can lead to equal opportunities in language learning for learners with special needs. The project extends over four years (one preliminary and three funded years) during which the investigation is planned to take place in three distinct areas: (1) experienced teachers' perceptions and practice regarding learners with special needs; (2) the learning process of students with special needs; and (3) the preparation of language teachers for dealing with learners with special needs.

In the present study the authors report on the results of the first round of preliminary investigations conducted among teachers of dyslexic language learners. The focus of the investigation was to identify the symptoms which characterise Hungarian dyslexic language learners as perceived by their teachers, and to come to a deeper understanding of their problems in foreign language learning. The authors are convinced that the prerequisite for any change in education and educational policy is awareness and a deep understanding of the issues. By providing a thorough and detailed picture of dyslexic language learners in their natural context, the authors hope to raise awareness of the existing problems, which might serve as the first step in initiating some of the necessary changes in attitudes towards this particular group of language learners with special needs.

For this part of the project the main research focus was broken down into the following research questions:

(1) How do the symptoms of dyslexia already documented in the literature manifest themselves in the foreign language classroom?
(2) What other symptoms do teachers 'at the chalkface' identify as indicative of the presence of dyslexia?
(3) What non-linguistic problems do the language learning difficulties of dyslexic learners occur in conjunction with?

In the following, a brief review of the difficulties of language learners with dyslexia as identified in the international literature will be provided to create the necessary backdrop for the present investigation. Following that, an interview study conducted among devoted and experienced teachers of dyslexic students will be described in detail, including the purposive selection of the participants, the development of the instrument, and the process of data collection. The results will be analysed qualitatively following the descriptive-interpretative approach. The qualitative analysis is going to lead to the conceptualisation of an emerging model of dyslexia in a foreign language classroom, which is presented in the final section of the chapter.

Difficulties of Dyslexic Learners in Learning Languages

Dyslexic students have been found to exhibit great difficulties in learning sequences, remembering names, interpreting sound-symbol correspondences, understanding abstract grammatical relations and being able to divide their attention (Pothos & Kirk, 2004; Ranaldi, 2003; Reiter et al., 2005). Since these skills are the key components of foreign language learning aptitude (Robinson, 2005), dyslexic learners are likely to encounter a large number of problems when learning foreign languages. Indeed in several studies conducted by Sparks, Ganshow and their colleagues (for a review see Ganschow et al., 1998) students with learning disabilities scored significantly lower on all the components of the Modern Language Aptitude Test (MLAT) (Carroll & Sapon, 1959). Not only is language aptitude an important determinant of language learning success, but also certain native language (L1) skills serve as a foundation of foreign language (L2) learning (Skehan, 1986; Spolsky, 1989). A number of linguistic skills that are considered relevant in L2 learning such as word recognition, spelling, pseudo-word reading, word and non-word repetition were also found to be impaired in dyslexic language learners (see Downey et al., 2000; Ganschow et al., 1998; Sparks et al., this volume).

Therefore, it is understandable that empirical studies comparing dyslexic and non-dyslexic language learners have found a number of differences between these two groups of students in performance on a variety of English language tasks (see Helland, in this volume). Helland and Kaasa's (2005) results indicated that Norwegian dyslexic children scored significantly lower on all aspects of an English language proficiency test specially designed for dyslexic language learners. The test included a listening comprehension test, an oral component consisting of a daily conversation and a picture narration task, a spelling, reading and translation task, as well as a component in which students had to formulate new sentences based on model sentences. Their study also revealed that dyslexic language learners who had good auditory skills only differed from the control group in the model sentences task testing the use of English morphology and in the English literacy tasks (spelling, reading and translation), whereas those dyslexic students whose auditory skills were impaired performed in every test component significantly worse than the non-dyslexic students. Helland and Kaasa's research is important in pointing out the differential success of dyslexic students in language learning.

Ho and Fong (2005) conducted their research with Chinese learners of English in Hong Kong in order to investigate whether dyslexic symptoms experienced in a language that uses a non-phonological orthographic system manifest themselves in learning a language with a phonological script, namely English. The results showed that the Chinese group of dyslexic students performed significantly worse in an English picture vocabulary test, in English reading tasks (testing both word reading and global comprehension), in English phoneme detection tasks and in a spelling and an English rapid naming task than the non-dyslexic control group. These findings indicate that Chinese students with reading difficulties also have difficulties learning a foreign language and that the severity of their dyslexic symptoms in Chinese is closely related to the extent to which they experience problems in reading in English as an L2.

Although the two studies described above provide a good overview of dyslexic students' overall L2 performance, we have very little information about how the students and their teachers see the language learning problems specific to dyslexia. Ormos (2003) examined the language learning difficulties of Hungarian students with dyslexia in a secondary school for students with special educational needs. Based on the brief questionnaires filled in by the students and interviews conducted with language teachers, she concluded that the most problematic area for dyslexic learners of English was spelling, which she argued was due to the non-transparent orthographic system of the language. On the basis of the language classes she observed, Ormos also found that students had serious problems with written and oral self-expression, reading aloud, vocabulary acquisition, pronunciation and understanding grammatical concepts. Sarkadi (this volume) investigated the vocabulary learning difficulties and strategies of a dyslexic teenager and concluded that the deep orthography of English was very challenging even for a relatively successful student, and that the confusion of similar-sounding words caused serious problems not only in written but also in oral communication.

Research Method

Participants

In our research we interviewed 19 teachers from five different schools in geographically and socio-economically diverse regions of Hungary (for an overview of the participants see Table 8.1). The five schools were selected from a pool of 12 institutions which participated in a project sponsored by the Hungarian Ministry of Education. In this project schools received a grant for enhancing their effectiveness of teaching foreign languages to students with special educational needs. The participating institutions were allocated resources to buy books, equipment and audiovisual materials, as well as to organise training programmes for their language teachers. The project also sponsored the development and implementation of a one-year-long compensatory language teaching programme of pullout classes for learners with learning disabilities.

We selected one elementary school from an economically disadvantaged small town in Eastern Hungary (School A) and one boarding school (School D) from the highly developed Western region of Hungary close to the Austrian border. The third school (School B) was located in a major city of Western Hungary and prided itself in its language teacher training program for students with learning disabilities. One of the schools (School C) was situated on the outskirts of the capital city in a less prestigious part

Table 8.1 An overview of the participants

School	Position	Years of teaching experience	Qualifications
A	Headmaster	19	Teacher of geography and visual arts
A	Special education expert	10	Nursery school teacher Teacher of special education Speech therapist
A	Teacher	20	Elementary school teacher Teacher of English with postgraduate certificate in teaching English to dyslexic students
A	Teacher	12	Elementary school teacher Teacher of English
A	Teacher	5	Teacher of English and biology
A	Teacher	5	Elementary school teacher with specialisation in English
B	Special education expert and Teacher trainer	35	Teacher of special education
B	Teacher Mentor teacher	11	Elementary school teacher with specialisation in English Teacher of English
B	Teacher Mentor teacher	11	Teacher of Hungarian and Russian Teacher of German

Table 8.1 Continued

School	Position	Years of teaching experience	Qualifications
C	Special education expert	20 years teaching 12 years in therapy	Elementary school teacher with a specialisation in Russian and visual arts Therapist of students with learning disabilities
C	Teacher	Approx. 25	Teacher of Russian and pedagogy Teacher of German
C	Teacher	26	Elementary school teacher Teacher of Russian Teacher of German
D	Headmaster	38	Teacher of special education Speech therapist
D	Deputy headmaster	Missing data	Teacher of mathematics, information technology, and crafts
D	Speech therapist	Approx. 30	Teacher of special education Speech therapist
D	Teacher	3	Teacher of German
E	Teacher	16	Teacher of English and Hungarian
E	Teacher	16	Teacher of Italian and Portuguese Psychologist
E	Teacher	Missing data	Teacher of English

of Budapest, whereas the fifth school (School E) was an integrated nursery, elementary and secondary (K-12) school that was maintained by a foundation related to one of the religious communities in Hungary. This private school was located in an elegant suburban area of Budapest.

All of the respondents in the interviews had a teacher's degree of some sort. Fifteen interviewees were content area teachers, three participants were special education teachers, and one of the respondents worked as a speech therapist in her school. From among the content area teachers, three participants were active in the management of their school (two headmasters and a deputy headmaster), seven teachers taught English, four German and one Italian. Many of our participants had a number of qualifications, and with the exception of one young teacher from School D, all of the interviewees had more than five years of school experience. The number of years our interviewees have spent in education ranges from three to 38 and averages approximately 18 years. Among the special education teachers, two participants also had training in speech therapy.

Out of the five institutions, four are renowned locally for their educational programmes for students with learning disabilities. School E does not offer a special programme for students with dyslexia, but it claims to be highly learner-centred, which, as the respondents explained, attracts a number of children with learning disabilities.

As the interviewees all noted, even before working in the school they are currently employed at, they frequently encountered dyslexic students in their teaching practice. Therefore, all the participants have an amount of experience working with students with learning disabilities that allows them to have a deep insight into the problems these children experience in the Hungarian school system. The respondents are also valuable sources of information due to their participation in the one-year long project on teaching languages to students with special educational needs.

The interviews

We conducted semi-structured focus group interviews in the five schools described above. The interview questions were compiled based on our previous review of the literature and on the detailed project reports the schools submitted to the funding agency concerning their language teaching programme. A contact teacher from each selected school arranged the interviews, and we obtained consent from all the participants. The interviews were conducted in Hungarian, the native language of all the participating teachers, and lasted for approximately two hours each.

The interview consisted of four main parts. In the first few minutes all the respondents were asked to introduce themselves and describe their school in detail. The next section inquired about the symptoms on the basis of which teachers can recognise that students are struggling with language learning due to some kind of learning disability. The questions were designed to elicit information regarding the difficulties in the areas already known from the dyslexia literature, such as writing, reading aloud, comprehension, learning words, dealing with structures, oral fluency and pronunciation. Our questions concerning this topic also covered related behavioural and first language (L1) problems. The remaining two main groups of questions were centred around the special language teaching program these schools developed in the framework of the project mentioned above, which, however, will not be discussed in this chapter.

Procedures

In order to maximise what we can learn from the interviews, we first reviewed the project documentation. This served two main purposes: it helped us compile the interview questions and allowed us to make informed decisions in selecting schools that were diverse in their profiles and educational programmes. In making our selection, we considered schools whose documents were the most informative in terms of the compensatory programme they provided. In addition to this, we aimed for maximum variety in our sampling in terms of geographical location, social circumstances of students and school-type.

Once the selection of the schools was made, the authors contacted the project leaders in the respective schools and arranged a mutually convenient time for the interviews. As in all the institutions special education and language teachers as well as speech therapists worked together as a team in the project, we decided to conduct focus group interviews. The advantage of the focus group interviews is that not only the views of individual interviewees can be recorded but also the exchange of ideas between the participants of a given institution.

All the interviews were recorded on a digital voice recorder and were also videotaped. The audio-visual and audio-recordings were both necessary to facilitate the transcription of the interviews. The interviews were transcribed by two trained transcribers, and the transcripts were checked by the authors.

The interview transcripts yielded about 60,000 words of data, which were first analysed independently by the two authors for emerging themes. Once the themes found relevant by both researchers were agreed on, definitions of the categories of analysis were worded based on the analysis of two of the five interviews. The authors then coded all the utterances separately, following which certain modifications were made in some of the categories, and the wording of the definitions was fine-tuned. Discrepancies between the analyses of the two authors were discussed until a full agreement was reached.

The four main themes that emerged from the data are as follows:

(1) Recognising the symptoms of dyslexia in the foreign language classroom.
(2) Personal factors observed by teachers as characteristic of dyslexic learners.
(3) Course management and organisational issues.
(4) Methods and materials for dyslexic learners.

Each of the themes comprised several categories which will be introduced below. Owing to the richness of the data and the constraints on the length of this chapter, however, here we restrict ourselves to the analysis of the first two themes, as they are the ones which lead to answers to the research questions presented above.

After establishing the main themes and fine-tuning their definitions, the emerging categories contributing to each theme were also identified and defined. The categories were numbered consecutively to ease the later coding and sorting process.

The following problem areas emerged as categories contributing to Theme One: 'Recognising the symptoms of dyslexia in the foreign language':

(1) Problems related to oral language, such as repeating utterances, constructing sentences orally, fluent speech, recitation, listening comprehension and comments including the comparison of written and oral speech production.
(2) Difficulties related to learning vocabulary, including problems with word classes, homonyms, and the rate of learning.
(3) Difficulties in reading, including reading aloud and reading for comprehension.
(4) Problems related to writing and copying, also including spelling difficulties and issues of legibility.
(5) Overall low pace and the need for extra time for performing tasks.
(6) Serial integration, including problems with letter and word sequences, lists, and series of instructions.
(7) L1 problems affecting L2 learning including problems with L1 speech production, orthography, limited range of vocabulary and little awareness of linguistic structures, for example, word order.

The problem areas identified as categories to contribute to Theme Two: 'Personal factors observed by teachers as characteristic of dyslexic learners' are as follows:

(8) Problems rooted in the family including low levels of socialisation, emotional problems resulting from lack of parental attention or lack

of physical contact in early childhood, and the lack of L1 communication at home.
(9) General cognitive abilities including IQ, attention span and reasoning skills.
(10) Motivation, including amotivation, demotivation, the effects of failure, and the teachers' perception of whether dyslexics can be motivated to learn languages at all.
(11) Behavioural problems, including negative class-participation, anxiety, need for attention and rejection by the group.
(12) Compensation, including survival strategies used by students, which delay the identification of the real problem.

After the independent coding phase, the two researchers compared their results and discussed the differences item by item until a final resolution was reached in each case. The length of each 'utterance' (data unit) was also agreed on.

During this coding phase the need for establishing two further categories emerged. First, it was felt that several utterances regarding problems with memorising and recalling bits of the language required a category of their own. This was established under the code '5B Memory', since in many cases the problem was linked to the overall slow learning process of the students represented by category 5. Second, there were a few utterances which seemed relevant but were too few in number to create independent categories, such as problems with perception or L1–L2 contrastivity. These were all grouped together under category '13 Mixed'.

Before grouping the coded utterances under their respective category headings, it was necessary to complement the category code with letter codes indicating the source of each utterance. The first letter of this code was identical with the code of the school, that is, A, B, C, D, E, and the further letters were the codes used for identifying individual teachers. Thus 2CGA stands for a unit in the Vocabulary category taken from the interview in School C, contributed by teacher G.A.

After a complete coding of the data, the coded utterances were grouped under their respective headings, and the number of units in each category was tallied. Table 8.2 displays the results. We can see that neither of the two themes dominated the interviews, and the participants had approximately equal amounts of information to share regarding each. A surface phenomenon, classroom behaviour leads the frequency chart, but nearly equal amounts of information were collected on the role of L1 and motivation and on a well known symptom of dyslexia: writing difficulties. In the following, the results are discussed according to the overarching themes. The data are presented in the authors' translation, and the data source is indicated after each quote as described above.

Table 8.2 The frequency of utterances in categories 1–13

Code	Category	Number of units in category
Theme 1		
7	L1 problems affecting L2 learning	19
4	Problems related to writing and copying	18
3	Difficulties in reading	15
1	Problems related to oral language	14
2	Difficulties related to learning vocabulary	14
6	Seriality	10
5B	Memory	9
5	Overall low pace and the need for more time	6
Theme 2		
11	Behavioural problems	24
10	Motivation	17
9	General mental abilities	15
8	Problems rooted in the family	14
12	Compensation	9
13	Mixed	9

Results and Discussion

Recognising the symptoms of dyslexia in the foreign language classroom

From our interview data it is apparent that teachers can recognise the symptoms of dyslexia in almost every aspect of language learning: in producing and comprehending oral language, in reading, in writing and in learning new vocabulary items. As the frequency chart presented in Table 8.2 indicates, writing problems were mentioned most often by our interviewees, but difficulties arising in other areas of language learning were also perceived very frequently by the participating teachers. Although our research does not allow for drawing statistically based conclusions due to its qualitative nature, it seems that in the teachers' view, symptoms of dyslexia manifest themselves with almost equal severity in the most important skills and abilities necessary for L2 learning.

As regards oral language, the interviewed language teachers, special education teachers and speech therapists unequivocally asserted that one of the most apparent symptoms of dyslexia that can be noticed at the beginning of the language learning process is that dyslexic learners cannot repeat foreign language words accurately after the teacher. This warning sign of dyslexia was described by one of our participants in the following way:

> In the first year we build on oral methods, and we can already suspect dyslexia when children cannot repeat the words the way they heard them. We can notice the exchange of sounds or the addition of similar sounds to the word already at this stage. From this we can infer [that the child is dyslexic] and our inferences usually prove to be correct... (1ABE)

Another related problem experienced by language teachers is that students with dyslexia find it difficult to pronounce sounds corresponding to letters. This problem was not only mentioned by English teachers but also by one of the participating German teachers ('... they find it difficult to pronounce sounds denoted by a series of two or three vowels or consonants' (1DLB)).

Teachers' views varied as regards the students' problems in producing continuous stretches of oral discourse. One of the interviewed German teachers said that her dyslexic learners can only speak by using given sentence frames, whereas other teachers remarked that some of their students can express themselves fluently but with a great number of mistakes. Other interviewees noted that they have dyslexic students who cannot express themselves in long sentences and that there are learners who are unwilling to say anything in a language class. The fact that teachers' views vary as regards the seriousness of problems dyslexic learners experience in producing oral language, can probably be explained by the differences in auditory processing skills among students with dyslexia (for a review see Fletcher *et al.*, 2007). Helland and Kaasa's (2005) research also indicates that dyslexic students whose comprehension skills are not impaired performed on an oral test very similarly to learners with no learning disabilities, whereas dyslexic learners with auditory deficits scored significantly lower on the oral component of the English proficiency test than their non-dyslexic peers.

One of the teachers working with young dyslexic learners emphasised that teaching the language through the auditory channel at the beginning of the language learning process is important because students with learning disabilities 'are also capable of learning certain things in a foreign language through listening: for example a nursery rhyme or a song' (1ABE).

In the teachers' view, another sign of dyslexia that manifests itself at the very early stages of L2 learning is that 'students cannot find the sounds corresponding to letters' (3DLB) and that they mix up letters while reading. Other reading problems mentioned by our interviewees are that 'students with learning disabilities are not able to read aloud and pay attention to what they are reading simultaneously' (3BPK), 'they have difficulties reading longer texts' (3BHZS) and that 'they have comprehension problems' (3ABE). The participating teachers also agreed that dyslexia can easily be recognised in a language classroom through the children's writing problems. Dyslexic learners 'cannot copy words from the blackboard' (4BHZS), 'leave out and mix up the order of letters, use capital letters incorrectly, sometimes mix Hungarian and English spelling' (4BHZS) and 'write down the words as they would pronounce them in Hungarian' (4BSZE). Not only do students experience spelling problems, but according to their teachers, they also find it difficult to fill in gaps in written texts. The reading and writing problems listed by our interviewees seem to be in complete accord with the results of previous studies in which dyslexic students' performance on various L2 reading and writing tasks were investigated (Helland & Kaasa, 2004; Ho & Fong, 2005; Ormos, 2003).

Our interview data reveal that students with learning disabilities not only experience serious problems acquiring writing, reading and spelling skills in L2, but also in learning vocabulary. Every language teacher from every school commented on the difficulties dyslexic learners have to face in acquiring L2 words. Some of these problems include students' mixing up similarly sounding words ('I have a student who is in 8th grade now but still mixes up the words lesen [read] and lernen [learn]' (2BHZS)) and words that have similar meaning. Teachers also noted that students find it difficult to memorise abstract words, and that they find it easier to learn nouns than verbs and adjectives. 'In the case of compound words, it happens that they either remember the first or the second part of the word' (2DPM) and that they cannot segment compound words. Learning the gender and plural form of nouns also poses problems for dyslexic learners of German. Another important problem mentioned by one of the teachers is that

> they might invest a lot of energy in learning in vain because for them the given sound and letter string might not be the same. Maybe when they are studying, they learn a different string, which is not the same as the one I taught. So they might have studied a lot, and we might not be able to understand why their performance is poor. Actually we do know that as long as they do not learn how to recognise a word independently and with certainty, they cannot study alone, and we cannot take our hands off them; we have to practice in class as long as they do not know this. (2CGA)

This quote suggests that dyslexic students' vocabulary learning problems are indeed serious, which might even hinder them studying alone at home up to a certain stage. The interview data also indicate that most of the learners' difficulties in memorising L2 words stem from the problem of homogenous inhibition, that is, dyslexic people's general tendency to mix up similar looking, sounding and meaning items (words, letters and sounds) that was first described by the Hungarian researcher, Ranschburg (1916, cited in Torda, 2004; see also Sarkadi, this volume).

Teachers also gave an account of symptoms of dyslexia that are related to learning in general, which include problems with the speed of learning, memory and seriality. As regards the speed of learning, our interviewees noted that in the very first lessons it becomes apparent that 'they have much slower pace [than non-dyslexics]' (5ACA), due to which in one of the schools students with learning disabilities are frequently called the 'PP group' where PP stands for 'paced progress'. The use of this term to describe dyslexic learners instead of the 'Slow Group' reveals the positive and sympathetic attitude of the teachers of the school. The problem of pace affects learning in a number of ways as explained by one of the participants.

> They need more time because they are faced with the problem all the time that they cannot finish the assignment. Thus they tend to give it all up thinking that they cannot do it anyway. They cannot pay attention for such a long time, their attention wanders away, and then they start talking and laughing ... (5ESZA)

Several teachers argued that due to this problem, dyslexic learners need more time for completing both high-stake language tests and classroom progress tests.

Not only were dyslexic learners perceived as slow in performing tasks, but teachers also told us that 'imprinting takes more time for them' (5ACA) than for non-dyslexic students. One of our participants used the following metaphor to describe this problem 'they don't have this net, we have to teach them again and again because there are holes in their nets, and we have to revise the material regularly because they forget it' (5CGA). The teachers' accounts support the findings of a high number of studies conducted with adults and children that suggest that dyslexics have problems memorising verbal information (for recent reviews see Pothos & Kirk, 2004; Reiter *et al.*, 2005).

Our interviewees also observed that dyslexic students do not only have general memory problems, but they find it difficult to recall and memorise sequences in an appropriate order, which has been documented in previous studies in the field of psychology (for recent reviews see Pothos & Kirk, 2004; Reiter *et al.*, 2005). In language learning this manifests itself in learning sound and letter sequences in the right order (e.g. 'They know that the letters T, H and R appear in this word but not in which order, and they write down these letters but not in the appropriate order' (6ESZA)). Dyslexic language learners also have problems memorising sequences of words, which can be observed in students' mixing up numbers (e.g. 34 with 43) and using inappropriate word order. Seriality problems also appear above the sentence level as students with dyslexia 'cannot memorise a series of three or four instructions. They lose the thread at the first instruction, and even though they would be able to do all of them, they halt and do not know what to do' (6APK).

The last symptom of dyslexia that our participants mentioned involves problems that are due to the effect of dyslexia on first language (L1) acquisition, which in turn influence the learning of foreign languages. One of these problems is that because dyslexic children tend to have a smaller range of vocabulary in their L1, they have problems learning L2 words. One of the interviewees cited the following example: 'today in [English] class we were talking about butter and margarine, and the children did not know what the difference is in Hungarian' (7ANO). Other examples mentioned by the teachers include the names of months, or the days of the week. The participants also observed that sometimes students face difficulties understanding grammatical relations in their L1, which means that teachers cannot rely on this kind of knowledge in the teaching of the L2.

Personal factors observed by teachers as characteristic of dyslexic learners

It is hardly any surprise that the frequency chart in Table 8.2 is lead by behavioural problems, since behaviour appears on the surface and is the first thing a teacher notices about a student. One cannot say that all types of misbehaviour signal the presence of dyslexia, but according to the interviewed teachers, a high number of dyslexic children produce some type of misbehaviour in class (*cf.* Sindelar, 2000).

In the teachers' view, the most characteristic sign is the students' need for attention. This is partly caused by the fact that dyslexic children are fully aware that their performance in the language is below their true abilities, but they still want to surpass the others in something. The most self-evident way of gaining the attention of others is to misbehave, to be funny or to play the class clown (Sunderland, 1997). Among the respondents, it is a widely held belief about students with special educational needs [SEN] that they misbehave, are hard to discipline, are disorganised, and that they argue with their teacher and resist orders. Our participants also share in this belief, 'children with special educational needs are believed to be misbehaving, untidy, and disrespectful; in sum, all the bad things you can say about children with behavioural problems characterize SEN children' (11ABZS). The same respondents linked this kind of behaviour to previous experiences of failure:

> By the time the child reaches grade 5 or 6, – we see and sense it in the upper primary mainly, but very often in lower primary, in grade 4

already – that this series of failures, that 'I can't succeed no matter how much I study,' and 'although my mother always makes me recite [the homework] ... ,' and 'I spend a lot of time with the language and I still cannot do it, I have no success, I do not get praised,' and 'my classmates ridicule me when I say something wrong,' so this repeated experience of failure develops a defence mechanism in the children who try to compensate somehow and they do so via misbehaviour ... (11ABZS)

The interviewed teachers explained that misbehaving children cause problems in the dynamic of the group as well and told us that often the group itself ejects those who cannot or will not fit in. One of our respondents considers this kind of misbehaviour a mask 'behind which there are very alive little souls hiding' (11CMM). The interviewed teachers also noted that cooperation and working together in a group is very difficult for dyslexic students. Children sometimes get physical; they fight or trip each other or just simply put obstacles in the way of the success of others only because they focus on their own individual needs and want the full attention of the teacher for themselves.

A different behavioural symptom common among dyslexic students is shyness and anxiety (Piechurska-Kuciel, this volume; Schneider & Crombie, 2003). Our interviewees observed that some students with learning disabilities lack self-confidence and withdraw completely. The teachers assume that dyslexic children are afraid of speaking up in front of the others because they are worried about saying something wrong. Several of our respondents asserted that these students are difficult to identify as having SEN because they do not call attention to themselves, and sometimes it turns out only in higher grades that the student's poor performance is caused by a so far untreated learning disability.

Language teachers are aware of the importance of motivation in language learning, and our data point to the fact that the lack of motivation is a major problem in the case of dyslexic learners. As the teachers reported, some of them do not even bring along the initial motivation from home to the classroom because the parents do not consider language learning important for a child with special educational needs. Other students were perceived to have lost their motivation and become demotivated due to the frequently experienced failures, the lack of praise from the teacher or the negative feedback coming from their peers. The respondents also noted that extensive error correction can have a detrimental effect on these learners. In the teachers' view, demotivation manifests itself in the student giving up performing a task, for example, reading a passage, even before trying, or in the lack of effort in trying to understand what the task is. One of the language teachers commented that unless these students get special attention and extra help, they fall behind the others to such an extent by the time they reach Grade 7 or 8 that it is impossible to rebuild their motivation. The frequent practice of waiving the foreign language requirement completely or issuing no grades in foreign languages to these students is also seen as a demotivating factor by our research participants:

> And another thing is the lack of motivation, that's what they bring from home to begin with, that they have been exempted from testing and assessment, and that is interpreted by the parents as they have been exempted from language learning itself, and that is their attitude that the children then do not have to study this subject. (10ABE)

An important element in our data is that the interviewed teachers do not consider dyslexic learners hopeless. Several responses point to the fact that with the right approach it is possible to motivate dyslexic learners and to develop a positive attitude to language learning. As one teacher pointed out 'the student who acted with resistance in the regular language classes, later in the compensatory class became the teacher's helper' (10BSZE). Another teacher from a different school made a similar comment:

> They do participate willingly, and I do not see the 'I don't want to' attitude, but that they do want to do it, and are proud of it, and I think they like coming here [i.e. to compensatory classes] in the afternoons. (10ANE)

Owing to their poor performance and low achievement, dyslexic students are often suspected of having poor cognitive abilities and a low IQ (Sparks *et al.*, 1998). One of our respondents, PK, for instance, got interested in dealing with dyslexic learners after having encountered some children with an IQ of 114 and above in a school for the mentally retarded. Such cases might occur in areas where screening is poor. In the schools where the interviews were conducted, the teachers occasionally encounter severely dyslexic students with good intellectual abilities, but most of their experience is with students of average or poor abilities. One of our respondents, however, emphasised the importance of realising that these students 'are not different from any other kid, they just require a different attitude' (9BSZE).

The interviewed teachers also noted that certain cognitive functions impaired due to dyslexia also cause several problems in the foreign language classroom. The teachers observed that the poorer the cognitive abilities of students, the sooner they seem to get bored of an activity. They also noted that dealing with grammatical concepts is difficult below Grade 5 or 6. Another problem mentioned by the participants was that dyslexic students find it difficult to move from one task to another promptly, which slows them down and makes them lag behind when the task requires switching promptly from one sentence to the next or from one activity to the other. This problem, which to our knowledge has not been documented in previous research, is described by one of our participants in the following way:

> Problems with memory and attention, flexibility of thinking. They get stuck at a previous task and, for example, the translation of the previous sentence is still in their heads and they cannot start translating the next sentence in a flexible manner. (9BPK)

Our respondents also discussed problems related to the family of a high number of dyslexic children. In their view, three related themes deserve special attention: the lack of physical and emotional contact in early childhood, the lack of attention given to the small child, and the lack of L1 communication at home. One of the speech therapists asserted that the lack of touching, stroking, and hugging in early childhood can add to some of the children's late development of sensing spatial relations (8DPM). The interviewed special education teachers and psychologists also explained that inadequate verbal contact with parents in early childhood can aggravate dyslexic children's L1 acquisition problems, since the development of vocabulary and speech comprehension can lag behind if mother–child talk, fairy tales and story telling are replaced by noises coming from the TV, the radio or the computer. A telling example of inadequate verbal contact within the family is presented in the following quote (the names have been changed):

> One time we were doing this activity with the dice, and anyway, what they had to do was to say their mother's first name. And when it came to saying the name of his own mother, this one child said, 'Now, what shall I say, she's Mrs Lang.' And he did not know whether his mother was called Kate or Mary or what. I was terribly shocked. [...] They were 10 to 11-year-olds. (8CSZSA)

A speech therapist at school D had this example:

> When I examine them, I always ask them about Cinderella. 'What do you know about Cinderella? [...] What does it mean to pick the lentils out of the ashes?' They simply do not know. They have never heard the fairy tale, they do not know what lentils are or other grain ... (8DPM)

As we have shown above, all these factors severely affect the students' abilities of learning a foreign language. One German teacher also made a direct link between the misbehaviour of children in the lesson and their unfulfilled need for communicating with someone and being paid attention to in the family.

Good intellectual abilities and support from the family can help the dyslexic child develop various survival strategies, which hinders the recognition of their dyslexia in the classroom. Our interviewees told us that a frequently applied compensation strategy is learning by heart (Sindelar, 2000). Sometimes dyslexic learners memorise sentences, and when asked to read out a sentence or a text, they pretend to be reading but actually recite from memory:

> Well, there was this child who had good abilities, the daughter of N.N. [a TV personality] did this, that up to grade 4 she 'read' magnificently because auditively she managed to memorise everything so perfectly. (12DPM)

The teachers observed that some dyslexic students recognise some elements of the sentence and their strategy is to guess what the rest of the words might be. The respondents also explained that sometimes the supportive family environment that in some cases surrounds the child who has been diagnosed as dyslexic, can do more harm than good. They told us examples when students learn full texts by heart with the help of a parent or a private tutor at home, and as a result students' reading problems are masked until Grade 6, when the amount of course material becomes too much for rote memorisation, and it turns out only then that the student actually cannot read. One of our respondents (12CCSZS) also linked some behaviour problems to compensation. She asserted that sometimes children make such an incredible effort to find an appropriate strategy for filling gaps and covering up their deficiencies that they develop psychological problems, which manifest themselves in negative class participation. Although our respondents agree that learning to find the strategies with which they can help themselves is beneficial for dyslexic learners, they also maintain that the use of compensation strategies which delay early recognition and early intervention can cause serious problems.

When asked about the benefits of participating in the Ministry's dyslexia project, the respondents confirmed that the greatest change they experienced took place in their thinking and attitude. Now they confidently reject the idea of exempting dyslexic children from participating in foreign language education and agree that dyslexic children should not be subjected to further disadvantages. As one of the head masters said: 'Unequal opportunities should not be further increased. This is not our job' (AKGY).

An emerging model of teachers' perception of dyslexia in the foreign language classroom

During the process of data analysis the strong interconnectedness of the emerging categories lead us to experiment with a graphic representation of the findings. This is how the model displayed in Figure 8.1 came about.

At the base of this three-stage model the two bubbles represent two of our categories: General cognitive abilities and Family. These are

Hungarian Teachers' Perceptions of Dyslexic Language Learners   209

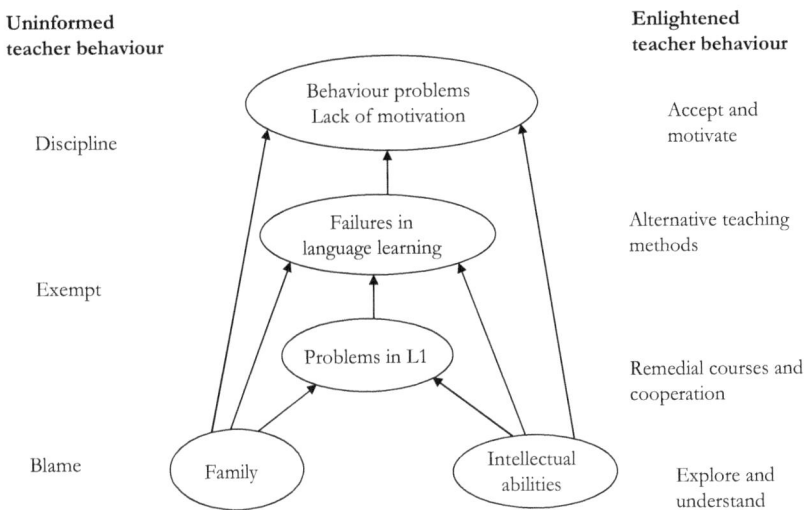

Figure 8.1 Teachers' perception of dyslexia in the classroom

factors that the teacher has no influence on, and the 'baggage' that a child brings to the classroom originates from these two sources. Both the children's abilities and their family background strongly influence L1 development. The L1 skills of children directly affect their school performance in all the subjects and provide a basis for L2 learning as well. As we tried to show above, besides indirect effects, cognitive abilities and family also exert a direct influence on foreign language learning in the classroom. The big central bubble contains the failures dyslexic learners experience in nearly all areas of language learning, for example, reading, writing, comprehension, oral production, vocabulary learning and the use of structures. The failures lead to the top level of the model where the single bubble comprises both lack of motivation and behaviour problems. By lack of motivation we mean both amotivation and demotivation. The first of the two means that the students are negatively tuned towards L2 learning initially, and the second term covers the situation when learners lose their initial motivation as a result of negative experiences in the classroom, such as negative feedback or lack of praise from the teacher, rejection and teasing from peers and overall poor achievement. These motivational problems feed directly into behaviour disorders, which appear on the surface, and all the other problems represented by the bubbles do the same, both directly and indirectly. It is misbehaviour with which students react to their failures, but misbehaviour is also caused by deeply rooted family problems, and by underdeveloped intellectual abilities, such as short attention span and slow processing speed.

The various stages of the model can also be linked vertically to two different types of teacher reactions. On the left hand side of the model, we present the reactions of an uninformed teacher, and on the right can be seen the behaviour pattern of the informed teacher as portrayed by our respondents. Teachers who are confronted by bad student behaviour are inclined to want to solve the problem by disciplining the child. A surface phenomenon triggers surface reaction. This can take several forms from reprimanding the children or isolating them to sending them out of the classroom. Teachers who realise that the poor behaviour of the child is actually linked to or caused by the poor performance in the foreign language look for solutions in taking administrative measures and might exempt the learner from being graded in foreign languages or initiate the waiving of the foreign language requirement completely. When looking for an excuse for not dealing with the students' problems more effectively, the child's assumed poor intellect or problems rooted in the family tend to be blamed.

If, however, teachers explore and understand all three layers of their students' problems, a different kind of behaviour can be realised which is displayed in the far right column in Figure 8.1. The enlightened reaction to the surface level problems would be accepting the child and making an effort to motivate him or her. Teachers who gain an insight into the middle layers of the problem will look for and develop different methodologies, materials and teaching techniques to match the needs of these learners. Understanding the interrelatedness of L2 and L1 problems should lead to compensatory programs in the L1 and to cooperation between L1 and L2 teachers. And finally, a new attitude is needed as regards the underlying layer as well. Instead of using the child's allegedly poor cognitive abilities and the family related problems as an excuse for doing little or nothing, there is a need to explore these areas and to gain a deep understanding of the issues by virtue of which action in the middle and top stages can take place effectively. It is only through this kind of exploration and understanding that the teachers' work in the classroom can be placed on solid grounds.

Conclusion

In this study the authors made an attempt at presenting the case of the dyslexic language learner from a new perspective: that of their language teachers. The fact that language teachers play a key role in the foreign language learning of a dyslexic learner is undeniable (McKay, 1997). Whether students drop out or persist, whether they end up with a waiver or a language certificate in their hands depends more on the teacher than on anybody else besides the students themselves. It is therefore of vital importance that language teachers be aware of the fact that a child or an adolescent is dyslexic and that they also know what difficulties this fact causes in the language learning process. From the results of the present study, it can be seen that teachers can do a lot of harm or a lot of good, and which way they go will depend on how prepared they are for the task (Ganschow et al., 1998; Schneider & Crombie, 2003).

The preparation of the teacher for the challenge of dealing with dyslexic learners must begin with awareness raising. Teachers must be aware of the basic problems dyslexic learners have which will affect their L2 acquisition. These include some general psychological and cognitive problems, and difficulties in the use of L1. In our model, we demonstrated how necessary it is that they interpret what they encounter in the classroom appropriately and react professionally. Teachers also need to be familiar with methods and materials with the help of which dyslexic learners can be taught in an interesting and engaging manner. It is the experience of teachers themselves that can best convince the rest of the profession that dyslexic learners can be taught foreign languages successfully if the right approach is applied.

In order to achieve some improvement at the chalkface, several conditions need to be fulfilled. The results of the present study highlight the importance of cooperation at various levels. It is imperative that language teachers cooperate with the school psychologist and speech therapist so that the development of basic functional skills and language skills can be coordinated. Equally important is cooperation with the L1 teacher because, as we have seen, the foreign language development of a learner is seriously hindered by underdeveloped L1 vocabulary, comprehension skills and grammatical awareness. Last but not least, the cooperation of the school management also needs to be obtained so that special compensatory groups can be formed for dyslexic learners where they can gain enough input, practice, knowledge, positive feedback and confidence before reintegration into their regular classrooms.

Since dyslexia affects about 7–10% of the school-age population, turning a blind eye and hoping that the problem will resolve itself is unacceptable. We hope that this study fulfils its purpose of presenting the teaching of foreign languages to dyslexic learners from an insider's perspective and leads to a deeper understanding of the problems teachers face in the classroom. This deeper understanding should encourage teachers and fellow researchers to further explore the options of dyslexic students for achieving success in foreign languages.

Note

1. This definition of dyslexia is different from that of the definition of the British Dyslexia Association, which does not make any reference to intellectual abilities (Johnson & Peer, 2002).

Acknowledgements

The authors are grateful to the TEMPUS Office, Budapest for making their files available for our research and for the support of all the participating schools and teachers. The research reported in this paper has been sponsored by the Equal Rights in Foreign Language Education project of the Hungarian National Bureau of Research and Technology (NKTH B2 2006-0010).

References

Carroll, J. and Sapon, S. (1959) *Modern Language Aptitude Test (MLAT): Manual*. San Antonio, TX: Psychological Corp.
Downey, D., Snyder, L. and Hill, B. (2000) College students with dyslexia: Persistent linguistic deficits and foreign language learning. *Dyslexia* 6 (2), 101–111.
Fletcher, J.M., Lyon, G.R., Fuchs, L.S. and Barnes, M.A. (2007) *Learning Disabilities: From Identification to Intervention*. New York: Guilford.
Frostig, M. and Horne, D. (1964) *The Frostig Program for the Development of Visual Perception: Teachers Guide*. Chicago, IL: Follett.
Ganschow, L., Sparks, R. and Javorsky, J. (1998) Foreign language learning difficulties: An historical perspective. *Journal of Learning Disabilities* 31 (3), 248–258.
Gordosné Szabó, A. (2004) *Bevezető általános gyógypedagógiai ismeretek [Introduction to Special Education]*. Budapest: Nemzeti Tankönyvkiadó.
Helland, T. and Kaasa, R. (2005) Dyslexia in English as a second language. *Dyslexia* 11 (1), 41–60.
Ho, C.S-H. and Fong, K-M. (2005) Do Chinese dyslexic children have difficulties learning English as a second language? *Journal of Psycholinguistic Research* 34 (6), 603–618.
Johnson, M. and Peer, L. (2002) *The Dyslexia Handbook*. London: The British Dyslexia Association.
MacKay, N. (1997) Study skills for dyslexics – How to help individuals without always giving individual help. *Dyslexia* 3 (4), 235–239.
Meixner, I. (1993) *A dyslexia prevenció, reedukáció módszere [Prevention and Re-education in Dyslexia]*. Budapest: Bárczi Gusztáv Gyógypedagógiai Tanárképző Főiskola.
Ormos, E. (2003) Teaching English as a foreign language to dyslexic children. Unpublished MA dissertation, Eötvös Loránd University.
Pothos, E.M. and Kirk, J. (2004) Investigating learning deficits associated with dyslexia. *Dyslexia* 10 (1), 61–76.
Ranaldi, F. (2003) *Dyslexia and Design and Technology*. London: David Fulton.
Reiter, A., Tucha, O. and Lange, K.W. (2005) Executive functions in children with dyslexia. *Dyslexia* 11 (2), 116–131.
Robinson, P. (2005) Aptitude and second language acquisition. *Annual Review of Applied Linguistics* 25 (1), 45–73.
Sarkadi, Á. (2006) A diszlexiás nyelvtanulók angoltanításának kérdései [Issues in teaching English to dyslexic language learners]. *Iskolakultúra* 8, 59–65.
Schneider, E. and Crombie, M. (2003) *Dyslexia and Foreign Language Learning*. London: David Fulton.
Sindelar, B. (2000) *Basic Functional Disorders. Reasons for Learning and Behavior Problems in Children* (1st English edn). Vienna: Verlag Austria Press.
Skehan, P. (1986) Where does language aptitude come from? In P. Meara (ed.) *Spoken Language* (pp. 95–113). London: Center for Information on Language Teaching.

Smythe, I. and Everatt, J. (2000) Dyslexia diagnosis in different languages. In L. Peer and G. Reid (eds) *Multilingualism, Literacy and Dyslexia* (pp. 12–21). London: David Fulton.

Sparks, R.L., Artzer, M., Patton, J., Ganschow, L., Miller, K., Hordubay, D.J. and Walsh, G. (1998) Benefits of multisensory structured language instruction for at-risk foreign language learners: A comparison study of high school Spanish students. *Annals of Dyslexia* 48 (1), 239–270.

Spolsky, B. (1989) *Conditions for Second Language Learning*. Oxford: Oxford University Press.

Sunderland, H. (1997) Dyslexia – What does it mean for ESOL teachers? *Language Issues* 9 (1), 17–19.

Torda, Á. (2004) A képességzavar mint különleges ellátási jogosultság a közoktatásban [Learning disability as a right to special needs education]. In Á. Lányiné Engelmayer (ed.) *Képességzavarok diagnosztikája és terápiája a gyógypedagógiai pszichológiában [Diagnosis and Therapy of Learning Disabilities in the Psychology of Special Education]* (pp. 153–164). Budapest: Akadémiai Kiadó.

Chapter 9
Teachers' and Trainers' Perceptions of Inclusive Education Within TEFL Certificate Courses in Britain

ANNE MARGARET SMITH

Introduction

Every year tens of thousands of new recruits to English language teaching (ELT) graduate from short intensive courses in Britain with an initial Certificate in Teaching English as a Foreign Language (TEFL) (Cambridge ESOL, 2007). Some of these new teachers stay and teach in private schools or the state sector in Britain, but many find their first posts outside the UK, so that the content of these courses has an impact not only in Britain but also around the world. This model for training teachers of EFL was developed in 1962, when International House ran the first four-week, intensive TEFL course. The emphasis then was on providing 'as much practical grounding and classroom exposure as possible' (Haycraft, 1988: 4), and this is still the norm today, over 40 years later. In what ways and how well this 'practical grounding' prepares new teachers to include a wide range of learners – particularly disabled learners – in their classes is the main focus of this study.

There are currently two bodies in the UK that award the majority of initial TEFL certificates: the University of Cambridge (Cambridge ESOL, 2007) and Trinity College, London. These organisations are by no means the only ones offering accreditation, but they are the best known in the British ELT community, and their international reputations provide a certain level of confidence for employers of new teachers worldwide. These organisations (and others) also offer further qualifications for more experienced teachers as well as for those who wish to work in the British state sector and who therefore need different qualifications.

A new route to TEFL-qualification is being developed which meets the national standards for British state sector teachers, and which teachers of

English to Speakers of Other Languages (ESOL) in the UK will have to follow if they are to continue teaching in Further Education (FE). This has raised a lot of issues for ELT practitioners including the question of whether the existing initial training for new teachers is adequate, and in what ways it could or should be improved (see e.g. Ferguson & Donno, 2003). The discussion in this chapter is confined to the current initial Certificate, which is often, though not exclusively, run as a four- or six-week intensive course.

One shortcoming of the intensive courses that has not received a lot of attention to date is the way in which the issue of inclusion is approached. Although this has been high on the agenda of state sector education providers for some years, it is only slowly making an impact on the largely private EFL sector in the UK. The term 'inclusion' or 'inclusive education' is interpreted in many different ways in different contexts, but generally the goals are to eliminate discriminatory practice, to minimise the barriers that some students experience in their learning and so allow access to education for all. One group of people who are under-represented in ELT are disabled people, both as learners and as teachers.

Over the last few years, the 1995 Disability Discrimination Act has gradually been amended with the result that all teachers now have a legal responsibility both to anticipate the needs of disabled learners and also to accommodate them, by making reasonable adjustments to the physical environment or curriculum. Unfortunately, the definition of what is 'reasonable' is still open to interpretation, so that organisations that are reluctant to comply can still exclude some learners. In the most recent legal amendments, disability is defined as 'a physical or mental impairment which has a substantial and long-term adverse effect on the ability to carry out day-to-day activities' (Disability Discrimination Act, 1995: chap. 50, Part 1, 1/1). This includes long-term illnesses such as Multiple Sclerosis and developmental learning differences such as dyslexia and attention deficit disorder (ADD), as well as sensory impairments and physical disabilities. Although it must be acknowledged that not everyone who comes under this definition would perceive themselves as being disabled, for the purposes of this study, the term 'disabled learners' is used to denote students who experience any of these barriers to learning. Since there is now an obligation to anticipate learners' needs, not just to react on an ad hoc basis to situations as they arise, it would seem that teachers and teacher educators require some kind of preparation in order to equip them to fulfil their duty in this respect. This, then, is the climate in which the question arose: Do British EFL/ESOL teachers feel sufficiently well prepared to accommodate different types of disability in their classrooms? This chapter reports the findings from the research project which sought some answers to this question.

Background

The focus of this study – teacher education for inclusive English language teaching – is a relatively under-researched area, and so it was necessary to draw on work done in several related fields of education in order to gain an understanding of the wider context in which the study is located.

In its purest form an inclusive approach to education looks beyond physical integration of disabled learners and those deemed to have 'Special Educational Needs' (SEN) into mainstream classes (i.e. state-funded education for 5–16-year-olds) and calls for a radical restructuring of education systems so that they will be equipped to accommodate all learners (Clough & Corbett, 2000; Frederikson & Cline, 2002). It offers a vision of participation and engagement in education which is accessible to all. This depends to a large degree on the willingness and ability of teachers to rethink their classroom practices and – crucially – their attitudes. Croll and Moses (2003: 742) found that the primary school teachers in their survey demonstrated 'a considerable degree of commitment in principle to the policy of inclusion' but warned that the reality might prove to be somewhat different. Where teachers were already supporting disabled learners, they were often happy to retain them as members of their class, so it seems that it is sometimes the fear of the unknown that leads to un-inclusive attitudes. Wedell and the British Educational Communications and Technology Agency (BECTA) Special Needs Team (2002) also report that secondary school teachers largely appear to support the principles of inclusion. However, they caution that in some cases what teachers actually support may be the so-called 'responsible inclusion' that Garner and Gains (2000, cited in Dyson, 2001: 27) reported, that is, something akin to a physical integration model, in which the onus is still on the learner to accommodate to the culture of the school.

The degree of acceptance accorded to different types and degrees of disability is a comparatively well-researched area. Alghazo and Gaad's (2004) study of mainstream teachers in the United Arab Emirates (UAE) showed that, like the respondents in other studies that they surveyed, students with physical disabilities were deemed to be the easiest to include in the classroom, followed by students with specific learning difficulties. Those with emotional or behavioural difficulties were the least welcome to the teachers in that study, but the more experienced UAE teachers (measured in years of teaching experience) were found to be much more accepting of disabled students than their novice colleagues. That teachers perceive disability on a sliding scale in this way should not be surprising, particularly in view of the fact that there appears to be a perception of a similar hierarchy amongst disabled people (Deal, 2003) in terms of how they relate to people with the same impairments as themselves or different ones.

The availability of initial and in-service courses that offer teachers the opportunity to explore these issues is key to fostering inclusiveness. Sadly, though, Booth (2003) notes that the barriers to inclusion in British teacher training institutions are numerous, and not least amongst them are the number of official initiatives and directives that have their bases in a variety of underpinning (and often conflicting) principles, which he suggests do little to contribute to the development of an inclusive culture; this does not bode well for EFL/ESOL in the current era of increased government regulation in Britain. Haug (2003: 106) notes, in relation to the failure of reform in Norwegian teacher education, that, 'to change teacher education you have to convince and motivate the lecturers [teacher educators]'. This resonates with the findings of the study reported in this chapter, which highlights the importance of having the trainers on board if there is to be any chance of change at a fundamental level.

Serving teachers and trainers have an enormous impact on the trainees that they teach and mentor in their placements, and it is important to attend to these professionals' continuing development as well as the new teachers' initial training. Florian and Rouse (2001) found that 78% of mainstream teachers in their survey reported having had no training in SEN in the previous five years, a figure which at first glance seems shocking. However, they suspect that many of their respondents may well have received training that was inclusion-oriented, but that the use of an inclusive discourse, rather than the more familiar discourse pertaining to SEN, meant that they did not fully realise how well prepared they were. This has clear implications for ELT professionals and the language that we use: it is important that we learn from the experiences in other branches of education with relation to the issues mentioned above, if teachers are to be enabled (and to feel confident in their abilities) to include disabled learners.

In the United States, Ganschow and colleagues have led the way in conducting research which considers the impact of disabilities and learning differences on foreign language learning; Sparks *et al.* (2005), synthesising their comprehensive series of research projects in the United States, reported that students deemed to have a disability do not necessarily perform worse in the language classroom than their peers, and that if they do experience difficulties, they are not different from the types of problems that students without such a diagnosis might encounter (see also Sparks *et al.*, this volume). In the UK the 'Learning for Living' project (Department for Education and Skills, 2006) looked into the experiences of ESOL learners with disabilities and learning differences, indicating a growing awareness that inclusion is an area that needs highlighting.

However, in terms of examining how well teacher education prepares new teachers for the inclusive language classroom, almost nothing has been done in the UK. This study therefore has a unique contribution to make to the ELT community's understanding of the issue of inclusion, particularly in Britain, but also in other countries where the influence of British ELT has been (and remains) significant. The way in which the study was carried out is presented in the following section.

Method

There were two phases to the project: one strand in the data collection was a postal questionnaire which collected quantitative and qualitative data concerning the respondents' preparation for, experiences of and attitudes to working with disabled students. To complement this, a series of semi-structured interviews were conducted, which sought to clarify and probe some of the issues that arose from the survey. In this chapter the qualitative data from both the questionnaire and the interviews are reported, and the quotations that appear in the results section represent the voices of both questionnaire and interview participants. However, the quantitative data also contributed to the formation of the overall conclusions and will be briefly summarised where relevant – all figures given pertain to these data from the questionnaire. (For a full report of the quantitative results of this project see Smith, 2006.)

Participants

For the questionnaire survey a sampling frame was constructed, based on the population of schools and academic departments that are accredited in the UK by the British Council and British Association of Lecturers in English for Academic Purposes (henceforth, 'BALEAP'). Stratified random sampling was used to ensure that there was a mix of type (private and state-funded) and location of schools. Schools that had been chosen for this stage of the study were then disqualified from the interview stage, to avoid overloading any single institution and repeating the same questions to the informants. The institutions chosen were approached first by e-mail, and then a follow-up telephone call was made, to establish personal contact with a named person who was to be responsible for distribution and collection of the papers. Ninety of the schools originally approached were willing to take part, and the timing and return date of the questionnaire was negotiated as well as the number of questionnaires that each institution could take; those who were unwilling or unable to take part were replaced by the next school on the sampling list.

In all, 194 ELT practitioners responded to the questionnaire: 120 (62%) of them women and 74 (38%) men. All the participants were UK-based professionals: 133 (69%) of these people were working in private language schools, 61 (31%) in the state sector, as illustrated in Table 9.1 below.

Age was not considered a relevant factor in this study, but rather the number of years of experience as a teacher of English, and the level of

Table 9.1 Questionnaire respondents (by gender and place of work)

	Women	*Men*	*Total*
Private institutions	81	52	133
State institutions	39	22	61
Total	120	74	194

qualification. Teaching experience ranged from one year or less ($n = 5$), to 40 years ($n = 1$) with a mean of 11 and a mode of 5. For 135 (69.6%) of the respondents, their first teaching qualification was an initial TEFL certificate, like the ones described above. Seven did not state their first qualification, but for the other 52, the most common entry to teaching was through a Postgraduate Certificate in Education (PGCE) ($n = 19$) or a Certificate in Education ($n = 13$), although other programmes were also cited, such as a first degree in Education or a Teaching Diploma. Of the 135 respondents who had done the initial certificate as their first teaching qualification, 81 (60%) had gained a further qualification. The most common further qualifications were a Diploma in ELT ($n = 71$) or a Master's degree ($n = 21$). Some of the respondents had taken more than one further qualification, including PGCEs and research degrees.

As regards experience of working with disabled learners, only 36 (18.6%) of the respondents reported that they had never worked with any learner who had any known disability. The most commonly encountered disability was a specific learning difficulty (dyslexia, or dyspraxia, for example), which 121 (62.4%) respondents had had experience of, in roughly equal proportions across both the private and the state sectors. The least common disability was severe autism, which only seven (3.6%) respondents had encountered.

The interviewees were first identified through purposive, maximum variety sampling, by building a typology to choose institutions which represented different types of educational provision in the same towns, and which followed different curricula in their training courses for new EFL teachers. In each case, the director of studies or head of department was contacted to ask if they and their staff would be willing to take part in the study, and a date was set for the interviews to take place. Only one institution declined to take part, on the grounds of time constraints. During the course of the study, the participants at the selected institutions also suggested other contacts who could provide valuable input, and so the sampling became more opportunistic in nature.

Altogether 15 ELT professionals from eight different organisations took part in semi-structured interviews, drawn from both the private and the state sector, as shown in Table 9.2 below. This was important because of

Table 9.2 Interview respondents

ID	Sector	Gender	Role/title	Years of teaching experience	Years of training experience
IP1	Private	Female	Chief Examiner	10	10
IP2	Private	Female	Chief Examiner	7	7
IS3	State	Female	EFL Co-ordinator	22	15
IS4	State	Female	Trainer	19	12
IP5	Private	Male	Director of Studies	13	5
IP6	Private	Female	Trainer	12	5
IP7	Private	Female	Trainer	5	0.5
IP8	Private	Female	Director of EFL	14	7
IP9	Private	Male	Trainer	10	3
IP10	Private	Male	Trainer	15	3
IS11	State	Male	TESOL Co-ordinator	23	10
IS12	State	Male	TESOL Co-ordinator	30	15
IS13	State	Male	Senior Lecturer	20	3
IS14	State	Male	Senior Lecturer	13	5
IS15	State	Female	Head of ESOL	20	15
Average experience				15.5	7.7

the different regulations that pertain to state education, in terms of how support is available to disabled learners who require it, and the different clientele that the two sectors generally attract.

All the interviewees were qualified in TEFL beyond Certificate level, holding at least a Diploma; six reported that they held higher academic degrees as well. The least experienced had more than five years experience of ELT, and the most experienced had been involved in English teaching for more than 30 years; the mean was 15.5 years overall. All 15 of the participants had had some experience of working with either disabled language learners or disabled trainees during their careers, a figure which reinforces the argument for preparing teachers early in their careers for this situation. Only one was able to say with certainty that she had had appropriate preparation for this aspect of her work; she happened also to be a qualified teacher of dyslexic learners so the training she had undertaken was not specifically related to ELT, but more generally to dyslexia.

All had English as their first language, although that was not a prerequisite for taking part, only that they should be involved in ELT in the UK. As well as teaching, they were involved in training new English language teachers, or designing training programmes. One was a newly promoted member of staff in her first year of being a trainer, and three had been involved in training for 15 years; the group mean was 7.7 years working in a training capacity.

Instruments

The questionnaire was designed to elicit both qualitative and quantitative information about the respondents' training and backgrounds, as well as their attitudes and experiences of working with disabled learners. Section A collected the personal background information about the respondents which is reported above. Section B elicited information about the respondents' initial teaching qualifications and training experiences while section C focused on the professional development that the respondents had subsequently undertaken. Section D investigated the respondents' experience of working with disabled learners, and section E explored the respondents' attitudes to supporting learners who have disabilities. The questions that yielded qualitative data (amounting to approximately 12,000 words in total) asked the participants to comment on their initial training course (B4), and on post certificate TEFL/TESL training or professional development (C5). One question inquired in detail about their first experience of teaching English to a student with learning difficulties (D3), and one invited the respondents to express their views on supporting such learners (E2).

A schedule of interview questions was devised, based on preliminary informal discussions in two institutions (which for reasons of space are not reported here). This was refined in the light of the data gleaned from the first questionnaires returned from the postal survey, for example, to include more explicit questions about their early careers and qualifications. The interview schedule covered the informants' experiences as teachers and trainers, their experiences of working with disabled learners and their views on training and staff development opportunities in ELT (see Appendix). Each interview lasted between 45 and 70 minutes, and the same topics were addressed in each, although the order in which they arose depended largely on the interviewees, and how they responded to each question. Because of the relatively free structure of the interviews, there is necessarily less uniformity in the data collected than would have been the case in structured interviews. However, the benefits of allowing interviewees to speak freely, and therefore to reveal information that the researcher may not have anticipated, far outweigh the difficulties of later analysing and comparing responses, and greatly add to the content validity of the study. All the interviewees were asked to speak on the same topics, and the interviewer refrained as far as possible from 'leading' them in their responses. In all cases the interviewees willingly opened up in response to the questions and appeared happy to discuss the issues candidly and fully.

Analysis

The analysis of questionnaire data was facilitated by pre-coding for the quantitative questions on the questionnaire, giving figures on which statistical tests could be run using the Statistical Package for the Social Sciences (SPSS) computer software, v.11. The interviews were audio-taped, and afterwards transcribed; these transcripts were sent to the interviewees for verification and correction where necessary.

About two thirds of the questionnaire participants responded to the open-ended questions in the written survey writing between one and four sentences to each. The qualitative analysis yielded themes such as *disabilities, course management*, for example, course length, course quality, *support and resources, time and money constraints, the teachers' qualifications, training and experience*, as well as their and their groups' *reactions* to students with learning disabilities.

The qualitative data gained from the questionnaire and the interviews were post-coded manually according to the common themes that emerged, using the first few returns to set up a 'grounded' coding frame. The researcher then returned to the data after a period of several months had elapsed and recoded them to ensure that nothing had been overlooked.

The checking of the transcripts by the participants ensured greater accuracy, since accidental slips on the part of either the interviewee or the transcriber could be eliminated. The use of two data collection methods was a further safeguard; the data gathered through the interviews were corroborated and contextualised by the findings of the questionnaire survey.

Each participant was assigned a unique code to ensure anonymity. The interviewees are differentiated from the questionnaire respondents by the prefix (I rather than Q) and the second character denotes the sector in which they work (P = private, S = state); the number indicates the order in which they were interviewed. The questionnaire respondents' codes consist of their employment sector (P or S), location (City, Large town or Small town) and an individual number. These codes are used in the following section of this report to protect the respondents' identities.

Results

The main themes that emerged from the data are explored here and can be characterised as belonging to three broad categories, the first of which is *institutional factors*, including the range of support resources available.

The second is *classroom management*, encompassing how other learners perceive their disabled peers, and how teachers manage diversity of need in their classrooms; the final category, and perhaps the most important, is *professional expertise*, relating to the content of training programmes, and the range of experience that trainers and teachers were able to draw on when working with disabled learners.

Institutional factors

The institutional factor that had the most direct influence on teachers' confidence in accommodating disabled learners, or how well supported they felt in their work, was whether they worked in the private or state sector. Encouragingly, section E of the questionnaire revealed that only a small number of questionnaire respondents (11.8%) felt that working with disabled learners should not be part of the job and the majority (67%) felt that classroom diversity was what makes teaching particularly rewarding. However, there was a strong feeling among private language school employees that they had access to fewer resources than their state sector colleagues, and that because they were 'not trained, prepared or equipped to deal with students with learning difficulties' (QPL6-1) as one respondent put it, additional support was not something that could be provided as easily as in state funded colleges. As another respondent expressed it: 'it is not possible for a small private language school to support the many and varied needs of "SEN" as is done in the state sector' (QPL15-1).

Whilst 63.9% of all questionnaire respondents agreed that some support needs could be met, the state sector response was more positive (86.8% compared to 53.4% from the private sector). Sixty-four percent of the state sector employees agreed that there was an established support system in place for all students where they worked, while most of the respondents from the private sector (86.5%) disagreed with that statement. Conversely, when asked to respond to the statements that there was 'no support available' where they worked, or that they 'did not know what support would be available', the private sector respondents were split roughly in half, while the state sector responses were clear disagreements (75.4% and 68.8% respectively). The majority of respondents (86.1%) from both sectors were united in agreeing that it was the responsibility of management to provide the necessary resources and support, rather than that of the teacher or the student.

It was interesting that there were no comments from respondents in the state sector referring to this difference between the sectors; however, one respondent who worked in both sectors was able to compare them thus:

> There is practically no support for students with learning difficulties [in this private school] because it is a private business and nobody really cares about individual students in the classroom ... The other

> school [I work in] is ESOL which gets money from the government, and the groups are much smaller, and more money for the teachers. There is support for the learners with difficulties and for the teachers, although it is often not enough. (QPC7-6)

As well as describing the support that is offered in different institutions, this teacher also touched on the issue of funding, which is crucial in allowing good practice to flourish.

Generally, then, the respondents in the private sector were less positive about the support available to them and their learners than their state sector counterparts, but this attitude was not shared by all. One state sector teacher and trainer reported that in her institution there was 'support [available], but not specific to EFL students' needs' (QSC4-4), a comment that echoed other informants' views, including the one above and some of the interviewees, indicating that all is not as rosy in the state sector as it might seem from the private school perspective.

From the point of view of the trainers who were interviewed, there seemed to be little difference between the two sectors in terms of preparation for supporting learners with disabilities. One private sector respondent reported that teachers relied on their abilities 'to adapt and react' (IP10) to learners' needs, and another thought that most were willing to do 'a bit of research: How bad is it? What do they do? What do they need?' (IP8) but all were unanimous in expressing a feeling of being underprepared and ill-equipped for this aspect of their work. Their state sector counterparts echoed this sentiment, in this trainer's words:

> It's just very much a case of having to think on your feet, and via a tutorial with those individuals enter into a discussion as to whether or not you feel that you are actually responding to their needs as an individual. Because basically you don't have that specialist support or training (IS14).

This reference to lack of specialist support may surprise respondents from the private sector, but although trainers agreed that on paper 'there are specialist counsellors ... there is a support network' (IS11), there was also a perceived problem that the support is rarely provided by staff who have a specialist background in language teaching, and so there may be discrepancies between what is needed and what can be provided, as the trainer quoted above went on:

> Within FE colleges, the reality is whilst there are learner support units ... they tend to be centred very much around the domestic market ... so when it comes to ESOL learners with any kind of difficulty, the reality is that your hands are tied, there's not very much you can do ... So in that situation I've found, in my experience, you're relying on the good will and collaboration of the fellow students to help them out. (IS14)

The important aspect of peer support is addressed later in this chapter. Another trainer agreed and added: '... if you don't know anything about [a student's needs] until the course has started, then the systems that operate here are so slow, that the course has finished by the time we get it sorted out.' (IS12).

Despite the imperfect support systems operating in many institutions, there were grounds for optimism for the future, with the trend being towards improved facilities and increased awareness of how to support learners. One highly experienced teacher in the state sector noted that 'it is becoming increasingly important' (QSC2-14), while another state sector teacher and trainer remarked that in the twelve years she had been teaching it had become 'much easier to support students with learning difficulties' (QSC3-7). Among the private sector respondents, too, there was an acknowledgement that 'there is an emerging need for TEFLers to focus on the area' (QPL20-2), which could lead to better resources becoming available. One respondent commented:

> Disability access to classrooms and facilities is generally poor especially in private language schools. These schools are inspected by the British Council which at present does not seem to cover disability access for overseas students. This serious problem needs to be rectified urgently to put private schools in line with universities and FE colleges. (QPC6-3)

Whilst this teacher acknowledges that it is an issue that needs attention, what is interesting here is that he is nominating the British Council as the overseer of good practice (something that two other respondents also suggest), thus suggesting that the responsibility for supporting learners should be borne not only by the teachers and managers but also by an external agency.

These institutional differences, whether real or imagined, are likely to be crucial in the campaign to create an inclusive system. Although most of the respondents felt that there was insufficient support available to them, there are grounds for optimism in the acknowledgements of the importance of the issue of supporting disabled learners which come from both sectors.

Classroom management

Most of the questionnaire respondents (88.1%) agreed that it is the teacher's job to accommodate different needs in the classroom. Students who experienced slight restrictions in their mobility were deemed by the questionnaire respondents to be the easiest to accommodate in an English language classroom, with 94.8% feeling confident that they would be able to participate in at least half the lesson (and none feeling that no participation would be possible). This group was closely followed by students with more severe mobility impairments (e.g. wheelchair users), with 88.6% of the respondents estimating more than 50% participation. Students with severe sensory impairment or autism were rated hardest to accommodate; only 7.7% of respondents thought that profoundly deaf students would be able to participate more than 50% (44.8% judged that they would not be able to participate at all) and only 6.2% rated students with severe autism as being able to participate in more than half of the lesson (40.7% estimated no participation at all).

Very few (4.6%) of the questionnaire respondents considered it 'a form of cheating' for students to receive support, and only a small minority (29.4%) agreed that disabled learners 'took teacher time away from the rest of the class'. However, the respondents who commented on the effect that students with learning difficulties have on the classroom environment mostly saw it as a negative influence, from which their other students should be protected. These respondents apparently failed to see the irony of statements such as: 'The attention given to them takes away from that needed for the others and is unfair' (QPL15-2). One teacher from this section of the sample argued, for example, that '... it is simply not fair [to anybody], least of all the students with special educational needs to mix students with severe learning difficulties with "able bodied" students' (QPL6-2), and two others recommended that teachers should discuss whether to 'contain them in special schools' (QPL7-3), thus segregating learners who already face barriers to participation on the grounds that '... the rest of the class are effected [sic]' (QPL14-6).

The attitude held by this minority can perhaps be partly explained by the report from one teacher who had had a bad experience with a young student deemed to have Attention Deficit/Hyperactivity Disorder who would 'run around the class, disturbing and threatening the other students' (QPS1-2), but this was the only report of actual disruption, amongst several accounts that students '... would lose patience listening to [a hearing impaired student]' (QPC6-2) or '... were reluctant to work in pairs/small groups with the [autistic] student ...' (QPS5-3) and that '[d]ifficulties included making them part of the group and well accepted' (QPL10-3). These comments seem to point to a problem for the teachers in managing the class (including the group dynamics) rather than a real problem for any of the learners; most teachers would agree that having a group which co-operates well makes teaching much easier. Poor group relationships were often put down to '... the other students who don't know how to react or work with these students' (QPL10-1). One teacher had found that the average age of the class was significant and that '... adult students [are] less accepting and tolerant of students in their class who can't keep up, for whatever reason. Young learners are more willing to integrate and help or support their peers' (QPL7-5). However, another, very well-travelled course leader believed that it was cultural differences in attitudes towards disability that were 'an added pressure which we can do little to influence' (QSC3-4). This voice from the state sector was backed up by another experienced teacher in the private sector who also felt that 'the problem is often with the attitude of the other students and this might be difficult to overcome' (QPL10-1). The issue of diverse international and cultural perceptions of disability is undoubtedly particularly pertinent in the ELT context, and should not be overlooked in initial training.

From the state sector there is some evidence that the situation is not as difficult for other class members or the teacher as the respondents quoted above feared. These teachers' comments show that the reality of including students with sensory impairments was not as taxing as they had anticipated. One of the teachers commented that 'I think I was more shocked than anything and it made it a bit strange for me, not for anyone else in the class. (QSC2-2)', and another one noted that:

> At first I found it daunting to teach someone with hearing difficulties, but he was well integrated into a class he'd been with for a long time. They made many allowances for him and he was good at seating himself where he could see me speaking ... (QSS2-2)

Nor were the other students – apparently – adversely affected. Indeed, one teacher went so far as to suggest that she would '... learn from these students and hope other members of the class do' (QSC2-9), and one highly experienced private school manager, although he reported having no direct experience of working with disabled learners, suggested that 'probably all students have a learning difficulty of one kind or another, to a greater or lesser degree. Focus in EFL on all aspects of learning difficulty will assist all students, therefore, and not just those with obvious difficulties' (QPS3-1).

Although it is worrying that some teachers seemed to be using an avowed concern for their learners' well-being as an excuse to exclude certain members of the class, these were not the majority of teachers. The lack of confidence exhibited by some of the respondents in their abilities to accommodate all their learners' needs is perhaps easier to understand in the context of the limited support and facilities available to them.

Professional expertise

Expertise (not to be confused with experience, as measured in years) can be considered as a combination of the knowledge gained in a range of professional situations, supported by on-going training and education. As regards the first formal training that many of the respondents had undertaken, the intensive certificate courses, there was a consensus among the respondents that there was little explicit coverage of disability issues. Only 21.1% of the questionnaire respondents agreed with the statement that they had felt 'competent in teaching students with a wide range of needs' after completing their Certificate. Overwhelmingly, the respondents felt they had needed more experience (78.4%), with colleagues' support and formal training was perceived as less important.

The trainers themselves recognised that disability is 'not something that's addressed from the special needs aspect' (IP7) in their courses, and even in the state sector it was acknowledged by one trainer that ELT professionals 'don't talk about "differentiation" as a buzz word' (IS4). Despite this, the interviewees were able to identify aspects of the training that would generally lead to an inclusive attitude towards teaching in the English language classroom. The language used commonly in this respect employs terms such as 'addressing learner styles, the learner needs' (IP5) and 'student involvement, student-centredness' (IP7), rather than the mainstream 'SEN' discourse. One state sector trainer summed it up thus, 'I think in the [certificate] training we are quite hot on: "Are you addressing individual students' needs?"' (IS4) and this certainly reflected the majority view. The onus, it seems, is on the teacher to be sensitive and attentive to the way in which each learner is developing. To foster this, it is common for courses to include an activity in which trainees are asked 'to develop case studies of particular learners who had a particular area of difficulty or whatever, and to research the barriers to them learning English' (IS13).

One of the questionnaire respondents spoke for many when he commented that: '[t]he topic of learning difficulties was not featured in my [certificate course] ... The wide range of needs covered were all concerned with language and cultural differences' (QPS8-2). There were indications that although courses might not include 'enough on emotional issues that can disrupt or impede a student's learning and progress' (QPC12-11), they might 'very quickly cover kinaesthetic, visual and oral [sic] learners' (QPC11-7), with a view to introducing the concept of the range of learning styles that learners bring to the classroom. The learning styles and needs of the trainees on the course were also sometimes exploited by the trainers to illustrate this point.

Following their initial training, 49.5% of the questionnaire respondents stated that they had never been offered the opportunity to develop their skills in supporting learners with disabilities, and only 13.4% had had formal training in this area. Some of the respondents felt that it was '... an area neglected in TEFL/TESOL' (QSC8-3) and generally 'ignored' (QSC8-1) by the profession. In terms of in-service training offered in the participating institutions, none of the interview informants was able to state definitely that supporting disabled learners was a topic that had appeared on the programme in their school, although one trainer reported that at his institution they had had:

> input on making sure classes are inclusive, to cater for shy people, extrovert people, making sure there's a variety of activities to deal with different learner styles, so we do it from that angle, but not really specifically to do with learning problems. (IP10)

This quote indicates a more holistically inclusive approach rather than a narrow concern for disability issues. Experience was widely felt to be the key in responding to need, as exemplified by this respondent, who, despite having undertaken no further training since his certificate, either general or specific, felt he had 'sufficient experience at this point in my career to cope with most of these teaching requirements' (QPC6-2).

Some respondents thought that training in disability issues should be mandatory for all, 'as part of the Certification courses for TEFL/TESOL' (QPC11-8) that is, the initial training for all ELT professionals. Others suggested that it was something that some teachers might choose to specialise in because (according to this state sector teacher) 'special teaching staff are required to teach these students' (QSL1-3) and that the solution was not 'a question of purposefully ignoring students with learning difficulties, but providing trained professionals to deal with difficulties' (QSC1-1). When asked to nominate an area of teaching in which they would like access to more training, a large proportion of the questionnaire respondents who answered (46 of the 112 responses given) indicated a desire to learn more about working with disabled learners (the extent to which this was an effect of their participation in the study is unclear). None of the interview participants was aware of any training opportunities being offered by outside agencies on the topic of working with disabled learners. It seems that this is an aspect of teaching in which it is hard to access specific training, even in the state education sector.

One typical response to the question about how well the interviewees felt their education had equipped them to work with disabled learners was this from a private school trainer: 'The first time I came across [dyslexia] I obviously didn't know what to do' (IP9). His director expressed the feeling 'that none of us here have any kind of training in dealing with this [working with disabled learners]. It's only through the odd experience of what we've picked up, teaching people' (IP8). Another private sector interviewee reported that it was not uncommon in EFL to be put 'into situations where you've got to go "right, well, I'll do it"' (IP10) without being adequately prepared or supported. All the private-sector interviewees were unanimous in expressing a feeling of being under-prepared and ill-equipped for this aspect of their work. Their state sector counterparts echoed this sentiment: 'I've got experience of having taught people with visual impairment... and I was never given any training or support on how to approach that' (IS14).

From the responses to this part of the interview it became clear that, although all of the interviewees had been in the situation of having disabled learners in their classrooms, only one had felt confident in her ability to respond appropriately, even drawing on all of their practical experience. Perhaps most surprisingly, even the participants who were working in the state sector, where support is theoretically available, had found it very difficult to accommodate their learners' needs satisfactorily. It is not surprising, then, that Certificate courses do not raise the issue of supporting disabled learners explicitly, if most trainers do not perceive themselves to be well-qualified to cover the topic.

These findings have some serious implications for the ELT profession in the UK, and further afield, if a commitment to inclusive education is to become a reality. The following section outlines these implications and makes some suggestions for how the present model of teacher education could be refined.

Conclusion and Implications

To summarise the findings of the study, it appears that working with disabled learners either in the language classroom or the training classroom is by no means an unusual situation, but it is one for which the majority of ELT professionals in this study consider themselves to be under-prepared. In terms of the institutional factors that emerged it appears that one factor that influenced the respondents' opinions concerning disabled learners was the amount of support that they received. This was affected by the sector in which they worked, but most teachers in both private and state schools reported feeling ill-equipped to offer the necessary support to their disabled learners. A minority of these teachers also thought that having disabled learners in the classroom had a negative effect on the other students. This, they explained, compromised their ability to manage the classroom situation, although this was qualified by the type and degree of disability in question. Significantly, the majority of teachers were convinced that their initial training had not adequately prepared them for the task of including all learners in the language classroom, and that it was only experience and (in a very few cases) further training that enabled them to develop the professional expertise necessary to meet the diverse needs of all their learners.

The most important implication of these findings is that the current design and content of the short intensive training programmes need to be reconsidered. It may be that inclusive practice is modelled and encouraged on many courses, but if teachers do not begin their careers feeling confident to support their learners, then more explicit coverage of the issues pertaining to disability and learning differences is evidently required. The findings of Florian and Rouse's (2001) study noted above in the Background section of this study are particularly pertinent here and must be kept in mind. While the use of 'Special Educational Needs' discourses should be avoided wherever possible in favour of inclusive language, it must be acknowledged that teachers need to be able to identify and discuss their learners' difficulties, in order to put in place systems that accommodate the full range of disabilities and differences.

This study has made a first attempt at examining an under-researched field, and it has inevitably raised as many questions as it has answered. British government policy with regard to ESOL and teacher education has changed several times in the last decade, and so this study was unavoidably carried out in a fluctuating climate. This meant that as the interviews were carried out over a period of a year, the later interviewees may have been influenced by different factors from those uppermost in the minds of the earlier interviewees. As it was a small-scale research project, looking only at the situation in the UK, it may be that considering ELT training systems in other countries would prove useful in finding solutions to some of the problems raised.

Several other avenues of potentially fruitful research have also been identified for the future. For example, it would be interesting to compare how the first graduates of the longer courses for FE-based practitioners feel about their professional preparation, compared to graduates of the intensive certificate courses. Specifically, it would be useful to gauge how confident they feel in supporting disabled learners, and to conduct longitudinal studies following graduates of both types of course to see how their careers, and their responses to the challenges they meet, differ. Unfortunately, it was not feasible to undertake a longitudinal study as part of this project, but other researchers who were able to forge firm relationships with the trainees on short courses have been able to obtain some information about their career progression (see Watkins (2006), who was a course tutor, and Hobbs (2006), who was a participant on a short course). The research models used in these studies could be exploited to find out at what stage of their careers teachers feel the need to supplement their initial training, particularly in the field of disability issues and/or learner support.

Further work could be done with the professional bodies in the UK (e.g. the British Council, who accredit many private language schools, or BALEAP, who accredit courses in the FE and university sectors) to ascertain in what ways they are already promoting inclusive practice, and how they could work more effectively with schools and colleges to ensure parity of provision across the country. One possible way forward could be to make the demonstration of inclusive practices and fully accessible curricula a pre-requisite for accreditation by the British Council or BALEAP, or for validation of teacher training courses. If implemented intelligently, this would ensure that inclusion remained high on the professional development agenda in any institution that required accreditation or validation of courses.

It seems likely that the building of an inclusive English language education system will be a cyclical and gradual process, beginning not only with initial teacher education, but at all levels of teaching simultaneously, from TEFL certificate courses to trainer training. Since ELT professionals demonstrate a strong preference for learning through experience, any number of reforms to the training courses will probably prove to be ineffectual unless and until they are backed up with practical experience. This means that more disabled students need to be encouraged into the language classroom, and more disabled trainees need to be recruited into the profession, so that the trainers gain the valuable experience of working with a wider range of trainees, and can then pass this on to the next generation of teachers. In this 'chicken and egg' process, the commitment that ELT professionals have traditionally shown to their learners' individual needs will be a most valuable asset in furthering the inclusive agenda.

References

Alghazo, E.M. and Gaad, E.E.N. (2004) General education teachers in the United Arab Emirates and their acceptance of the inclusion of students with disabilities. *British Journal of Special Education* 31 (2), 94–99.

Booth, T. (2003) Views from the institution: Overcoming barriers to inclusive teacher education? In T. Booth, K. Nes and M. Strømstad (eds) *Developing Inclusive Teacher Education* (pp. 33–58). London: Routledge Falmer.

Cambridge ESOL (2007) University of Cambridge ESOL Examinations: CELTA. On WWW at http://www.cambridgeesol.org/teaching/celta.htm. Accessed 06.05.07.

Clough, P. and Corbett, J. (2000) *Theories of Inclusive Education – A Students' Guide*. London: Sage.

Croll, P. and Moses, D. (2003) Special educational needs across two decades: Survey evidence from English primary schools. *British Educational Research Journal* 29 (5), 731–747.

Deal, M. (2003) Disabled people's attitudes toward other impairment groups: A hierarchy of impairments. *Disability and Society* 18 (7), 897–910.

Department for Education and Skills (DfES) (2006) *It's Not as Simple as You Think: Cultural Viewpoints Around Disability*. London: The Stationery Office.

Disability Discrimination Act (1995) London: The Stationery Office.

Dyson, A. (2001) Special needs in the twenty-first century: Where we've been and where we're going. *British Journal of Special Education* 28 (1), 24–29.

Ferguson, G. and Donno, S. (2003) One-month teacher training courses: Time for a change? *ELT Journal* 57 (1), 26–33.

Florian, L. and Rouse, M. (2001) Inclusive practice in English secondary schools: Lessons learned. *Cambridge Journal of Education* 31 (3), 399–412.

Frederikson, N. and Cline, T. (2002) *Special Educational Needs, Inclusion and Diversity*. Oxford: Oxford University Press.

Haycraft, J. (1988) The first International House preparatory course: An historical overview. In T. Duff (ed.) *Explorations in Teacher Training – Problems and Issues* (pp. 1–10). London: Longman.

Haug, P. (2003) Qualifying teachers for the school for all. In T. Booth, K. Nes and M. Strømstad (eds) *Developing Inclusive Teacher Education* (pp. 97–115). London: Routledge Falmer.

Hobbs, V. (2006) Examining the effectiveness of the four-week ELT training course: Change or no change? Paper presented at the 2006 IATEFL Conference, Harrogate.

Sparks, R., Javorsky, J. and Philips, L. (2005) Comparison of the performance of college students classified as ADHD, LD and LD/ADHD in foreign language courses. *Language Learning* 55 (1), 151–177.

Smith, A.M. (2006) Inclusion in English language teacher training and education. PhD thesis, University of Lancaster.

Watkins, P. (2006) Pre-service training and the first year of teaching. Paper presented at the 2006 IATEFL Conference, Harrogate.

Wedell, K. and the BECTA Special Needs Team (2002) Points from the SENCo-Forum: All teachers should be teachers for special needs – but is it possible yet? *British Journal of Special Education* 29 (3), 151.

Appendix: Interview Questions for Trainers and Course Leaders

Section 1. Overview of ELT career:
(1) Could you tell me briefly how you got into ELT?
(2) What was your first teaching qualification?
(3) How many years have you been teaching English?
(4) Where have you taught?
(5) What kinds of situations have you taught in?
(6) How did you get into training?
(7) How long have you been doing training ?
(8) How did you learn to be a trainer?
(9) How do you see your career developing?

Section 2. Experience as an ELT trainer:
(1) What do you see as the main needs of trainees on the course?
(2) What would you say are the main aims of the course?
(3) How have the changes in ESOL training (the new ESOL certificate) affected you or your institution?
(4) What other changes would you like to see?

Section 3. Students with 'learning difficulties':
(1) Have you ever worked with English learners or trainee teachers who had (or seemed to have) any 'learning difficulties'?
(2) Do you feel that your training or experience had/would have prepared you for that situation? (in what ways?)
(3) If a student who had a recognised learning difficulty were to arrive at this institution, whose responsibility would it be to organise the support s/he needed to complete the course?
(4) Does this institution offer any in-service training (or professional development courses) on this issue to teachers? Or do you know of any other providers offering courses in this field?

For Product Safety Concerns and Information please contact our EU Authorised Representative:

Easy Access System Europe

Mustamäe tee 50

10621 Tallinn

Estonia

gpsr.requests@easproject.com